ROUTLEDGE LIBRARY EDITIONS: INTERNATIONAL SECURITY STUDIES

Volume 15

A PREFACE TO PEACE

A PREFACE TO PEACE

HAROLD CALLENDER

LONDON AND NEW YORK

This edition first published in 2021
by Routledge
2 Park Square, Milton Park, Abingdon, Oxon OX14 4RN

and by Routledge
52 Vanderbilt Avenue, New York, NY 10017

Routledge is an imprint of the Taylor & Francis Group, an informa business

First published in Great Britain in 1944 by George Allen & Unwin Ltd

All rights reserved. No part of this book may be reprinted or reproduced or utilised in any form or by any electronic, mechanical, or other means, now known or hereafter invented, including photocopying and recording, or in any information storage or retrieval system, without permission in writing from the publishers.

Trademark notice: Product or corporate names may be trademarks or registered trademarks, and are used only for identification and explanation without intent to infringe.

British Library Cataloguing in Publication Data
A catalogue record for this book is available from the British Library

ISBN: 978-0-367-68499-0 (Set)
ISBN: 978-1-00-316169-1 (Set) (ebk)
ISBN: 978-0-367-70687-6 (Volume 15) (hbk)
ISBN: 978-0-367-70689-0 (Volume 15) (pbk)
ISBN: 978-1-00-314754-1 (Volume 15) (ebk)

Publisher's Note
The publisher has gone to great lengths to ensure the quality of this reprint but points out that some imperfections in the original copies may be apparent.

Disclaimer
The publisher has made every effort to trace copyright holders and would welcome correspondence from those they have been unable to trace.

A Preface to Peace

by
Harold Callender

London
George Allen & Unwin Ltd

Copyright in the U.S.A.

First published in Great Britain
in 1944

ALL RIGHTS RESERVED

---

to
B.S.C.

Printed in Great Britain
by Bradford & Dickens
London W.C.1

CONTENTS

| PREFACE | VII |

Part One: *Looking Forward*

I. THE USES OF VICTORY	3
II. TIME, SPACE, AND POWER	11
III. WHAT IS PEACE?	23

Part Two: *America in the Mediterranean*

IV. PRELUDE TO INVASION	34
V. OUR FRENCH ALLIES	56
VI. OUR BRITISH ALLIES	79
VII. FRENCH VERSUS FRENCH	93
VIII. ITALY'S SURRENDER	102

Part Three: *Democratic Failure*

IX. SPAIN DIVIDES AMERICANS	113
X. WASTED VICTORY	130
XI. INVITATION TO AGGRESSION	150
XII. OUR EXTREME NATIONALISTS	168

Part Four: *After Victory*

| XIII. GERMANY AFTER DEFEAT | 180 |
| XIV. THE ENIGMA OF RUSSIA | 201 |

CONTENTS

XV.	BRITAIN'S POLICY AND OURS	213
XVI.	WHAT WILL AMERICA DO?	226
XVII.	OUR SOUTHERN NEIGHBORS	248
	APPENDIX A	269
	APPENDIX B	273
	APPENDIX C	277
	ACKNOWLEDGMENTS	289
	INDEX	*follows page* 289

PREFACE

Though designed for the average American who has had little personal contact with the world abroad, this book is equally applicable to the average Englishman. They are the final arbiters of the destinies of their respective countries, and perhaps of the destiny of the world.

The United States held aloof from foreign affairs while a preventable world war developed. Recently she has taken the first steps towards a policy of actively preventing another great war. This can be done only with the aid of the power and influence of the United States. I believe that the American citizen is ready to see that power and influence so used.

In the following pages I have tried to indicate, in Part I, some of the tasks which victory imposes; in Part II the development during the war of our policies, military and political; in Part III the errors of the democratic powers, including the United States, in the two decades between the wars—errors which helped to bring on the Second World War; in Part IV the viewpoints and needs of the great Allied Powers and the problems the United States face in future relations with Latin America.

Much of the material has been derived from personal experience in Europe during fourteen years, in Latin America during one year, in Washington during a year. Much comes from indicated documentary sources.

An effort has been made throughout to be objective in presenting opposing views on controversial points. I have not offered any final formula for peace nor any design for a new world, but rather have tried to sketch some important parts of the "background" of the issues of the present and future, so closely resembling those of the past.

My own view—which I trust will be differentiated from

the various other views presented—is : (*a*) that an enduring peace is possible ; (*b*) that it can be achieved only with the active aid of the United States ; (*c*) that the process of achieving it, and of fully uniting the Allied Powers to achieve it, will be long and will require great patience and far greater statesmanship than was displayed the last time Europe was saved from German domination.

Most of this book was written before the Moscow Agreement of October 1943 supplied new hope of lasting unity among the victors, and parts of it reflect the skepticism of 1942 and 1943 regarding that unity and regarding Russia's policies. I have let those parts stand. For they may have a certain historical interest touching the situation in those months ; they indicate attitudes which will linger for a long time ; and they show, by reference to the obstacles to be overcome, how great a diplomatic achievement full agreement with Russia would be. They form part of the record of an unhappy past, whose influence it is our task to overcome.

It is the task not only of the national leaders and diplomats but of the average American and Englishman. For those who strive to avoid this time the sins and follies of the last post-war period can succeed only with the support of public opinion in these countries.

I believe that support will be forthcoming, in spite of occasional signs of the narrow nationalism which would rely upon American strength alone instead of upon a union of peaceful nations, in spite of the isolationist obscurantism that still survives in limited spheres.

I am grateful to the *New York Times* for permission to draw upon articles I have written for that newspaper ; to Mr. Lester Markel, the Sunday Editor, for whom I first began to write in Europe ; to Mr. Edwin L. James, the Managing Editor, for numerous foreign assignments. I desire to thank Mr. Arthur Krock and Mr. John McCormac for reading the manuscript, and the Library of Congress, the British Information Services and representatives in Washington of the French Committee of National Liberation for supplying documentary material. I thank my wife for her advice and encouragement. My gratitude also goes to hundreds of officials and private individuals in some thirty countries for contributing to my enlightenment regarding their particular regions or subjects in the years that I have passed abroad as a correspondent.

HAROLD CALLENDER.

PART ONE: *Looking Forward*

I

THE USES OF VICTORY

Hopes and Doubts

VICTORY is above all an opportunity to make further victories unnecessary. The opportunity was missed the last time Germany was defeated — when a mere twenty-year interlude between wars followed, which was not much in relation either to the cost of victory or to the far longer interlude after Napoleon's defeat.

Whether it is missed this time will depend upon the continuance after the war of the unity among the Allies which was a strictly wartime achievement, a unity created by the enemy and not easily maintained after the pressure of the enemy disappears.

The reason the last victory was thrown away was that the democratic powers — who could have been, but declined to be, masters of their destiny — destroyed their unity the moment the enemy was vanquished and not only permitted but encouraged the revival of German military strength and the expansion of Japanese. It was natural and inevitable that those two powers should eventually join in revolt against the positions and even the existence of the democracies, who in a sense invited them to do so.

The failure of Britain, France and the United States to make good their victory after 1918, though all three were Western powers with related cultures and visible common interests, augured none too well for continuing co-operation of

Britain, the United States and Russia, since they exhibited neither the similarity of culture possessed by the three victors of a quarter-century ago nor so obvious an identity of interests.

When one recalled that the Western democracies divided and dissipated the unique power they then enjoyed, one was constrained to wonder whether the two remaining great democracies, Britain and America, would in the long run attain not only agreement between themselves but agreement with the great Eurasian power, Russia, who has her own special outlook and has not always been convinced that her interests lay with the Western powers.

These misgivings seemed to lose much of their justification when the British, Russian and American leaders finally agreed in general terms upon a program for co-operation after the war, to which China also subscribed and in which the other United Nations certainly would be disposed to join. It appeared in the Autumn of 1943 that the Western democracies and Russia, who until then had fought related yet essentially separate wars without fully co-ordinating either their military strategy or their political aims, were at last in accord regarding a grand design for peace which would achieve all that the victors had failed to achieve after 1918. A new era in the relations of nations seemed about to open. Both the United States and Russia seemed ready to abandon their former isolation in favor of leadership in a concert of powers determined upon creating the collective that had been sought half-heartedly and vainly after the First World War.

In the early nineteen-twenties many Britons and Americans thought that France had become a militaristic menace and felt sorry for the prospective victim, Germany. At the same time they thought that Japan might become a pleasant companion to the democratic world if only we let her keep a chain of strategic islands pointed our way and assured her naval supremacy on her side of the Pacific (which we thought we were rather clever to get her to accept). A decade later many influential persons in the advanced and enlightened democracies, or at any rate in the two greatest democracies, be lieved that the saviors of Europe would be Adolf Hitler and the eager, vigorous, athletic German youths whom he had taught to get bronzed in the sun and to march with shining spades and to hate Jews and Communists.

It seems unlikely today that we shall again be quite so easily misled about where the danger lies, or about the character of such healthy, outdoor German movements for revenge as may be marching and singing their way to power in future years.

Origins of a Conquest

AT FIRST the Nazi movement was regarded as a counter-revolution directed against Communism and against Russia — and the Russians will not soon forget the favor it won in the Western democratic world as a result. Conservatives both in Germany and west of the Rhine long looked upon it with tolerance if not with approval and hope. This was the attitude of at least some German industrialists, who feared Communism in Germany and saw in the Nazi Party a bourgeois-proletarian force which, if conservatively guided, might reestablish German power, wipe out the German foreign debt and restore the prosperity they sought. It was in this way that Herr Fritz Thyssen, the German industrialist, explained to me at Essen in 1932 why he had supported Hitler.

The name "National Socialism" did not frighten German conservatives as it did foreign conservatives; for — as Oswald Spengler explained in his essay, *Deutschtum und Sozialismus* — Germans associated Socialism with the Prussian military state which on the whole they admired. Nor did state control of economic life shock the German industrialists as it does those of the United States, since German industry has never been so free from that control as ours has been and the extreme economic and political individualism characteristic of America hardly existed in Germany.

So it was that Hitler's movement became not only a revolution against what he called the Versailles system — the peace imposed by the Allies in 1919 which they soon showed they had no serious intention of maintaining; it became also a revolution against the economic practices of the democratic world, especially after the world-wide depression in the early nineteen-thirties gave rise to an extreme economic nationalism which provided precisely the setting required for Hitler's militarized economy geared mainly to preparation for war.

It was not surprising that Hitlerism commended itself to the 6,000,000 German unemployed whom it thus put to work, and to the impoverished middle class whose sufferings in the inflation had not created enthusiasm for capitalism or democracy or the German republic. Nor was it surprising that Communists in Germany in 1931 and 1932 joined with the Nazis against the main German party, the Socialists, who seemed linked with the capitalist-democratic world to which both the Communists and the interests of Germany seemed opposed. Communists and Nazis within Germany became revolutionary rivals who were agreed in their eagerness to throw out the Socialists.

Thus Hitler's conquest of Germany was made possible by the fact that economic discontent and the sense of national frustration left by defeat merged in a single violent emotion.

It is important to remember the character of the Nazi movement as we face a future which seems certain to present similar situations and similar emotions, and in which economic and political decisions again will often be inseparably linked in their consequences.

Although for the United States the Second World War was a greater threat than the First, and was so recognized, it was carried on more dispassionately. It produced none of the hysteria which during the previous war had caused the German language to be outlawed in the schools, German music to be banned, freedom of speech to be systematically infringed. This absence of hysteria was an encouraging sign, for it suggested that we might face the victory with less cheering and more reflection. Let us therefore note the limited character of the improvised Allied coalition against the Axis and the nature of the task we shall face in striving to make better use of this victory than we made of the last.

Negative and Positive

WE WERE fighting against the domination of Europe and other parts of the world by Hitler, and against the conquest of Asia and the Pacific by Japan — not having had the foresight or the collective will to prevent those violent onslaughts against us, as we could have done with far less effort than was required to defeat them once they had begun. The Axis had struck first, and we had responded because the Axis had set out to do certain things which we could not permit. The Axis were the attackers, we the defenders. The Axis leaders knew what they wanted. We knew what we did *not* want.

Even in this respect the anti-Axis powers were not fully agreed; for there was long a dispute as to which we should fight first and most, Hitler or Japan, and as to whether Russia would fight Japan at all. But when the question was asked what we *did* want, divergence became more marked and no very specific or positive answer could be given.

So far was the democratic or anti-Axis world from real agreement, even about what it should oppose, that Hitler could attack the more civilized western rim of Europe nation by nation without much more than local resistance. Belgium and Holland received little aid. Norway fought almost alone, as Poland had done, as Yugoslavia and Greece were to do, as Russia was to do on land for more than a year. Japan could invade not only Manchuria and China proper but Indo-China as well without facing the active opposition of any great power, which she faced in fact only when she herself attacked the great powers. For a full year — from the fall of France in June 1940 until the Nazi attack on Russia in June 1941 — Great Britain was the only great power engaged in resisting the Axis. The Axis conquests had gone on for two years and three months before the United States entered the arena and insured an Axis defeat. Thus the mobilization of the anti-Axis world was a slow and piecemeal process. Its unity was created only by the blows of the enemy and was never so complete as to give much assurance of permanence.

It is therefore accurate to say that the Axis powers were

fighting for positive ends — their domination of two regions of the earth — while the Allies were fighting for the negative end of defeating the Axis program.[1] The Axis had a scheme for organizing the world on new lines. It was an unacceptable scheme, but it was a scheme, a design, a plan.

The Germans, inveterate planners, had it all worked out both philosophically and technically and no doubt reduced to a perfect card-index system. The Japanese had their part equally worked out. The German design looked to a consolidation of Europe under the rule of Berlin, and it conformed to certain non-German conceptions in Europe at least in the sense that it offered in one form the unity of Europe which for so many had long seemed a desirable goal. The Japanese design for uniting Asia under Tokyo conformed to non-Japanese conceptions in the Orient at least in proposing to liberate Asia from Western rule and tutelage.

The barbarous behavior of Germans and Japanese in the war should not be permitted to blind us to the fact that they had plans — pernicious plans, yet plans — for organizing two major parts of a much too disorganized world, while we on the Allied side had no equivalent plans.

The collapse of the Axis leaves a vacuum, consisting not only in the breakdown of the armed power which, after a fashion, was ruling and controlling the large areas of Europe

---

[1] It will be said that we were fighting for the liberty of this and other nations, which is certainly true, even if some Americans were rather late to concede it and opposed our fighting at all. It may be said that we were fighting for individual rights as against a form of government which denied such rights. This was true. But to some those rights meant the right of an employer to hire or dismiss whom he pleased and to manage his business without interference from the government; while to others they included the right to uninterrupted employment and security, both of which entail interference by the government with business. In America and Britain those rights included the right of free speech, but in Russia that seemed irrelevant, just as it did in Nazi Germany. Thus the liberties, national and individual, for which the Allies may be said to have fought meant different things to different people and did not at all imply agreement upon any given kind of society or international system, especially in the field of economic relations where agreement was most necessary.

and Asia conquered by the Axis before the democracies had begun to resist successfully, but also in the absence of any general plan to take the place of the plans which the Axis powers were in process of applying. The two Axis conquerors had begun to organize their respective regions on fixed lines favorable to their domination. The defeat of their attempt to do so raises in imperative form the question what is to replace the Nazi "new order" in Europe and the Japanese "co-prosperity sphere" in Asia.

We may condemn or ridicule their plans, which were oppressive and ruthless, but we cannot ridicule the idea that plans were necessary. We may rebel at Hitler's way of uniting Europe by slaughter and starvation, and at Japan's way of organizing Asia by comparable methods; but we cannot deny that Europe required some kind of unity and Asia some kind of organization.

Moreover, the vacuum left by the collapse of Axis power is the consequence of a vacuum that already existed before the war and that had been due to the failure of the democracies to solve the problem of forming a politically and economically co-operating community. We had not seized the opportunity offered by our earlier victory over Germany to provide a workable alternative to the over-lordship which was Germany's proposed solution. Hitler did seize the opportunity to try once again to put Europe under German dominion, an opportunity which probably would have been seized sooner or later even had Hitler not appeared. The question may therefore be asked whether we shall leave it to Germany to fill the vacuum again — or perhaps to Russia.

Thus our victory is negative in the sense that it marks the defeat of another German onslaught on Europe, accompanied by a pre-arranged and co-ordinated Japanese onslaught on Asia, and the frustration for the moment of a revolution within the community of national powers.

It is potentially positive in the sense that it gives us the opportunity to do more than to beat back an aggressor, more than to crush a kind of revolution against the existing order of power and wealth, more even than to insure peace by overwhelming armaments. Like victory itself, none of these things can be enough because none can be permanent and none is positive in the sense of being constructive. All were necessary because of the short-sightedness of the democracies in the twenty inter-war years regarding their own security in terms of military power and regarding their own and the world's welfare in terms of the economic prerequisites of genuine peace.

We need overwhelming armaments as a sheet anchor, so to speak, in the disturbed and unsettled period that surely lies ahead; but we should not consider them more than a steadying factor; we must not imagine that they solve any of the fundamental questions upon which peace depends. They are the indispensable first step. With them as a safeguard, we may face more hopefully the larger task of creating the kind of world in which can be eliminated, not the combative instincts of men, but the economic incentives that help make those instincts dominant.

II

TIME, SPACE, AND POWER

Revolution in Geography

THE world we shall now have to live in and somehow come to terms with has substantially changed, and very probably will change still further in the near future, not only in its political and economic aspects but even in its geography. I refer not to such new frontiers and colorings as the maps may require but to what may be called new scales of time and space which seem destined to revolutionize our thinking about the position and strength and needs of the United States in relation to the rest of the world.

For all practical purposes it would be true to say that the proportions of the world have altered — that its land masses, particularly those that most directly concern this country, have been thrown closer together. If we could forget the flat maps and the ideas based upon those maps and upon pre-aviation concepts of distance, we should more readily appreciate the transformation that time and space have undergone.

Take a globe and turn it so that you look at it as if you were directly above the North Pole. Below lies a huge ice-cap which we learned at school was an impassable barrier for all but a handful of intrepid explorers, who had only recently succeeded in reaching the Pole. Below the ice-cap the three principal continents of the world, Europe, Asia and North America, approach one another; two of them almost touching; yet they seemed to be permanently separated by that forbidding polar barrier.

That barrier today is neither impassable nor so very forbidding. Not only has it been flown over experimentally and for purposes of exploration; there is abundant evidence that it will soon be crossed by the principal aerial highways of the world and thus become as populous as the North Atlantic sea lanes have been.[1]

With a bit of string and a globe anyone may measure how much closer New York and Moscow will be when the line between them passes over Greenland and the North Cape instead of following the water-and-land route of the past; how much closer the British Isles when reached via Greenland and Iceland; how much closer China and India and in fact the entire Northern Hemisphere.

When these short cuts to all the principal parts of the civilized world are fully utilized, it is likely that the northerly forests and frozen wastes of Canada, Alaska, Greenland and Spitzbergen will be drawn out of their chilly isolation and become parts of the thriving, populous world. For in those now remote areas will be ports of call and emergency stations for air-liners carrying hundreds of people and hundreds of tons of freight. Hotels, warehouses, repair shops, and new towns will appear in those wastes. The experiments of the Russians in the region of Murmansk seem to have demonstrated that scientific ingenuity can create in the hitherto forbidding North all the necessaries and even the comforts required for building industries and cities there.

Boarding a stratoliner at New York one night and changing to a Pacific Clipper next day at Los Angeles, I landed, after approximately sixty hours of flight, in New Zealand — as far south as Buenos Aires and as far west as Midway Island. Yet I had traveled at an average of a mere 160 miles an hour, which a few years hence will probably seem much like the speed of the "horse-and-buggy age" to those who move through the stratosphere at, let us say, twice that rate. From New York, Western Europe will be a flight of a few hours; while, via the polar short cut, China and Persia will be substantially nearer in time than New Zealand was by what seemed to me an almost miraculous journey. It will be as if the polar ice-cap had been washed away and the three great northern continents had moved into close proximity. The re-

[1] See article "The Polar Route to Victory" by Earl P. Hanson in *Harper's Magazine* for November 1942.

motest jungles and tundras and deserts will have ceased to be inaccessible, and many a small island where ships hardly ever touched will find itself on a main line of international travel.

Meanwhile the warmer oceans, like the polar ice-cap, have narrowed in terms of time. In a very real sense the Atlantic coasts of Europe and Africa have moved closer to the once splendidly isolated Western Hemisphere, whose Pacific outposts have for the first time been attacked by an Asiatic power.

Yesterday's Axioms Are Today's Illusions

AGAINST such an attack in future we shall require not only bases in Hawaii and the Aleutian Islands but a chain of strategic points in the Mariana and Caroline and Marshall islands stretching far into the southwestern Pacific — the chain we permitted Japan to retain under a mandate at the end of the First World War when the oceans still seemed rather broad; the chain from which she organized her attack against Pearl Harbor in 1941.

To the eastward we found it desirable even before we were at war to occupy Greenland and Iceland for the protection of our shores, and later we used as defensive points Great Britain, North Africa, and Dakar, as well as the tip of Brazil.

For us the Atlantic ceased to be a protective moat the moment Germany threatened to break through the barriers, first of France, then of Britain, and to menace the shores of this hemisphere, now so near in South America to the bulge of Africa and in North America to Europe via the northern islands. It was in fact the second time that in those circumstances the Atlantic ceased in our estimation to be an adequate natural defence, and that we sought security by the defeat of Germany. It will be, of course, still less of a barrier in the still more shrunken world of the future than it was in either 1917 or 1940.

Those who in 1940 thought the Atlantic still an effective barrier, and who believed we had gone to war for other than defensive reasons in 1917, were examples of the mental time-lag which occurs when the axioms of yesterday become the illusions of today. We, like the British, were victims of that time-lag.

For nearly nine centuries Britain's moat of salt water, narrow though it was, sufficed for her security so long as her fleet could dominate it; and her Empire was safe (as we were) so long as her naval power could drive an enemy from the seas. For her, wars were usually remote affairs overseas into which her ships could throw small armies but in which her survival was not involved. For this reason she became an unmilitary and consequently a politically free country. In the eighteenth century Laurence Sterne could travel agreeably in France without always being quite sure whether his King and France's were at war or not.

The same lazy feeling of aloofness and security developed in America, living behind a still broader moat. To Americans for nearly eighty years war has seemed, as it seemed to the British in *their* days of isolation, essentially a foreign adventure into which we entered or not as we thought fit. So it seemed to the members of the American Legion, whose gay, schoolboyish reunion in Paris in 1926 amazed the French, to whom war was not at all an adventure or a joke. Even as recently as 1941 the question was debated whether we should enter the war or not. It was very generally taken for granted that we could do as we liked about it. Before Pearl Harbor few Americans had dreamed that we might fight for our own survival; that instead of offering our assistance to other powers, we should be equally in need of theirs.

Long before the war Lord Baldwin, speaking of his own country, said fatalistically that the bomber would always get through. But it was not until the bombers did get through that the British fully recovered from the illusion of security created by their island position which for nine centuries *had* been secure.

With the rise of air power Britain, in a strategic sense, ceased to be an island; and with the increased range of that power the United States, in the same sense, ceased to be a continent. What the Germans did to London and Coventry and Plymouth, what the British later did even more devastatingly to Hamburg, Essen, Cologne and Wuppertal, could be done in a future war to New York, Detroit, Chicago or Washington. As Lord Baldwin said, the bomber will always get through — if we are ever again so foolish as to permit it to start.

The shrinkage of space, as if in obedience to some new Einstein theory, has already revolutionized our conceptions of strategy. But its implications go much farther. Time as well as space has shrunk. Neither we nor the British can rely in the future, as we have done in the past, upon our natural moats to give us the margin of time necessary to turn unmilitary nations into military nations and peace production into war production. We can no longer assume that the possession of a navy gives us time to create an army and an air force after war has broken out, as we did from 1940 onward. We can no longer wait until the enemy has struck at us before even preparing to strike back. Though the suggestion may shock some people, we should be prepared if necessary to strike first, thus turning to our advantage the shrinkage of space and the value of initiative which we have hitherto left to the enemy.[2]

---

[2] In Europe in the nineteen-thirties, when Hitler's power was steadily expanding and it was perfectly clear how he intended to use it, the phrase "preventive war" was whispered diffidently, as if it were something immoral. Yet in 1935, when Hitler violated the Treaty of Versailles by instituting conscription, and in 1936, when he marched into the Rhineland, demilitarized by that treaty, there was every legal justification for forcible restraint, which then would have been quite easy for the large French Army moving against the small German Army. There would have been little bloodshed compared with that which was to come because the democracies preferred a world war to a small and relatively painless preventive war. The logic of this experience seems to be that when we next disarm Germany, we should not only retain at least a massive air force in readiness to strike but should not shrink from striking the moment Germany (or Japan) breaks the bounds set by the victors. What this would mean in practice would be that, our intention being known, there probably would be no need to strike and hence no bloodshed at all. Consequently preventive war, so used, not only is not immoral but is as humane as it is wise.

Only Three Great Powers

WHILE THE earth itself has in effect shrunk to smaller and mechanically more manageable proportions, the constellation of power has meanwhile diminished in membership. Whereas at the beginning of the First World War there were seven great powers in the world, and at the beginning of the Second there were six (excluding Italy and including Japan at both periods), if German power is destroyed there will be only three great powers — Britain, Russia, and the United States. China cannot be counted as a great power until she achieves a strong national state and greater industrialization, since by definition a great power is one whose population, economic resources, and organizing ability enable it to enter the first rank of nations in a military sense.

There will remain only three great powers until China rises into that category, or until Germany or Japan or France recovers the strength to qualify for re-admission into the company of the giants, or until some newly developing nation proves that it possesses the requisite combination of wealth, energy, and strategic advantage to be included in the first rank of powers.

No new candidates, excepting China, are likely to appear in the near future; so the possible changes in the constellation of power relate principally to the future of China, Japan, Germany and France. The advance of China, with liberal Western financial aid, might be rather rapid. The revival of France, which Hitler deliberately sought during three years or more to cripple and weaken permanently as a nation by reducing its population, may not be so long delayed as those imagine who write her off as a great power for another half-century or more. Her return even as a second-class power would vitally affect the situation of Europe. For otherwise — so long as Germany remains excluded from the class of great powers — there will be, for the first time since great powers have existed in the modern sense, no single great power that is strictly European.

Though that part of Russia's territory which is geographically included in Europe formed in 1939 some 45 per cent of what the maps designate as Europe, this is a case (like that of the Mercator Projection) where geography misleads. For Europeans do not regard Russia as European but rather as a ponderous mass lying on the margin of Europe which has been subject to European influences yet remains more marked by the impress of Asia, into which its domains sprawl out to more than three times the extent of Russia-in-Europe. Russia, with a foot in each continent, should be called Eurasian rather than European.

Nor is Britain a European power, in spite of the maps. Britons, like Americans, think of Europe as an alien continent overseas and of the British Isles as a separate "little world," as Shakespeare called it. Politically the term "splendid isolation," first applied to British policy and only later (without the adjective) to ours, expressed a British desire — which Americans will readily understand — to hold aloof from European quarrels save as they resulted in threats to Britain. This was Britain's policy through the nineteenth century, from the downfall of Napoleon until 1903, when the German naval threat led to the Entente with France.

During that period, and again after the First World War, the British would have liked nothing better than to practice complete non-intervention towards Europe. But they found it impossible — as, in fact, we also did. For a power grew up in Europe which menaced Britain and, by menacing her and the Atlantic world (in Mr. Walter Lippmann's phrase), menaced us as well. Whenever that happens, the British will emerge from whatever degree of isolation obtains at the moment and fight against the menacing power. And, to judge by the history of the last quarter century, so shall we — even if we should again elaborately pretend, and so in effect inform the intending aggressor, that we shall do no such thing.

Our Defence Area Widens

IN RELATION to Europe the United States, of course, is more marginal than Russia, which is partly in Europe, or than Britain, an island anchored off the shore of Europe. Yet in view of the general shrinkage of distances, in view of the fact that Europe has moved closer to us both by way of the North Pole and by way of the Atlantic, the presence or absence of aggressive or potentially aggressive powers in Europe seems destined to assume for us something of the direct and vital importance which it has had for Great Britain in past centuries. The fact that our margin is broader than hers dwindles in importance in the light of the far more significant fact that both margins have narrowed and very probably will continue to do so.

As regards Asia, all three great powers possess territories either in that continent or in the islands adjoining it or stretching out from it. It was once thought that by liberating the Philippines we should liquidate our commitments in Asia and practice towards that continent the policy of isolation which we tried to practice towards Europe.

Today the trend is in the opposite direction. Our naval strategists insist that for defence purposes we must hold not fewer but more islands in the southwestern Pacific. Meanwhile the view seems to be growing that American security is involved whenever, either in Europe or in Asia, an aggressive power appears which might move beyond those continents — as Germany threatened to do in 1917 and 1940, and as Japan did in 1941. Such a power on either side of us may now leap across the ocean barriers. The Pacific as well as the Atlantic has shrunk. The Pacific will never again appear so vast to Americans as it did before the attack on Pearl Harbor.

Among the three great powers — the United States, Britain and Russia — the United States is not the largest but, in territory and population, is the smallest. As compared with the approximately 130,000,000 inhabitants of continental United States, Russia contains something like 165,000,000 and the British Empire perhaps 500,000,000. As compared with our 3,026,789 square miles of continental territory, Russia embraces 8,073,185 square miles and the British Empire not far from a quarter of the land area of the globe. The United States is richer in some raw materials like petroleur and iron (though it has had to import many strategic minerals from Mexico, Brazil, Bolivia, and Canada), and just now it enjoys superior industrial capacity, though other nations, notably Russia, are rapidly becoming industrialized. It is not easy to measure the war potential of nations, which consists in their productive power, their populations, their military skill, and the qualities and training of their peoples. But it is well to remember that the United States has an enormous strategic area to protect with limited man-power and wealth.[3]

When Coalitions Dissolve

IF ONE of the three great powers were to become antagonistic to the others, it would be to its interest to encourage the growth or resurrection of a fourth or a fifth great power. If Britain and Russia should come to look upon each other as potential or probable enemies — as they did as late as 1938, when there were British hopes of a German-Russian conflict, and in 1939, when Russia hoped to stand aside in a German-British conflict — one or the other might turn to Germany as a possible ally. I have met Germans in this country who believed that after the Second World War Britain would rearm Germany as a barrier against Russia, and we know that after the First World War Russia and Germany developed a relationship that continued or was resumed even under Hitler, the avowed enemy of Bolshevism. In Germany, the dominant

[3] "The area of American defensive commitment is not quite 40 per cent of the land surface of the earth. But it contains a little less than 25 per cent of the population of the earth. The Old World contains 75 per cent of mankind living on 60 per cent of the land of this globe. Thus it is evident that the potential military strength of the Old World is enormously greater than that of the New World. . . . The only arsenal of the New World is in North America; and Canada, which provides an important part of it, is an independent state which has strong ties of interest and of tradition outside the area of our commitments. The Old World, on the other hand, comprises the military states of Britain, Germany, France, Japan, Italy and China — all of them arsenals or potential arsenals and each of them with a population used to war and the carrying of arms." Walter Lippmann: *U. S. Foreign Policy* (Boston, Little, Brown & Co., 1943).

hope of the military men and the conservatives, or whatever group succeeds Hitler, will be that the fear of Russia in Britain and the United States will induce us to forget Germany's crimes and to restore her power in the belief that it will be in our interests to do so. Nor can we assume today that there will never be Britons or Americans who will entertain this suggestion; some did so after the last war when they thought France too powerful, and some did so in 1937 and 1938 when they feared Russia more than Germany.

It will be the permanent interest and policy of the defeated powers to divide the great powers, for only so can they hope to regain the positions they will have lost. It will be the constant temptation of one or another of the great powers to yield to the pleas of the defeated if by doing so it can gain even a momentary advantage for itself. The temptation will grow in proportion as the hope of mutually advantageous unity among the victorious powers diminishes.

It will be the constant aim of Germany to play Russia against Britain, or Britain against Russia, or the United States against either or both, as occasion may offer, but always in the interest of Germany; for a populous, industrious, gifted, energetic Germany will not accept defeat but will immediately plan and work for the recovery of the power she has lost. It will be the constant aim of Japan to incite Russia against China or against the English-speaking powers, or India against Britain, or Asia generally against the West — to stir up dissension wherever it will contribute to the strengthening of her own position. For the Japanese, too, are numerous, prolific, industrious, energetic, and they are unlikely to accept defeat permanently, however severe it will have been.

We cannot assume that the defeated states will stay defeated or that any powerful state will become a benevolent institution instead of an aggregation of interests. We cannot assume that the victorious powers will always be as averse to war as they will be on the morrow of a hard and costly war. We cannot assume that the conduct of any other power will be restrained by the peculiar and unusual esteem for human life and happiness and liberty which exists in the United

States, the British Commonwealth, and the advanced states of Europe west of the Rhine and north of the German frontiers. We must assume that conceptions of national interest, ruthlessly pursued, will continue to dominate the affairs of nations, and that if the three great victorious powers get on together it will be not because of charters or covenants or ideals but because their principal interests so dictate.

Reasons for Continuing Unity

IT IS HERE that we must find such ground for hope as there is, and it is here that the best ground exists. For the immediate and probably for a protracted future it seems clear that the aggregate interests of Britain, Russia, and the United States counsel agreement among them in spite of past differences and suspicions and in spite of obvious clashes of minor interests. Such clashes must be expected always to go on within such a vast concert of powers, but so long as the primary interests of each state are best served by the concert, its survival should be assured.

The primary interest of the United States in world affairs is that no power shall again arise which will threaten our shores, our overseas possessions, or this hemisphere. Two such powers have arisen in recent times, Germany and Japan. We have fought two wars against the first and one war against the second. Our interests demand that neither of those states or any other state that might threaten us should become strong enough to do so.

Since strength is relative, this means that we must never again become as weak as we were in 1917 and in 1940, and that neither Germany nor Japan must be permitted to become as strong as they formerly were. This suggests the retention of powerful armament on our part, especially on the sea and in the air, and the survèillance of Germany and Japan over a long period to prevent — by force, if necessary — their rearmament.

It will likewise be in the interest of Britain and Russia to insure that neither of those states recovers its aggressive power, in spite of apparent differences of view on this point. Whatever may be Russia's continuing suspicions towards Britain or her doubts about the United States, the simple facts are that she has fought two great wars against Germany and one against Japan, who has long been regarded as her predestined enemy of the future. Neither Britain nor the United States has been so regarded, except as the entire capitalist world was once conceived as desiring to destroy Soviet Russia. American and Russian interests have largely coincided throughout our history, in spite of our dislike of Russian governments, Czarist or Communist. Russia sent naval squadrons to San Francisco and New York in 1863 as a warning against British intervention in our Civil War. Russia helped defeat Germany in the First World War and more notably in the Second. Britain and Russia have clashed in the Crimea and in Persia, and "the bear that walks like a man" was once a bogey to the British. But that was before the rise of German power, which has made Britain and Russia allies in two desperate wars and given them a common defensive interest for the future. These historic trends have been obscured in recent years by ideological differences, as they are called. But policies must be based not upon prejudices or emotions or even class interests but upon major and continuing national interests.

III

WHAT IS PEACE?

A Skeptical Age

UPON what positive, constructive, enlightened forces can we count to win the victory that is as important as victory over the Axis — the victory over the ignorance, prejudice, inertia and obscurantism within our own and other countries which may threaten to nullify the victory in war?

Desperately though they needed one, Europeans and Americans alike seemed to lack in the last two decades any conspicuous or exciting interest or ideal that was remotely comparable to those which in revolutionary ages of the past, like the Elizabethan period and the eighteenth century, lifted life to new levels, endowed men with exceptional powers and energies, stimulated the pursuit of new knowledge, new worlds to explore, new societies to build. Both those dynamic periods revived men's confidence in themselves and their future, in what eighteenth-century Utopians called human perfectibility.

Nobody uses such language today, not only because ours is a less philosophical age but because it is a more skeptical age. Few believe profoundly in anything whatever. There was little to inspire new faith during the two inter-war decades when, as the late Mr. Frank Simonds put it, a post-war period turned into a pre-war period. The currency and debt structure of the world, laboriously pieced together from the wreckage of the First World War, collapsed in the depression of 1931. Britain, having lost her supreme position as an exporting nation, readjusted her economy quickly and successfully after departing from the gold standard, but at the cost of a new closed Empire tariff system. The United States suffered more sveerely and recovered less rapidly. France, internally divided, saw her power declining but was unable to meet her responsibilities. The time and efforts of statesmen were consumed by talk of collective security and disarmament, the only result of which was that the democratic powers were unready when Germany struck at them. It was hardly surprising therefore that faith in democracy and in democratic civilization was undermined.

Not only in defeated Germany but in the victorious countries as well there was a bewildered pessimism born of a sense of helplessness and doom which led to speculation about "the decline of the West," as Oswald Spengler called it in a depressing historical treatise under that title. In the United States, where we believed in prosperity as a kind of perpetual motion, even if we believed in nothing much else, the depression destroyed not only investments and bank accounts but also that reassuring even if naïve and materialistic doctrine. In so doing it shook Americans' faith in themselves, which was inseparable from their faith in the new society they had created as a kind of by-product of the laboratory, a passion for machinery and the pursuit of wealth.

When America Seemed a Menace

CRITICAL European minds, notably in France where other ideals prevailed, had already questioned the human value of that prosperity and of the American society which it had transformed. They had looked with a consternation approaching horror upon our excessive industrial productivity and the resulting cult which they thought was shaping both the social life and the mind of America.[1]

The subordination of the individual to the machine seemed to be taking place not only in the assembly lines of industrial plants but throughout our society. For all aspects of our na-

---

[1] *America Comes of Age* by André Siegfried and *L'Europe ou l'Amérique* by Lucien Romier represented these views, while *Visions de la Vie future* by Georges Duhamel is an impressionistic version of the America which shocked the esthetic sense of some Europeans as well as inspiring their social criticism. These and similar books about the wild new world appeared in the nineteen-twenties.

tional life, including entertainment and mental processes, appeared affected by the mechanization and standardization that found such fertile ground in this exceptionally "extroverted" country, where the European cultural tradition had grown feeble and the restless and physically creative spirit of the pioneer seemed to have moved into the laboratories and the machine-tool industry.

What this indicated to Europeans was that the United States was abandoning the individualism which was the deepest foundation of European civilization. The United States was being transformed in such a way that, by European standards, it was growing less and less civilized. At any rate we were creating a kind of society which, whether civilized or not, would not represent the same civilization or the same human values as those represented by Europe's tradition.

In this sense America was compared to Russia. Both were vast and populous and energetic. Both were growing increasingly un-European as they pursued their respective Utopias, which were so different in theory yet so similar in practice and results. Both were passionately mechanical and socially regimented — Russia by a totalitarian state, America by the uniformity imposed by its mass-producing industrial apparatus. Fear of Russia in relation to Europe was consequently linked with fear of the United States. For both were regarded as apostates from the European tradition and way of life, and as threats to the humanistic culture which Europe had inherited from Greece and Rome. Their mechanized societies represented competitive power in the economic and military spheres, while the examples of their fabulous productivity were likely to inspire imitation in Europe.

It is ironical today to reflect that the immediate threat to European civilization came not from America but from Europe itself, where regimentation had taken political and military forms which civilized Western Europe had been slow to resist, and that France will owe her escape from enslavement to the military power resulting from America's persistence in the sin of mass production which French intellectuals had denounced.

The conclusion to be drawn is not that the French critics of our national life were mistaken in suggesting that dangers were inherent in a mass-produced civilization, but rather that neither in highly mechanized America nor in the older society of Europe did there exist the intelligence to perceive or the will to eliminate the destructive forces which immediately threatened all the values of our contemporary life.

The misgivings of the French critics are shared by one of the greatest living historians, Professor Arnold Toynbee, who is not at all sure whether our increased control over the physical world, which is the foundation of our high productivity, is a sign of growth or of decay. He suspects that the prosperity we have so overvalued may accompany, and perhaps conceal, an actual decline in the strength and durability of the society in which we live.[2]

At any rate, our failure to master our political and social environment in spite of unique scientific powers and produc-

[2] "An empirical study has left us doubtful whether there is any ascertainable correlation at all between the historical variations in the degree of a society's control over its environment and the historical change in the fortunes of a society whose growth is cut short by a breakdown running into a disintegration. And the evidence, so far as it goes, suggests that, if some correlation did prove to exist, we should find that an increase in command over the environment was a concomitant of breakdown and disintegration and not of growth. It looks, in fact, as though the internal struggles within the bosom of a society which bring the society's breakdown about, and which become more and more violent as its consequent disintegration proceeds, were actually more effective than the activities of genesis and growth in promoting the extension of the society's command both over the life of other living societies and over the inanimate forces of physical nature. . . . Since the vulgar estimates of human prosperity are reckoned in terms of power and wealth, it thus often happens that the opening chapters in the history of a society's tragic decline are popularly hailed as the culminating chapters of a magnificent growth; and this ironic misconception may even persist for centuries. Sooner or later, however, disillusionment is bound to follow; for a society that has become incurably divided against itself is almost certain to 'put back into the business' of war the greater part of those additional resources, human and material, which the same business has incidentally brought into its hands." (A Study of History, V, pp. 15–16, New York, Oxford University Press, 1939.)

WHAT IS PEACE?

tive capacity has certainly not filled us with confidence in our future. That failure explains the search, not only in totalitarian countries but in democratic countries, for some new doctrine or creed or system which might offer greater assurance and hope. The fanatical devotion of German youth to the Nazi state, an emotional force powerful enough to provoke a world war, owed something to distinctively German qualities, but it also owed much to the instinctive need of youth everywhere to believe intensely in some cause or creed.[3]

(This is not merely an inference from events. It is a vivid impression resulting from travels throughout Germany in 1930, 1931, and 1932, when the Nazi movement was gathering momentum in the universities and the majority of students were being swept along by its emotional appeal. I talked with hundreds of those students in those years. I met some of them again in Munich, Vienna, Danzig, Berlin, and Hamburg in the summer of 1939, when they had become full-fledged Na-

---

[3] "If a considerable part of the younger generation in many European countries came to believe that either Soviet Russia or Nazi Germany held the key to the future, this was because both those countries propounded new economic systems based on new principles and therefore opening up a prospect of hope, whereas the political and intellectual leaders of the satisfied countries appeared to offer no solution of the economic problem but a return to a past whose bankruptcy had been sufficiently demonstrated," writes a severe British critic of the era of democratic dominance in the twenty years between the world wars. (Edward Hallett Carr: *Conditions of Peace*, New York, Macmillan, 1943.)

American writers have passed equally sharp judgments, for instance Professor Frederick L. Schuman, who wrote: "The fall of the West exhibits on the grandest scale the comic-tragic drama of a whole culture done to death by the deeds of those entrusted with its protection, with each step toward doom plausibly presented and gladly accepted as the only means of salvation. . . . Security in the relations between men cannot be enjoyed by those who live in a world of endless flux, unless they are capable of reordering their collective existence according to some design which will recover in new forms the satisfaction which rapid social change destroys." (*Night over Europe*, New York, Alfred A. Knopf, 1941.) Professor Schuman wrote at the darkest period of the war, 1940, when the "fall of the West" seemed a rather more apposite phrase than it seems today.

zis, trained at *Fuehrerschulen* and eager for the coming war, which we discussed frankly and at length for hours as we sat in cafés or Nazi party offices. I argued that they would lose their war because Britain would fight when they invaded Poland, and the United States would fight when Britain was in danger. But they were not convinced of either statement — nor was Hitler.)

A Peace We Can Believe In

IT IS IMPERATIVE, therefore, that the peace shall be one that young men can believe in. It must be a peace that will recreate the hopes that were destroyed by the last peace and by the subsequent, and consequent, depression. It must provide some reason for believing, in spite of all the evidence to the contrary, that civilized men can manage the society which — perhaps in a fit of absent-mindedness — they have created.

The last great peace was denounced and opposed in the victorious countries only less than in the defeated countries. The will to enforce or defend it was impaired from the moment of its signature — and Hitler was the result.

Peace should not be conceived merely as a fat document signed and sealed with red ribbons by elderly gentlemen who will soon pass from the scene, or as a fixed and rigid structure that will stay put only until the repressed forces of growth or revolution smash it to pieces, or as a kind of insurance policy for our possessions and our social order which might, with luck, be valid for another twenty years. Nor should it be some new League of Nations Covenant in which governments solemnly proclaim principles that they have not the slightest intention of carrying out. We have been oversupplied with officially expounded ideals, which often only deepen cynicism and seem almost to justify the desire of those who are afraid of life to set their feet upon solid ground by seeking in the irrecoverable past less inspiring goals like that which the least inspired of all our Presidents called "normalcy."

Such a desire existed in this country a quarter-century ago, after a much less arduous and less revolutionary war than the second German world war. It was almost as if in the prosperous but unhealthy nineteen-twenties the youthful, venturesome spirit that had made America had given way to a kind of elderly caution. The desire to withdraw from the world in order to keep out of trouble accorded ill with the daring, enterprising mood so conspicuously displayed in American history. America, once so filled with energy and confidence, seemed to have become a decrepit old gentleman with hardened arteries and quivering fingers who lived bent over a safe-deposit box counting his securities.

But we soon found that we could not set the clock back; that "normalcy" was the most impossible of all goals; that we did not find security in isolation; that we did not keep out of war.

"Eppur si muove"

THE FAIRLY obvious fact that the world can no more stop evolving than it can stop revolving disturbs nations and classes and individuals who have large investments in a particular stage of its evolution and wish that it could be halted and frozen at just that agreeable point, which they would no doubt call "normalcy."

Much of our nationalism has been animated by this fear of change and by the assumption that, if we could somehow cut ourselves off from the world, we could escape the changes and ills to which it is subject. Isolationism in the United States has been inspired not only by fear of war as such but equally by fear of the social changes that accompany it,[4] and

[4] This attitude was similar to that of the conservatives, in Germany and in the democracies, who supported or tolerated the Nazi movement and the Hitler régime on the theory that, being against Communism, the Nazis must represent a slightly odd and exotic but recognizable version of the impulses and emotions animating, say, the National Association of Manufacturers. The fears of social change, some examples of which are cited in Chapter XII below, were intensified to the point of morbidity by the New Deal which, oddly enough, was extremely nationalistic in its early stage of currency experimentation (tantamount to American secession from the monetary community) but

in some cases by fear of contamination by the "Socialism" of the instinctively conservative British.[5]

So far as this fear of the world is a relic of the early days of this Republic, when we were in danger of being pounced upon by greater powers, it is a mark of our national immaturity, and its persistence today betrays distrust of our fitness for leadership and reluctance towards our assumption of the rôle of great power for which events have cast us. So far as this fear represents a rugged and unyielding conservatism defying the currents of modern thought abroad, it takes on a Bourbon quality which, if dominant, might soon place the United States in the category of backward nations.

Americans have long regarded Europe as a restless and explosive continent, incurably warlike, perversely opposed to such peaceful and unfortified frontiers as that between this country and Canada — which Americans sometimes commended to the attention of Europeans. When I was in Europe in the nineteen-thirties, an American editor asked me to write an article answering the question: Can Europe settle down? It seemed an odd question to be put by the nervous, migratory, motorized New World to the Old World of Europe, which some thought much too stagnant and conservative and which Americans had been known to call effete. The question was a tribute to Europe's energy and vitality, then about to burst its framework of frontiers, which spoke of reserves of primitive strength rather than of the exhaustion of which Europe had so often been thought a victim.

Europe is a dynamic part of a disconcertingly dynamic world which moves ever onward, possibly towards higher forms of social life, possibly towards another dark age, but which cannot "settle down" or freeze into a reassuringly

---

later came to be associated with internationalism under the influence of President Roosevelt's developing foreign policy. The doctrine of cooperation with other powers against aggression or for a world order has now been dissociated from the doctrines of the New Deal, bitterly disliked by conservatives; though the economic implications of that cooperation — as regards our tariff, for example — are not yet fully appreciated.

[5] See Chapter XII.

static state — even under the influence of those who feel that it is not quite up to the world we should have got if the Republican Party and the Chamber of Commerce of the United States had been able to submit specifications in advance of its creation.

The younger generation, who will bear the burden of the peace and of the next war to end war, would not care for such an immobile universe even if one were available. They accept, not with resignation but with eagerness, a world that vibrates with life and growth and is full of risk and adventure and scope for creative achievement.

Let us then beware of the statesman-like habit of talking of peace in terms of stability or security or order or isolation from a too restless world. For these are all negative goals suggestive of stagnation, reaction, immobility — even defeat. The response they evoke from the young and healthy minds which should be engaged, not in debating whether it is worth while to fight for King and country, as Oxford students once did, but in making their indispensable contribution to a civilized society, is like the attitude towards the League of Nations expressed by Peter in *Joan and Peter* by that major prophet, Mr. H. G. Wells. The novel was written in 1918, when the League was only a blue-print drawn in a wistfully hopeful mood, but of it Peter, a 25-year-old war veteran, says:

We don't want a preventive League of Nations. It's got to be creative or nothing. . . . A world peace for its own sake is impossible. . . . It's got to be a positive proposal. . . . No peace, as we have known peace hitherto, offers such opportunities for good inventive work as war does. There's no comparison between the excitement of making a real, live, efficient submarine, for example, that has to meet and escape the intensest risks, and the occupation of designing a great big, upholstered liner in which fat swindlers can cross the Atlantic without being seasick. War tempts imaginative, restless people, and a stagnant peace bores them. . . . I'm all for the end of flags and kings and custom houses. But I have my doubts of all this talk of making the world safe — safe for democracy. I want the world made one for the adventure of mankind, which is quite another story.

Is Peace Tolerable?

WILLIAM JAMES, to the end of his life not only one of the greatest but one of the most youthful minds of his time, had expressed much the same idea eight years earlier in discussing what he called a moral equivalent of war — that is, a form of activity that would satisfy the instincts to which war appeals and that would also call forth the human qualities that war demands.[6]

James thought that the militarists and the believers in war as a divinely ordained necessity of the race had had the better of the argument with the pacifists. He thought it useless to emphasize the horrors and bloodshed of war because "modern man inherits all the innate pugnacity and all the love of glory of his ancestors," and hence "The horrors make the fascination. War is the *strong* life; it is life *in extremis.*" Men lived under a "pain-and-fear economy" and the whole atmosphere of contemporary Utopian literature tasted "mawkish and dishwatery to people who still keep a sense for life's more bitter flavors." In the United States — James was writing in 1910 — where was "sharpness and precipitousness, the contempt for life, one's own or another's?" "We must make new energies and hardihoods continue the manliness to which the military mind so faithfully clings. Martial virtues must be the enduring cement; intrepidity, contempt of softness, surrender of private interest, obedience to command, must still remain the rock upon which states are built — unless, indeed, we wish for dangerous reactions against commonwealths fit only for contempt and liable to invite attack whenever a centre of crystallization for military-minded enterprise gets formed anywhere in their neighborhood."

James suggested that if instead of military conscription there were a conscription of the "whole youthful population to form for a certain number of years a part of the army enlisted against nature," something like a moral equivalent of

[6] See his essay *The Moral Equivalent of War*, in the volume entitled *Essays on Faith and Morals* (New York, Longmans, Green & Co., 1943).

war would result and the "military ideals of hardihood and discipline would be wrought into the growing fibre of the people; no one would remain blind, as the luxurious classes are now blind, to man's relations to the globe he lives on and to the permanently sour and hard foundations of his higher life."

Thus to James peace did not mean ease and softness and relaxation and "settling down" and "normalcy," but the deliberate exposure of men of all classes to the "more bitter flavors" and the risks and adventure of life which Peter feared might be eliminated from a safe and therefore intolerably dull world.

Such young people, men and women, who are not half so interested in wealth or security as in doing something interesting and satisfying, constitute a positive, constructive, civilizing force that never yet has been adequately utilized. To them war, manipulating electrons, fighting endemic diseases, building dams, exploring wastes, creating international machinery, and a hundred other enterprises are all fascinating fun; and if the world is not rebuilt for the fun of it, it is not likely ever to be rebuilt.

They are willing to accept the universe, as Margaret Fuller put it, with all its faults, its capriciousness, its combination of growth and decay and whatever implications this may have for our own society, if only the positive, creative forces within our battered civilization are permitted to have their chance. They do not insist upon an unbreakable, fool-proof, guaranteed peace with no risks left. They are content to take an imperfect one full of cracks and flaws (which is what they will have to take) and try what can be done with it. All they ask is that moderate scope be left for human intelligence and for the human emotional requirement of something to believe in, even if it is only the most tentative and experimental of working hypotheses.

PART TWO: *America in the Mediterranean*

IV

PRELUDE TO INVASION

Our Frontier in Africa

IN the absence of a positive, authorized policy our diplomacy, when the war began, labored under heavy handicaps. In Europe it encouraged resistance to the Germans without being able to offer to nations fighting for their lives much more than moral support and the vague hope of possible eventual military assistance if they could hold out long enough. In the Far East it faced the dilemma of denying American strategic materials to Japan at the risk of precipitating her attack on the Dutch East Indies oil region, or of continuing the supplies and strengthening her for the aggression that was to come. In Latin America it had to persuade the many doubters that, although Britain was fighting with her back to the wall and we were neutral, someone somehow was going to defeat Hitler.[1]

As for France, we were in the singular position of propping

---

[1] This was indeed the decisive task of our diplomats and military attachés and good-will emissaries down to the end of 1942. For if he assumed that Germany would win or retain control of the Continent, the Latin American was inclined to see more reason for being on good terms with Germany than for being on good terms with the United States, since Europe was a major market for Latin America. That assumption was hard to shake, especially on the part of the military men who play such a disproportionate rôle in Latin American affairs.

up for two years a defeated nation and spurring her by appeals and threats to sustain a resistance to the Germans which was in our interests but in which we were neither willing nor prepared to participate actively.

Few Americans in 1940 and 1941 perceived clearly the relationship between the French Fleet and American security. But the eyes of our strategists were upon the Mediterranean, where the balance of naval power was uncertain, and upon Africa, where the French-controlled territories formed stepping-stones for air and sea power in the direction of South America.

If Hitler should get those African bases from the French, he would cut off Britain's sea routes to the Far East, thus leaving the United States as the sole defender of the whole Pacific from Alaska to Singapore; and he would be within aerial striking distance of the coasts of South America, whose safety was closely related to the security of the Panama Canal and hence of the United States. It was one of the purposes of our Good Neighbor policy towards Latin America to obtain the assistance of the republics to the south in protecting those coasts.

The Secretary of State, Mr. Cordell Hull, called a meeting of military and naval officials to describe to them the German threat to Africa as he saw it.[2] He told them that, more than ever before, Hitler had the "whip hand among his outlaw associates" and that he might at any time order "a general advance from London to Tokyo in the air, on the sea, and on land." That is, he might strike hard at Britain in an attempt to conquer her while at the same time moving against Egypt and the Suez Canal. Should the Axis gain control of other continents, said Mr. Hull, "they would next concentrate upon perfecting their control of the seas and of the air over the seas and of the world's economy; and they might then be able with ships and planes to strike at the communication lines, the commerce, and the life of this hemisphere."[3]

[2] This took place on October 15, 1940.
[3] In a conversation with Viscount Halifax, the British Ambassador, on July 9, 1941.

After Hitler's invasion of Russia Mr. Hull again emphasized the link between Germany and Japan and the strategic possibilities it might involve. He suggested that the Japanese planned to invade the Indian Ocean, including China, and to move on the Suez Canal, the oil regions of the Persian Gulf, and even the Cape of Good Hope, thereby blocking Britain's trade routes and cutting off many of her supplies.[*] What the United States could do to prevent such a Japanese move would be affected by Britain's position in Europe and the American aid she might need at the same time.

Trade with Ulterior Motives

FOR THESE reasons the attention of American officials was concentrated upon Africa from the moment of the fall of France, and towards the end of 1940 plans were made to keep a still closer watch upon the French territories there which it was feared might fall into Hitler's hands or under his influence. This watch was carefully prepared in connection with — one may even say under the guise of — a trade agreement, and it was maintained until the Allied invasion of those shores, for which it paved the way.

The economic aid rendered to North Africa was never great, being in all less than 10 per cent of what was asked. At that time no other aid could be promised. We operated, so to speak, "on a shoestring." Our visible assets were absurdly small, yet the profits we hoped for were the effective defence of North Africa against Hitler in the interest of the security of the United States.

Our consular and special vice-consular watchers sought to persuade French and Arabs that the United States was arming and that our industrial power would turn the scales in the war. But the thin trickle of American supplies that came

---

[*] This view may seem exaggerated in the light of subsequent events; but it must be remembered that at that time Britain was fighting alone, that her naval power was very thinly spread round the world, and that few felt certain that Russia would be able to prevent Hitler's forces from reaching the Middle East where they might have joined Japan.

mostly in four French ships at irregular intervals, while Germany was overrunning the Balkans and much of Russia and the British were retreating in Libya, was hardly the most eloquent evidence either of our productive resources or of our determination to defeat the then triumphant Hitler. Our consular officers longed for more impressive signs of American power; and Mr. Robert D. Murphy, in charge of our official staff in North Africa, suggested a visit to Casablanca by an American naval squadron to counteract German influence.[5] The British at various times proposed that Casablanca and Dakar be seized to insure their safety from the Germans. That seemed logical, but it could not be done until after the Japanese attack on Pearl Harbor.

Meanwhile it might almost be said that we were holding North Africa with a few tankers of oil and a few tons of tea and sugar, fighting Hitler with coal, tar, cotton cloth, binder twine, spare machine parts — and whatever broader implications those goods might convey regarding the potential but still latent power of the United States. Those implications did not greatly impress officials of the British Ministry of Economic Warfare, who winced and grumbled at every ton of oil that passed through the blockade. Nor did it seem a huge contribution to America's war economy to bring from North Africa cork and tartar, red squill and coriander, six tons of thyme, two tons of rosebuds, 1.25 tons of perfume essence, 45 tons of horehound, 59 tons of snails.

But none of those products, domestic or exotic, was carried across the Atlantic for economic or gastronomic or esthetic reasons. The purpose of the trade was political, and indirectly military. The supplies sent to North Africa had a certain value as evidence of American solicitude and as a factor, however small, in preventing social unrest that might have weakened the French control there. But the motive in sending them was above all to enable the United States to keep a close watch on that region — on Germans, French, Arabs, ships, railways, armaments, power plants, hospitals, and in fact everything that might be important to the defence

[5] Message sent in April 1941.

of North Africa by diplomacy or possibly one day by an American military force.

The watch was kept by Mr. Murphy, the regular consuls and a dozen special vice-consuls authorized by the trade agreement. The vice-consuls, some of whom were Army and Navy officers chosen for this work, were to inspect ships and railways to make sure our goods did not go to the Germans. They were also to keep an eye on many non-economic activities. They became in effect an advance guard for the expeditionary force, though when they were sent none knew there would be an invasion since the United States was not at war.

Support for Weygand

THIS ADVENTURE in diplomacy may be said to have begun on November 15, 1940, when Mr. Murphy, counselor of Embassy at Vichy, was ordered to Algiers, where he arrived on December 18. General Weygand had gone there in October from France as Delegate General of the Vichy Government assigned to do what he could to protect North Africa. That purpose evoked lively American sympathy, and it was Mr. Murphy's mission to assist.

Word had come a few weeks previously that General Noguès, the French Resident General in Morocco, feared that the half-dozen German divisions then reported on the Franco-Spanish frontiers might move into Morocco. In view of the demobilization in French Morocco, there seemed little to stop the Germans if they came. The French believed that Germany desired control of Morocco, especially the naval and air bases there. Meanwhile the French had sent word through American intermediaries that North Africa badly needed oils and gasoline, normally imported from France but now unobtainable, as well as coal, mining machinery, spare parts of all kinds, sugar, tea, coffee, textiles, and consumers' goods generally. There were two tankers at Casablanca able to transport 18,000 tons of oil, and there were said to be available in Morocco for export 58,000 metric tons of manganese, 90,000 tons of iron ore, 25,000 tons of lead,

PRELUDE TO INVASION 39

2,860 tons of cobalt, 50 tons of graphite, 27 tons of vanadium. If the United States would not trade with North Africa, North Africa would be compelled to send those products to Germany. But imports from the United States might prevent social and political trouble in North Africa and so help to maintain French authority there.

General Weygand thought economic relief a factor in preserving the territories for the French Empire, and that by permitting moderate shipments from the United States to pass the blockade, the British could help to prevent economic paralysis. The impression was that Weygand would not break with Vichy but desired to unite the North African territories under his authority to save them from the Germans. He was reported to have expressed amazement at the British defence of their island during the heavy German air attacks of September, and to believe that Britain now could hold out. That conviction at any rate seemed to spread with Weygand's arrival in North Africa, and it served to encourage those who thought economic aid was politically and strategically worth while. The British Government itself seemed willing to consider such a policy. Britain needed phosphates for fertilizer and desired to get them from Morocco in return for grain, tea, and sugar, which the Arabs needed. Britain seemed prepared to relax the blockade for shipments to and from the United States so long as this involved no payments to France and no re-exportation of the imported goods.

The American view was that there was a chance that the hard-pressed Vichy Government might move to North Africa, that the Germans might menace Tunis and that Weygand would at least not co-operate with them, and that Weygand's hands should be upheld by economic aid. The United States was considering sending food to unoccupied France also, in spite of criticism from Britain, in the belief that support for Pétain and Weygand might prevent their replacement by more pro-German leaders.

This American policy of stiffening the Vichy régime in order to forestall more complete domination of France by the Germans never met more than reluctant and qualified British agreement. Having taken a sterner line towards the French Fleet, having tried unsuccessfully to seize Dakar, the British had incurred the special enmity of the French Navy and of Admiral Darlan and had no official relations with Vichy or North Africa. It was a natural consequence of their differing relations with Vichy that the American Government strove to sustain and encourage such resistance as seemed possible on the part of the defeated French, while the British made less distinction between Frenchmen who collaborated willingly and those who did so unwillingly. The British were the more insistent upon their blockade because it could not be complete and they were reluctant to do anything to weaken it further. They were prepared to consider exchanges with North Africa and between North Africa and unoccupied France, but only with strict safeguards against the accumulations of French balances abroad and the transfer of incoming goods to Germany.

The failure of British negotiations for phosphates from Morocco in exchange for green tea and sugar was attributed in London to interference by the Germans, who themselves wanted phosphates. Thereupon Britain granted credits for tea and sugar to Spain in exchange for some of the phosphates which Spain desired from Morocco for her 1941 harvest. The British pointed out that British ships were held in Moroccan ports under orders of the German Armistice Commission there, and they wanted those ships before opening trade negotiations. There had been no trade between Britain and Morocco since the French armistice, and the British were unwilling to reopen it unconditionally.

The British did not share the apparent confidence in Washington that Weygand would oppose the Germans, and they were somewhat doubtful about strengthening North Africa, where they feared the French might turn against Britain. A large part of the products being shipped to Marseille from North Africa were reaching German and Italian hands, British naval power being insufficient to stop this trade. But the British Government was willing for the United States to reopen trade with Morocco, including Tangier and Tunisia, if

British ships detained there were released, if American officials were stationed at ports and railway points to prevent shipments from the United States reaching the enemy, and if excessive stocks were not acquired in North Africa. The British suggested that their consuls might return to North Africa.

The Americans conceived North Africa as a quite separate problem and did not relate it, as the British did, to the question of food for unoccupied France or to conciliation of Spain and Portugal. They argued that if the Germans occupied and exploited Morocco, as they apparently desired to do, they would be in a position to influence Spain and Portugal and to threaten the South Atlantic. Therefore, without insisting upon the release of the British ships or the return of British consuls, the American authorities accepted the agreement made between General Weygand and Mr. Murphy on February 26, 1941, for trade between the United States and North Africa. But that agreement embodied the other safeguards proposed by the British — that excessive stocks would not result, that the imported goods would be consumed in North Africa and neither they nor similar goods would be reexported in any form, that the American Government would appoint control agents in ports and on railways, that if reexportation took place the whole agreement would terminate. The United States agreed to release funds from the "frozen" French credits in this country to finance purchases for North Africa. This agreement did not include petroleum products, which were subject to special permits for each cargo.[6]

The Vichy Government likewise accepted these terms and

[6] General Weygand's memorandum of the conversation between him and Mr. Murphy, signed by them both and ratified by Vichy on March 10 and by Washington on June 3, follows in its essentials:

(1) Que le ravitaillement de l'Afrique du Nord n'aura pas pour résultat la constitution de stocks excessifs, (2) que des dispositions seront prises en vu d'assurer que ces produits et les produits similaires seront consommés en Afrique du Nord Française et ne seront réexportés sous aucune forme, (3) qu'en vu de réaliser ce qui précède, le Gouvernement Américain sera autorisé à designer des représentants chargés du contrôle dans les ports et sur les chemins de fer, (4) qu'en cas de violation de l'accord relatif à la non-réexportation, la co-opération écono-

submitted a list of urgent requirements of North Africa.⁷ General Weygand appointed M. Paul Guérin, Assistant Director of the Moroccan Railways, as his representative in Washington for this trade. M. Guérin had gone to Washington in September 1940 to seek American supplies.

Under the Neutrality Act American ships were unable to enter the war zone, and the Germans in the armistice had obtained control of the French merchant fleet. So the four ships used in this trade were French vessels that had taken refuge in American ports prior to the armistice and were released for service through an understanding with the Germans via Vichy. Washington had decided that the *Léopold L.D.* and the *Ile de Ré* might carry flour to France if they returned immediately to American ports. Vichy agreed. But when the ships reached Marseille the Germans refused to release them unless two others were permitted to sail from the United States. The *Ile de Noirmoutier* and the *Ile d'Ouessant* were therefore released at New York and Baltimore to proceed to Casablanca. These four continued to move between North Africa and the United States, two always being in North Africa while the other two were in American ports. Thus two of the four were always within reach of the Germans.⁸ The *Aldébaran* substituted for one round trip.

British Misgivings

BY THIS time — March 1941 — the British were alarmed by Admiral Darlan's threat to convoy French supply ships across the Atlantic and from French African ports, which they

mique entre les Etats-Unis et l'Afrique Française du Nord prendra fin automatiquement et définitivement.

Il fut entendu que le Gouvernement Américain est disposé à faciliter le ravitaillement du Maroc français ět aussi de l'Algérie et de la Tunisie en produits essentiels, ainsi qu'a débloquer à cet effet les fonds nécessaires sur les avoirs français aux Etats-Unis, si les conditions précédentes sont respectées.

⁷ These included 30,000 metric tons of sugar, 15,000 metric tons of gasoline, 12,000 metric tons of gas oil, Diesel oil, and light fuel oil, 2,000 metric tons of lubricating oil, 60,000 metric tons of coal.

⁸ Léon Marchal: *Vichy* (New York, Macmillan, 1943).

feared might cause open war between Britain and France, and by German infiltration into North Africa, which they thought might be followed by a German military move from Tripoli to take Spain in the rear and compel her to join Germany. The British authorities questioned whether our trade agreement would suffice to stiffen Vichy's feeble resistance to German demands. They proposed instead that the French request for 5,000,000 to 8,000,000 bushels of wheat for unoccupied France be granted on condition that guarantees be given against re-exportation, that American and British observers be permitted in unoccupied France and North Africa, and that Marshal Pétain put a stop to German infiltration into North Africa. The British also suggested that the French warships at Toulon be moved to Casablanca or Dakar, and they urged the United States to send as many observers as possible to North Africa to check German influence and encourage armed resistance by the French.

Since the Prime Minister believed Darlan to be an enemy of Britain and to be completely in the power of the Germans, this proposal seemed designed to challenge the Vichy Government by asking it to do what was impossible. Yet the British seemed to expect that American observers and even British consuls might be permitted in North Africa. They apparently suspected that their proposal of a wheat ration for France would fail but that the United States, adhering to its policy of treating North Africa as a problem apart, would proceed with the Weygand-Murphy agreement. That, at any rate, is what happened; and the British were pleased, or at least consoled, by the presence of American observers to watch the movement of goods within and out of North Africa, and by the American promise that products sent to North Africa would be bought only in the United States and only with the consent of the United States Government. They seem to have overestimated the proportions of German infiltration and to have underestimated the possibilities of the American method of counter-infiltration. Being at war, as we were not, they attached greater urgency to the protection of Africa and were loath to take chances. The danger was closer to them than to us, and they were naturally more impatient.

The British thought our officials overestimated Vichy's freedom of action. Their interpretation of the situation in April 1941 was that Germany's armistice with France, based upon the assumption of a British defeat, had ceased to satisfy Germany, who now sought bases in North Africa and might take them by force. The arrival of German troops in Tripoli lent substance to this view. The British contended that Pétain's bargaining power, such as it was, was declining rapidly and that the French Fleet had lost its value to him. They thought Weygand would be unable, even if willing, to defend the French Empire; that in any case economic aid was not enough and that the time had come for Britain and America to seize Dakar and Casablanca.

From London came the suggestion on April 29, 1941, that only the United States could save the situation, and Washington was urged at least to send warships to Dakar and Casablanca for their steadying effect. The British authorities feared that Pétain would be unable to stop German penetration into the French Empire and that the Germans would move through unoccupied France and Spain. They wanted, through American channels, to warn Pétain and to urge the French to resist in France and in North Africa while there was yet time. Our officials thought such a warning would become known to the Germans immediately and might precipitate the dangers the British feared. How could Pétain resist, they asked, when the Fleet was at the disposal of Darlan? They advised playing for time, meanwhile stiffening Pétain as much as possible.

A similar sense of urgency animated Mr. Murphy in North Africa who had made seven days earlier the same proposal the British made — the sending of American warships to Dakar and Casablanca. He reported that the British reverses in Libya had weakened the morale which Weygand had built up among French and Arabs in North Africa, and he thought such a naval move would counteract the growing German influence there.

Meanwhile the economic program was still in the preliminary stages. The twelve control officers, who were to watch the movement of goods in North Africa and to report on German activities there, had been designated. The first crossed in April, others following in May and June. The Treasury had agreed, on April 18, 1941, to release $7,000,000 of frozen French funds in this country ($6,000,000 of French Government funds and $1,000,000 of the funds of the State Bank of Morocco) to finance purchases for North Africa. By April 23 a list of goods to be permitted to pass through the British blockade had been agreed upon by the Americans and the British.

On the same day that the Treasury promised to melt the frozen funds, word came from Vichy that some 200 more Germans were moving into North Africa, and four days later it was reported that Germany was increasing her Armistice Commission in North Africa from 65 to 200, ostensibly to replace some 450 members of the Italian Armistice Commission who were departing. The British thereupon suggested holding up the supplies which were to be sent from New York.

Shortly afterward — on May 15 — Marshal Pétain made a declaration in favor of collaboration with Germany, which brought from President Roosevelt on the same day a public statement warning Vichy against a "voluntary alliance" with France's conquerors which would let Germany get the French North African territories "with the menace which that would involve to the peace and safety of the Western Hemisphere."[9] Meanwhile the second tanker of oil sailed for North Africa in May, the first having gone in March. On July 1 the first of the cargo ships, the *Ile de Noirmoutier*, left New York

[9] To the French Ambassador, M. Henry-Haye, Secretary Hull on May 20, 1941, said that although about May 4 Marshal Pétain had assured the United States that the armistice terms would be maintained, the impression then abroad was that the pro-Hitler officials of the French government had got control. He said that military aid to Germany beyond the armistice terms was an attempt indirectly to "slit the throat of the United States."

for Casablanca carrying sugar, condensed milk, cotton goods and other supplies; and on July 6 the *Ile d'Ouessant* cleared at Baltimore with 7,000 tons of coal.

Africa and Pearl Harbor

BY AUGUST 1941, the atmosphere was one of doubt and pessimism. Such qualified confidence as there had been in the men of Vichy, even in Weygand, had dwindled almost to nothing. In April it had been expected by some officials in Washington that Weygand, having apparently become more friendly towards the Americans and the British, would fight the Germans if they crossed into French North Africa, for he had requested munitions from the United States. But by August the same officials practically gave up hope. They even suggested that Weygand might join the Germans, as French officials had joined the Japanese when the latter entered French Indo-China.

From North Africa the official reports were that the French, including Weygand, were growing cool towards us because the economic aid had not come in the expected quantities. Our observers there reported that the French regretted their armistice now that they saw Britain was not beaten, but that they "have no fight in them." Still it was deemed desirable to keep the door open to the American observers, whose uses were more than merely economic, and for this reason to send supplies. But by September 1941 only two ships had reached Casablanca from New York carrying American goods, and only two tankers of oil had gone. Meanwhile two shiploads of cork had reached the United States from Casablanca.

Whether related or not to the fact that cargoes of American supplies had at last actually appeared on North African docks, reports in September were that Weygand was growing more independent and using his influence at Vichy against the German desire for bases in Africa. At the same time, via the War Department, came news that the defences of Dakar were being strengthened and the French forces there increased. This was being encouraged by the Germans, who feared an American occupation of Dakar; and the German

Armistice Commission was consequently reported to be giving back to the French some of the war material it had confiscated earlier.

In October 1941, British misgivings about the economic plan seemed to be growing. There was criticism in Parliament. Permission for many commodities was made subject to conditions difficult for the French to meet. Argument about details of quotas caused long delays. Oil caused the greatest suspicions, for the British were fighting Rommel and Libya adjoined French Tunis. Yet some in Washington thought the British were seeking to link the economic scheme too closely with their war policy and to use it to wring concessions from the French. After all, there were American observers to examine French ships and railways to prevent the American oil reaching the Germans. Washington wanted to expedite the supplies.

The British suspicions seemed borne out by the dismissal of Weygand, under German pressure, on November 18, and the American authorities ordered the supplies held up pending indications as to how far Vichy now intended to go in yielding to the Germans.

But the sins of Vichy were forgotten nineteen days later when — as Mr. A. A. Berle, Assistant Secretary of State, put it — the Axis dropped the other shoe and Japan attacked the United States. Little attention was then paid to the four French cargo ships and three tankers that were sustaining our intelligence system in North Africa.

Yet the map of the Atlantic remained unchanged. Africa retained its strategic importance, which indeed was illumined by the glare of the fires in Hawaii. We were at war with Japan, Germany and Italy; and our Navy, with eight battleships put out of action, had two oceans to guard. Our observers in North Africa became more useful than before, and soon the cargo ships began moving again.

In January 1942 the North Africa trade committee meeting in the Department of State received from Vichy the report that the two ships that had reached Casablanca from New York could now depart again, contributing cork and tartaric acid to the American war economy and bringing back coal, tea, condensed milk, cotton piece goods, second-hand clothing, nails, baling wire, and sugar.

The German Armistice Commission had generously told the French that the ships might deliver the indicated cargoes to Germany's new enemy. But we must send them back promptly, said the French — or the Germans speaking through the French. Otherwise the North Africans would think we were letting them down, while the Germans would argue that with no cargoes to supervise we needed no official observers. Thus Americans and Germans, for their respective reasons, were in agreement that the ships should continue, and the two that were in New York soon sailed with 5,000 metric tons of refined sugar, 1,497 tons of cotton textiles, and other goods.

Britain now agreed, in spite of her former misgivings, that there were political and military gains to be had from the American policy of maintaining relations with the Vichy Government, although Britain was committed to a different course. She approved the work of our official observers as set forth in their reports, and agreed that the trade should go on so that those officers might remain until the time came for military operations in North Africa. But criticism of our policy in Britain continued, and the story was circulated that some of the gasoline we had sent to North Africa had been sold to Marshal Rommel. This caused bitter resentment in Washington, where officials felt sure that the presence of the observers averted any such possibility.

Yet it was clear that the German Afrika Corps was getting gasoline through French North Africa, whatever its original source, and getting food and trucks as well. The United States Government bluntly told Vichy that unless this traffic was stopped French North Africa would get no more petroleum from us.[10]

---

[10] Members of the Near Eastern Division of the State Department, including Mr. Henry S. Villard, assistant chief in charge of African affairs, are firmly convinced that the oil Rommel received did not come from the United States and that no proof was available at any time of

PRELUDE TO INVASION 49

The Vichy reply on April 8, 1942, was ingenious. It was that if we would sell petroleum to North Africa, none would go to the Germans. But we had suspended the trade agreement when Weygand was dismissed; so when the Germans happened at that moment to ask for "certain deliveries" of oil for Marshal Rommel's tanks, Vichy could not refuse on the ground of the agreement with us, as it had done in March 1941 when the Italians had asked for 5,000 metric tons of gasoline from Algeria. Vichy now turned to the Germans and explained that the Americans were about to resume shipments and therefore Vichy would like to sell Rommel only 3,600 metric tons instead of the greater amount he had requested. To this the Germans agreed, and Vichy whispered to us that it hoped to cut this down to the 1,500 tons already delivered — on the assumption, of course, that we would send along the loaded tankers from New York. This, at any rate, was Vichy's story as told to our Embassy. (Oil, though not included in the trade agreement, was sent, like the products covered by the agreement, on the understanding it would not be re-exported.)

The trade with North Africa was now regarded as a kind of economic warfare; so that when Vichy descended to the level of accepting Pierre Laval as Prime Minister, we nevertheless renewed the trade, though imposing conditions befitting the new conception of its purposes. Not only did we want to keep the Germans out of North Africa: we wanted to keep North African strategic minerals out of Germany. Washington thought cobalt and other minerals might be shipped to the United States. Vichy said the German Armistice Commission would not permit this, but it agreed to "freeze" existing stocks and see that none went to Germany. When the trade agreement was suspended, the Vichy authorities had agreed to ship 500 metric tons of cobalt to Germany, and the Germans had asked for 1,000 tons more by June 1942. Vichy, however, agreed to stop before shipping the 1,000 tons. The

violation by the French of their accord with us. They agree, however, that petroleum was sent from Marseille to Algiers and Tunis and there released to the Germans.

50   A PREFACE TO PEACE

annual North African production of cobalt averaged about 6,000 metric tons. It is used with tungsten and molybdenum for hardening steel.

By mid-1942 a new purpose began to take definite shape. At the meetings in the State Department to push the French vessels back and forth through the red tape, allusions were made to the possibility that these preparations might help save American lives. The economic-warfare specialists, British and American, still talked of keeping North Africa poor and disorganizing its transport to prevent goods from getting to France and the Germans, and as late as September representatives of the Office of War Information wanted to repack a shipment of sugar and tea in order to apply American labels for their propaganda value. Admiral Leahy then indicated that we were playing for far greater stakes, that meanwhile the object was to placate the French and not argue with them. Plans for the invasion were then being made.[11]

North Africa's Aid to Germany

AT THIS time — August 1942 — a summary was made of the estimated economic value that North Africa had had for the Axis in 1941. From those territories via France the Axis was believed to have received in that year more than 2,000,000 metric tons of phosphates, more than 50,000 metric tons of manganese ore, some 6,000 metric tons of zinc, 300,000 tons of fruits and vegetables, 5,000 tons of hides, 6,000 tons of wool (desperately needed by Germany in her first winter of war in Russia). Germany had received small but important amounts of cobalt and molybdenum. Her iron-ore shipments from

[11] On August 3, 1942, at a meeting in the office of Dean Acheson, Assistant Secretary of State, attended by representatives of the State Department, the Treasury, and the Board of Economic Warfare, Admiral Leahy appeared with an order from the White House written in ink and signed simply "F. D. R." Mr. Acheson held it in his hand as he introduced the Admiral. The order was to hasten shipments of consumers' goods to North Africa as a means of producing a favorable effect upon the population there. It represented part of the plans for the invasion in the following November.

North Africa had not been great in 1941 but by mid-1942 were 16,000 tons a month, though 50,000 tons a month had been agreed upon in January 1942. At Marseille, Germany had requisitioned an average of about 80 per cent of all imports, 100 per cent of the minerals and dried vegetables, 80 per cent of the cereals. The war against Russia had increased German interest in North African supplies, and all the wool clip and the leather stocks for 1942 were being requisitioned by the French authorities under pressure of the German Armistice Commission.

From French North Africa Marshal Rommel's army had received wheat, wine, olive oil, livestock, vegetables, fruits, petroleum products requisitioned from French military stocks, trucks from France, second-hand motor cars, and construction materials shipped from France to North Africa and then to Libya. Oil from Germany and Italy for Rommel was sent in French ships to North Africa, whence it moved eastward to the German army in Libya. Large shipments of trucks from Marseille to Algiers, thence to Libya, indicated that the Germans were sending them through France and across the Mediterranean in French ships. In March and April 1942, thirty-seven ships left France for North Africa carrying partial cargoes of war materials; and a total of 103 French ships were known to have made 169 voyages from French Mediterranean ports to North Africa loaded with armored vehicles, armor plate, munitions, and even freight cars for Rommel. Italian vessels up to 500 tons were admitted into Tunisian ports, flying sometimes the French or the Tunisian flag. Most of 302 motor vehicles unloaded at Tunis between January and May 1942 were Italian trucks, some containing small tanks. Sixty railways trucks were reported to have been shipped to Tunis containing light tanks for Rommel.[12]

[12] Mr. Harry A. Woodruff, a member of the State Department's staff who acted as a control officer in Tunis from January 1941 until November 1942, tells me he questions the reports about railway trucks, munitions, and freight cars having been sent to Rommel's forces. He says that either from or through Tunis the German army received a large number of motor vehicles, some from the French Army, some sent from France, but mostly from North Africa. He estimates the to-

These facts seemed to remove whatever doubts may have remained as to the meaning of "collaboration" between the Vichy régime and the Germans, who probably did not have the forces and transport facilities for an invasion of those vast territories but got from them a substantial amount of economic aid apart from the use of French ships to pass the British naval patrols.

In February 1942, the United States learned of a Vichy agreement to send in French ships to Tunisia materials for the Axis forces, including fuel oil. Washington asked for assurances that Vichy would discontinue this kind of aid. Vichy replied that it would not give military aid or permit the use of French ships "for purposes of war." Washington then asked that Vichy promise not to transport fuel, food, trucks, etc., to the Axis in North Africa, whatever their original source. Vichy agreed, save for the food supplies and trucks then in transit or soon to be delivered, thus admitting that this type of military aid was even then being rendered to the Axis.

Friends in Totalitaria

ROMMEL'S ADVANCE into Egypt and the German advance in Russia in 1942 perhaps stimulated the trend towards collaboration in North Africa. At any rate reports from North Africa to Washington told of growing hostility towards the Allies, of German and Vichy propaganda to the effect that an Allied victory would bring Bolshevism. Axis reports that the United States was particularly friendly to the Jews and had agreed that Lebanon should become a Jewish national home apparently turned French and Arabs against us. In June 1942, Noguès, Resident General of Algeria, told Mr. Murphy he would co-operate with the pro-German Vichy Premier, Pierre Laval, and that it would be folly for the Allies to land forces in North Africa. French Fascist organizations — the

---

tal at 1,500 to 2,000. He says Rommel got wheat from Tunisia, paid for in France by Italian wheat, and that from Zarzis the Germans got 400 tons of olive oil. They took all the supplies they could get from North Africa.

Service d'Ordre de la Légion and the Parti Populaire Français — formed a kind of Gestapo in Morocco which searched out and informed upon Allied sympathizers and threatened a reign of terror. Many supporters of General de Gaulle, the Fighting French leader, were arrested. Axis propaganda seemed to be effectively reaching all classes. It was therefore hardly surprising that it was the troops in Morocco who offered the greatest resistance to the American expeditionary force the following November.

Yet Mr. Murphy continued to regard the majority of the French in North Africa as friends or potential friends of the United States, in spite of the British doubts. The Germans seemed to share Mr. Murphy's view, or at any rate to fear we had too many friends there; for reports from Vichy told of German concern about our observers in North Africa who were suspected of making an alarming number of contacts with persons hostile to Germany, and the German-controlled Parisian press violently denounced the American consular officers.

On October 29, 1942, the North African Trade Committee in Washington discussed reports that in August and September the Germans were getting petroleum, even aviation gasoline, from French North Africa in apparent violation of the Vichy Government's promises to the United States. But the topic had now become purely historic, for nine days later Allied troops landed on North African shores and our troubled and artificial relations with Vichy — with what Secretary Hull later referred to as "the so-called Vichy Government" — were at an end.

The trade agreement had done its bit. Between July 1, 1941, and August 11, 1942, ten shiploads of American goods, apart from oils, had moved to North Africa and ten shiploads had come to this country.[13] Throughout that period the Vichy officials in North Africa were engaged in traffic for the Germans as well as with us, but it is believed the Germans received in 1942 fewer of the strategic materials which they

[13] For details of cargoes carried see Appendix A at end of this volume.

got in such substantial amounts from North Africa in 1941. Meanwhile our observers had traveled over the French territories, kept in touch with their populations, made invaluable technical and strategic reports, and found a goodly number of Frenchmen who were ready to risk their jobs and their skins to help the Allies beat the Axis. It was for this that the ships had been kept moving, by fits and starts, over protests of the skeptics and to the recurrent rhythm of renewed assurances from Vichy. Their work is to be measured not in tons of goods but in the less ponderable but far more vital service rendered by the observing vice-consuls, and by the regular consuls and their chief, Mr. Murphy.

These officers acknowledge particularly the assistance of General Weygand, who they think checked German penetration; Admiral Fenard; the Governor General of Morocco, M. Ives Chatel; Generals Béthouart and Mast, who risked their lives and careers to aid the Allies in Morocco, the leaders of the Youth Camps who mobilized their boys to help the Allied landing operations, and many anonymous Frenchmen who may have been Vichy employees or officials but were not Lavals.

One result of the enforced conformity of the totalitarian state is that within the ranks of the ruling groups the opposition continues, surreptitious yet irrepressible. Dissent is not abolished; it is merely reduced to silent deviousness. So it was with the Vichy régime, which imitated the Nazi state. Among its officials were many who aided the American agents to move about North Africa, who always found gasoline for them even when it was scarcest, who found seats for them in airplanes, who guided them to friends and away from enemies, who steadily practiced passive resistance to the Germans — the only resistance they could practice. Vichy officials were taken out of Africa because of their friendliness to Americans (doubtless under German pressure), but those who replaced them were just as friendly though a trifle more discreet. The agents soon discovered who was really Vichy and who was pseudo-Vichy. They found, for example, that the staff of the aviation company Air France in North Africa, though Vichy-controlled, were pro-American to a man and proved it, as did other Frenchmen.

Or, rather, they were pro-French in the sense that they were ready to act when it seemed that action against the conqueror might be worth while; and it was one of the main tasks of the American agents to persuade the isolated, Vichy-misled French population that Germany had not won and would not win the war, and that the Allies brought them hope.

Thus did our diplomacy operate in a strategic region in that curious interval of transition between neutrality and belligerency, when we were not yet at war but were no longer neutral; when we were fighting against the Germans with every weapon but the military; when we were openly arming Britain, trying to stiffen the French and publicly proclaiming that German penetration into French Africa would be a menace to us, though we had not yet reached the point of taking up arms against that menace.

Few Americans then understood, and few understand today, the game our State Department was playing in that equivocal period when we seemed to be feeding North Africa with oil while the Germans were in turn drawing upon it for supplies. It looked odd to those who could not see and who could not be told the purpose of the policy, necessarily shrouded in secrecy. It is an historic episode that is worth describing and emphasizing today for two reasons. It illustrates the handicaps under which our foreign relations had to be conducted because we were not as yet prepared either mentally or physically for adequate defence of our interests. It also reveals the extent of those interests in terms of the geography of defence.

V

OUR FRENCH ALLIES

We Collide with the French Problem

THE moment our troops landed upon the beaches of North Africa we encountered two problems, one political, the other military. They were so closely linked as to be inseparable and to form in reality a single problem. But they had to be arbitrarily divided in practice and must be so divided for purposes of discussion.

The military problem was solved fairly expeditiously, for it was mainly physical and manageable. The political problem, less ponderable or measurable, is not solved as these lines are written, and indeed it may never be really solved. For it involved such issues as freedom and authority which have divided modern France ever since the Revolution and have divided her still more since her defeat and enslavement, which were made possible largely by that very absence of social and national unity.

These issues lie behind the conflict of persons which, like the secondary plot of a play, developed along with the military conflict in and from North Africa and seemed likely to continue long after the military struggle had ended. For these or similar issues will arise again and again as occupied territories are liberated and as Allied power is extended provisionally to the Continent of Europe. They will arise wherever new states take form or old ones revive, in friendly or hostile countries. They will play their part in peace-making and reconstruction, and our policy towards the French will be cited as an example and precedent which will affect our relations with France and with Europe.

North Africa is not Europe but a colonial appendage of Europe, though Algeria is technically a part of metropolitan

France. It has been assumed in this country that the Vichy régime in North Africa was simply a projection there of the Nazi system. In some ways it was. Yet the "national revolution" of Pétain, associated with the Nazi system because it came into power in a time of defeat and "collaboration," was not a Nazi or a Fascist system. It represented old, and even antiquated, French conceptions of a highly Catholic state, corporate in form, authoritarian and anti-parliamentarian, but exalting the family and religion and tradition. In this sense it was the antithesis of the Nazi state, which opposed family and church in the interest of a kind of nationalization of youth and of religion. The Pétainist state more closely resembled in its inspiration the older, religious, paternalistic community preserved in French Quebec, a much more old-fashioned and more Latin type of authoritarianism.

It has become customary to call this conflict ideological, and so it was. But in using that term one should remember that there is an authoritarianism of the Right as well as of the Left, and that both are enemies of the now perhaps old-fashioned liberal democracy which has been the "ideology" of Americans. Leaders proclaiming the rights of man, nowadays chiefly his economic rights, are not necessarily averse to using the technique of propaganda and organization and concentrated power characteristic of Fascism, which itself professed to be a revolution on behalf of the proletariat. Americans were amazed to find in North Africa Frenchmen who, for various reasons, were pro-Nazi and even pro-German, and it seems not at all unlikely that equally startling phenomena will appear as German power recedes and the curtain rises on the post-war drama which will emerge.

In the shock caused by the transaction with Admiral Francois Darlan, in the controversy that arose between the partisans of General Henri-Honoré Giraud and General Charles de Gaulle, military issues were the immediate stakes. But, circumscribe them as we might, these issues also touched the future of France, the future of Europe, and the future of American foreign relations. It was a mistake to define our policy as if it had nothing to do with these broader questions.

Military versus *Political War*

Two THESES confronted each other, often in sharp opposition. One was the military thesis, simple, limited, narrow in scope and immediate in its urgency; the thesis that the war came first, that nothing whatever should be permitted to hamper military operations, that political questions must take second place in importance and in time, that the future of France, about which the French professed such concern, required above all the military victory which was the sole aim of the High Command. To the responsible military authorities, and to the political authorities in Washington who supported them, it seemed incredible that the French should not fully accept this view of the primacy and the urgency of driving the Axis out of North Africa and should not be willing to suspend political strife pending that achievement.

The opposing thesis, which may be called the political, was that the democratic character of the war must be accentuated even while it was in progress; that we were fighting not only the Axis armies but also the Axis mentality within French North Africa. This must be made clear, it was argued, to advance the unity and win the support of the democratic forces fighting underground within France and Europe, and to reassure Europeans and skeptical Americans that our aims in the war really were democratic. Doubts had arisen or been revived in some minds by our acceptance of Admiral Darlan as an instrument of military success, an act which was interpreted by the critical to imply possible further dealings with Fascist-minded leaders, transactions reaching beyond the military sphere.

It was a part of this thesis that our good name in Europe and the purity of our cause required that we dismiss or have dismissed the military and civil officers in North Africa who had served under the Pétain régime, some of whom had resisted the Allied landings and all of whom were regarded as untrustworthy associates of the democracies. We were urged to wipe out the Vichy laws and practices and to facilitate the transition from a semi-authoritarian system to a republican one. These were the professed aims of General de Gaulle, and advocacy of such a course was associated in many minds with the placing of General de Gaulle in power in North Africa instead of General Giraud, who had been taken there by the American Army to command the French forces in co-operation with the Allies and who, after the assassination of Admiral Darlan, acted as chief of the civil authorities.

Thus the political thesis came at once into sharp conflict with the military thesis. General Eisenhower, the American Commander-in-Chief of the Allied forces in that theater — advised in political affairs by Mr. Murphy, representing the President and the State Department — not only insisted upon retaining General Giraud; he also opposed the dismissal in the middle of a military campaign of the Governor of Algeria, the Resident General of Morocco, and scores of civil and military officers even though many had obeyed, and apparently in some cases also admired, Marshal Pétain. To some of the General's advisers it appeared that de Gaulle and his supporters — some of whom were Americans and British — proposed nothing less than a political revolution behind the military lines. They wanted to dismiss from office many who, whatever their political philosophy, were keeping order and maintaining civil life and labor along the communication line vital to the Allied forces sent out to fight the Germans thousands of miles from their home bases. To a soldier nothing is quite so important as the line of communications upon which lives depend, and to the military mind nothing could seem more fantastic than pressure at that critical moment for a political purge of officials who could not readily be replaced in those colonial territories where trained Europeans were not numerous.

The soldier was not inclined to inquire into the political creeds or the past records of officers who were doing their jobs, which he thought was all that mattered. Even those Frenchmen who had fought against Americans were welcomed as allies afterward, and the fact that they then were satisfactorily fighting Germans seemed more important than that earlier some had fought Americans with equal courage.

The de Gaullists, on the other hand, were inclined to draw a sharp line from June 18, 1940, the date of the appeal for an armistice, and to judge every Frenchman by his subsequent behavior. If he had ever followed or accepted Pétain, he was suspect unless he could prove he had acted under pressure or in the interests of Frenchmen. The de Gaullists displayed a doctrinaire, revolutionary rigidity which inevitably conflicted with the more pragmatic standard of the Allied commanders.

Search for a Leader

ALTHOUGH LATER our officials sometimes spoke as if this political argument had no validity because of the supreme importance of military requirements, and President Roosevelt went so far as to say there was no France because 95 per cent of the French people were under the German heel,[1] the fact was that the United States Government had considered the political aspects of the North African venture long before the invasion took place and had examined the possibility of a French leadership which might rally behind it the French patriots of all classes and groups, whatever their past political allegiance.

It was not believed by our officials that General de Gaulle had done this or was capable of doing it. To them he seemed unfitted for the rôle for four reasons: (a) he was regarded as a somewhat artificial figure bearing the trademark of London, where he had been "built up" by the British radio and financed by the British Treasury; (b) he was a military man, and the French for at least two generations had distrusted military men as national leaders; (c) he had been little known in France outside military circles before the war; (d) his usefulness in North Africa was considered limited because his troops, allied with the British, had fought other Frenchmen at Dakar and in Syria, and this had aroused bitter feelings towards him in the French Fleet and parts of the army in North Africa.

[1] President's press conference July 9, 1943.

It was hoped for a time in 1942 that M. Edouard Herriot — former Prime Minister, still nominally President of the Chamber of Deputies, elder statesman, and democrat — might escape to North Africa and there contribute a representative character to the temporary régime that might come into being when those territories should be brought into the war on the Allied side. He could speak for the Chamber, which had been the source of French authority until it was cast aside by the "national revolution" of Vichy, and he could thus establish both a link with the Republic and that thread of legality which is so important to French minds.

But M. Herriot would not go, saying he preferred to stay with his suffering people; and Washington had to rely upon a military leader, who might command the armed forces and so express the French will to drive out the invader but who could not be said to represent France in any other sense. For General Giraud was a man of the Right, an opponent of the Republic, a professional soldier, not a popular political leader. He might speak for the army but not for the nation. In North Africa he could speak for nobody until the army was induced to accept him as its chief after Admiral Darlan had brought peace between the French and Allied forces and paved the way for their co-operation.

The absence of a representative French leader like M. Herriot and the apparently accidental or at least unexpected presence of Darlan, with his power to command the French forces, put an end for the time being to the hope of making North Africa not only a military base but also a provisional and non-partisan rallying point for French patriotism. On the political side the adventure was marred by the lack of representative French leaders universally known and respected in France and by the necessity of dealing instead with agents of a régime that had grown out of France's defeat.

Our first great step towards the liberation of France was thus deprived of its full dramatic quality. Instead of carrying to the French nothing but inspiration and hope, it carried confusion as well. The arrival of the Americans in company with Darlan, who a week earlier had been Hitler's collaborator, required so many explanations that its moral effect was diminished.

These explanations could only be military. Thus we were thrown back upon the strictly military thesis and the doctrine of pure expediency which, however justifiable, were infinitely less inspiring for Frenchmen or Americans than would have been the spectacle of an American expeditionary force appearing upon French soil in association with French leaders whose patriotism had never been doubted.

In obedience to this thesis, our authorities hesitated to suggest or press for the removal of outstanding Vichy officials and even permitted General Giraud to bring in another such official from South America (Marcel Peyrouton) to help him administer Algeria. Consequently the military thesis seemed to involve us in a cynical association with the reactionary French groups dominant in North Africa and with men who had become known previously, both in France and in North Africa, as more or less willing agents of the Axis.

How Much Intervention?

THERE WAS not only the question of undertaking our invasion under suitable political auspices, which unfortunately proved impossible. There was also the question how far we were responsible for the inevitable political repercussions of our military action — how far it was true to say that while we must be responsible in the military sphere, even for what the French did, we left the political field entirely to them.

No military power operating in foreign territory can be indifferent to the political government of that territory while its armed forces are there. In North Africa we were conducting a huge military operation which extended along those shores and beyond them into and across the Mediterranean. We required harbors, communications, and freedom of transit all the way from Casablanca to Algiers and into Tunisia. We required labor and supplies from the region. We therefore required social and political tranquility and should have been obliged to guarantee it with our armed forces if the

French authorities had been unable to do so. From this point of view the political principles or the personal integrity of those in power in North Africa mattered little to us so long as our military requirements were met.

Thus our military position was deemed to entitle us to intervene as far as we thought necessary, even to the point of a straight-out military occupation and military government, as applied in conquered regions. We did not want to assume that responsibility if it could be avoided. We preferred that the French manage their own affairs while we carried on the war, with the assistance, if possible, of their military forces and their political authorities.

But this involved the least possible disturbance in the political field pending the completion of the campaign against the Germans in North Africa; and it was for this reason that General Eisenhower approved political decisions that bewildered Frenchmen, Americans, and Britons — such as the retention in power of General Noguès in Morocco even though he had ordered his men to fire on the Americans, and such as bringing across the Atlantic M. Peyrouton, who had served in a Vichy cabinet (his administrative merit being a knowledge of North Africa). Probably a commanding general in these circumstances would have sanctioned putting in office the greatest of political rogues if he had been convinced that it would further his military campaign. He would, at any rate, have been justified in so doing.

But it would have been inexcusable to intervene beyond the period or scope of our military requirements — either to compromise the freedom of the French people to choose their own government after their liberation, or to sustain totalitarian devices like concentration camps and anti-Semitic legislation merely because they were of no direct military disadvantage to us.

President Roosevelt quickly perceived this. Nine days after the invasion he said that the future French government would be chosen by the French people. At the same time he requested the liberation of all those in North Africa who had been imprisoned "because they opposed the efforts of the

Nazis to dominate the world" and the abrogation of all laws and decrees "inspired by Nazi governments or Nazi ideologists."

In asking these legal measures he was, in a sense, intervening, but intervening against the heritage from an unrepresentative régime established in France and carried into Africa when France was defeated and powerless. Strict non-intervention would have favored this Fascist régime — as it had done in Spain six years earlier.

In that statement the President recognized what we have called above the political thesis. He "understood and approved" the feeling in the United States and Britain that "no permanent arrangement should be made with Admiral Darlan," as he expressed it; and to remove any misunderstanding caused by that "temporary arrangement" he proceeded explicitly to dissociate the Allied cause from the taint of Fascism that had left its mark upon North Africa during two years of Vichy rule.

Yet the President apparently approved, or at any rate did not disapprove, the appointment of M. Peyrouton which took place while Mr. Roosevelt was at Casablanca and in connection with which the President later said he and Mr. Churchill had given some advice. At the same time the President commended a statement to the *News-Chronicle* of London in which General Giraud said he had called in M. Peyrouton because he knew the country, and the General added: "There are good men, decent men, who have worked for Vichy, and it is folly to call them men of Vichy merely because they have held office. Peyrouton is no man of Vichy in that [the invidious] sense. If he had been I should not have sent for him." [2]

Thus it seems clear that while the President recognized and took into account the political thesis that our acts in North Africa must be judged partly by their effects beyond the military sphere and that we must avoid the appearance of extending our Vichy policy into the French Empire, he nevertheless shared the military thesis that we should not condemn and refuse to co-operate with everyone who had taken orders

[2] President's press conference, February 2, 1943.

from Vichy. His attitude was that we might do much on grounds of military expediency that we should not otherwise do, so long as we made it clear that those were the grounds upon which we acted and that the actions were temporary and without bearing upon our policies for the future.

Let us note where this reasoning leads. If we were justified in intervening, as we did, on military grounds or to remove the vestiges of a Fascist régime unrepresentative of France, we should be equally justified in using our influence against any individual or group that might hamper military operations or that might be regarded as unrepresentative. This is what we did in opposing interference with the military command by General de Gaulle and in disapproving his efforts to control the French Committee of National Liberation, which it had been hoped would become a collective rather than an individual instrument.

Some Americans in Algiers protested that the American Government was intervening in French affairs "to frustrate General de Gaulle."[3] That phrase was revelatory: they did not object to intervention as such, but to intervention on what they considered the wrong side. They apparently believed that de Gaulle was representative of France, and to a great extent he was, especially as a symbol of resistance; but neither he nor Giraud had been chosen by the French people, and our government saw no adequate reason to regard either as an authorized representative of France. In a sense the Vichy régime was linked with Germany, de Gaulle with Britain, and Giraud with the United States, since our agents had placed him upon the African scene. At any rate Vichy represented the desperation of a defeated France now ruled by reactionaries, de Gaulle represented the hope of liberation and recovery, Giraud represented the military instrument of that liberation.

The military men were right in saying there would be no free France unless the Germans were beaten. The de Gaullists were right in saying there would be no free French institutions unless the Fascist and reactionary forces among

[3] Dispatch to *New York Times*, published July 8, 1943.

Frenchmen were overcome. The military men were right in saying that a political war ought not to be started in a theater of active military operations. The de Gaullists were right in saying that the political war must be fought out some time, and the sooner the better.

So the two theses really represented two wars that must be fought, one in the military field, one in the political field, to attain the aims for which the democracies were struggling. One can readily define the purposes of the first, but not so readily the purposes of the second. The military war sought to destroy the power of the Axis; that is, of Fascism as a physically conquering force. The political war seeks, let us say, to destroy Fascism as a creed and crusade by creating a more just and free society than the defective society of capitalistic democracy against which Fascism and Communism both had arisen in rebellion.

The conflict in North Africa therefore reflected these two wars, the one advancing triumphantly towards its goal, the other only then gathering momentum. The argument really was as to which of the two should have priority in North Africa. It was settled, so far as it was settled, by permitting the two to move forward at the same time; for on March 7, 1943, while the campaign in Tunisia was still going on, General Giraud as head of the military and civil authority severed all connections with Vichy, and on March 17 he announced that all legislation adopted under the Vichy régime was null and void in North Africa.[4] He also restored in Algeria the munici-

---

[4] One Vichy action which was not annulled was the abrogation of what was known as the Crémieux Decree of 1870 which declared native French Jews in Algeria to be citizens of France. Vichy had suspended that decree in 1940, placing the Jews of Algeria on a legal level with the Moslems. Giraud left this Vichy measure in effect, presumably because Moslems compromised the overwhelming majority of the population and formed some 70 per cent of the armed forces in North Africa, and it was thought undesirable in war-time to risk provoking them by reinstating legislation which had been, in form at least, discriminatory in favor of the native Jews as against the native Moslems. Baron Edouard de Rothschild and others protested vigorously, the Baron saying that Giraud's action "proves the desire of some of the

pal and departmental councils of the Republic. Political prisoners were gradually liberated, though after long delay.

The Shock of Darlan

IT ALARMED many Britons and Americans to find that at the moment we began our first great offensive in the European theater we were still, or again, dealing with the "men of Vichy" whose collaboration with the Germans, whatever the degree or the animating motives, had made them doubtful allies, to say the least. Actually in North Africa our military and civilian agents dealt with both de Gaullists and Vichy officers to prepare for the Allied landing, de Gaullist youths having led the way along the beaches and an arch-Vichy official, Admiral Darlan, having induced the French forces to cease firing. Before dealing with Darlan, General Mark Clark had sought an armistice through General Giraud, only to find that Giraud's orders would not be obeyed while Darlan's would be. In the circumstances, concerned for the lives of American soldiers, General Clark was more interested in the effectiveness of an armistice order than in the moral standing of him who signed it.

Our forces went to North Africa not to fight Vichy, nor to aid Vichy, but to drive the Axis out with the aid of anyone who might help, whatever his political antecedents or preferences. The end justified any, or almost any, means. Darlan was such a means. The French Army was so Vichy-minded or so legally-minded or so loyal to Pétain that its guns could be silenced only by Pétain or his deputy. The political consequences, or rather the psychological repercussions, of the

leading personalities in Algeria to attempt to maintain anti-Semitism in North Africa," which he thought would have a detrimental effect upon the prosecution of the war. (*New York Times,* March 19, 1943.) Meanwhile on April 26, 1943, the Overseas News Agency, New York, published in a copyrighted article the text of what purported to be an order issued to the army by General Giraud in January, 1943, discriminating against Jews in the armed forces. The General did not deny that such an order had been issued. The Committee restored the Crémieux Decree in October, 1943.

pact with Darlan were intensified by the dramatic quality of the situation which his accidental presence in Algiers created. The shock might have been less sharp had General Clark made an armistice with some obscure Vichy commander instead of with the notorious leader in "collaboration." Darlan's presence doubtless simplified that military task and thus saved many lives. But, in the absence of Darlan, General Clark would have dealt with lesser "men of Vichy." Agents of Vichy were in command and with no one else could he deal, save in the underground manner in which Americans dealt with the illegal de Gaullist movement. Therefore the decisive fact was not the presence of Darlan but the Vichy-controlled situation in North Africa.

This being little understood in England and America, the appearance of Darlan, collaborator with the Nazis, in the rôle of collaborator with the Allies bewildered many people. It seemed a blot on our 'scutcheon that our military men had even exchanged words with a Darlan, to say nothing of setting him up, as it seemed, to rule in a region of Allied military activity. Though the President explained that it was an act of pure military expediency without broader implications, some feared that Darlan's position might make him the chief of a provisional government for France and give him power over the French Army.

When Admiral Darlan was assassinated, after rendering in the last six weeks of his life what the War Department regarded as a distinct service to the Allies — whatever his motives may have been — the suspicion that his name had cast over Allied policy, especially American policy, lived after him. General Giraud, who succeeded him, was a soldier and a hero who had escaped from Germany and whose name apparently meant something in France for this reason. But he was regarded as anti-republican and, while not himself a Vichyite, he came to enjoy the support in North Africa of those who had followed Pétain. It had been stipulated before Giraud left France that no "outside elements" should participate with him in the American expedition. This condition formed part of the agreement made in France between Giraud and Mr. Murphy. Admiral Darlan took the same attitude when the question arose, at British suggestion, of bringing General de Gaulle to North Africa. Thus it appeared that in dealing with those two Frenchmen, one a Vichy man, the other not, the American Government had become committed, or further committed, against dealing with de Gaulle in relation to North Africa.

Since General de Gaulle regarded himself, and was regarded by many Britons and Americans, as the principal or the only legitimate voice of the imprisoned French people, this seemed to mean that we dealt with North African French territory without relation to France or independently of France. In one sense this was true, since France had no chosen representatives and we were in any case obliged to treat with the authorities actually in control in Africa, legitimate or not, representative or not. We were not able to deal with France. We assumed there could be no French Government pending France's liberation, and we made it clear that we would not regard any French group or organization in the Empire as a government but only as an instrument of co-operation with the Allies on the part of whatever Frenchmen were free and willing to co-operate. Yet the partisans of de Gaulle in Britain and America, viewing the situation in its political rather than its military aspects, bitterly resented what appeared to be a rejection of de Gaulle's aid in Africa in favor of that of numerous Frenchmen whose political past had been at least highly equivocal.

American de Gaullism

ONE REASON why these suspicions of American policy became so marked and so vocal was that they had existed for about six years and seemed confirmed by what happened after the Allied landing in Africa. They had their origin in the Spanish Civil War, beginning in 1936, when American sympathies were sharply, even bitterly, divided, partly on religious lines; when the supporters of the Republic believed the United States Government to have been unduly influenced in favor of the pro-Axis and partly Fascist rebellion of General Francisco Franco. The recognition of the Vichy régime, which took on a Fascist tinge, appeared to repeat the policy towards Spain; and the pact with Darlan and later with Giraud, which seemed to exclude de Gaulle, appeared to repeat the policy towards Vichy. A chain of official acts seemed to be forming which might project itself into the future and commit the United States to the support of other Francos and Pétains and Darlans in countries as yet unliberated. Such was, in substance, the reasoning of the critics of our official policy in this country and in Britain.

General de Gaulle consequently became a symbol of all the suspicions and criticism that had accumulated in the years since 1936 — a symbol charged with the emotions of those who had vicariously fought the Spanish Civil War on the anti-clerical, anti-monarchist, anti-Fascist side, and of those who had grown wrathful towards the Vichy group of collaborators with Germany.

De Gaulle thus became far more than a French figure. He and his movement became a domestic issue in the United States and in Britain, and a point of contention between the United States and Britain. In France, where he was little known save as a radio voice from Britain, de Gaulle gained a large following as the outstanding exponent of resistance by all possible means against the invader, the chief spokesman of those Frenchmen who looked to a British and later an Allied victory for salvation and less and less to Vichy. In the United States, where he was not known even as a radio voice, de Gaulle acquired ardent defenders who wrote letters to the State Department and to the press protesting against the slightest aspersion upon him.[5]

[5] On several occasions dispatches I have written to the *New York Times* from Washington explaining official views of de Gaulle, which (odd as it may seem) I thought were news of importance and therefore of interest to readers of all political faiths, have brought me numerous letters, in one case several hundred, protesting with varying degrees of vehemence that I was maligning de Gaulle. I had expressed no opinion whatever about de Gaulle but had merely presented views which, because of the circles in which they were held, had a bearing upon our foreign policy.

The feelings animating these American de Gaullists were made up partly of admiration of the Frenchman who in the hour of defeat had not given up hope or given up Britain, even though some of our military men had done so. But they were made up even more of the intense emotions engendered by the controversies in recent years over Fascism, Communism, and democracy; by the appeasement policies of the democracies towards Hitler, Mussolini and Franco; by the defence of Fascism and the defence of Communism in this country; by the changed but persisting antagonism between what used to be called Right and Left — though these terms have lost some of their validity from the fact that Fascism and Communism have been essentially rival revolutions against capitalistic democracy. So the de Gaulle-Giraud controversy became not a *cause célèbre* between two groups of Frenchmen but an epitome of basic political and ideological divisions throughout the world. The American de Gaullists were not so much champions of de Gaulle as antagonists of the Department of State.

Dubious Company

It was into an oddly exotic atmosphere that the Allied forces stepped when they entered North Africa. It was not at all a projection of France. In many ways it was more like a projection of Germany, or at any rate of totalitarian, Nazi-dominated Europe. It was an appendage of the Vichy régime where the so-called "national revolution," a French version of totalitarianism which was one manifestation of Vichy's collaboration in a conquered Europe, had been carried out in the form of Fascist laws, secret police, concentration camps, and hostility toward Britain, who alone could save France. It was presided over by colonial officials and army and navy of-

---

The letters I received came from various parts of the United States. This seemed very strange, since the complete confidence with which the writers pronounced judgment upon the slightly complicated French problem would otherwise have convinced me they dwelt in occupied France or at least in North Africa. Perhaps they all had just come from the one place or the other.

ficers who represented a peculiarly narrow and bureaucratic and often reactionary side of France. Some of the soldiers there had fought against the British and the de Gaulle forces in Syria, and some of the naval crews had fought against the British at Mers-el-Kebir and at Dakar in 1940. Hence there were special and recent sources of anti-British and anti-de Gaulle feeling. Long after the Allied landing the predominant attitude in parts of North Africa towards that decisive stroke against the German oppressors of France was one of indifference.

Opportunistic officials and traders were impressed above all by the success or the prospective success of the Allied blow, and many who had collaborated contentedly and profitably with Vichy and the German masters of Vichy were ready to shift to the Allied side with the turn in the fortunes of war. Darlan may have been one of these.[6] General Noguès may have been one. There apparently were businessmen who had dealt with the Germans and were equally prepared to deal with the Allies, and some who even imagined that the "national revolution" could be conserved with American assistance in North Africa.[7]

With some of these people, whose political philosophy was far from that of the American tradition and whose personal principles were far from impeccable, our diplomatic and military officers co-operated, cynically or not, for the practical ends of the invasion. Some critics apparently thought that course was wrong. Perhaps they thought it wrong for General Clark to bluff Darlan into an armistice by making him a prisoner and threatening military occupation when the Ameri-

---

[6] General Marie-Emile Béthouart, who aided the Allies in Morocco, tells of visiting Admiral Darlan in December, 1941, when the Admiral said he was perfectly willing to modify his policy, and that if the United States would guarantee him several hundred aeroplanes and tanks at Marseille he would be willing to change radically. Darlan seems to have been a highly mercurial person capable of swift changes of view and conduct and it is difficult to decide how much significance could be attached to his words.

[7] Pertinax: *Les Fossoyeurs* (Editions de la Maison Française, New York, 143), p. 281.

cans then ashore were probably inferior in numbers to the French forces in North Africa. But military exigencies, which justify killing people, may be regarded as excusing departures from strictly moral associations or strict veracity, such as those involved in accepting the aid of doubtful characters and in bullying successfully a French Minister of State.

The fact that the landings and the expulsion of the Axis forces from Africa succeeded is a point of some consequence in this connection.

Revolutionary Nationalism

AGAINST THIS underworld of cold opportunism and blind hostility towards those who alone could save France, against this backwash of imperialism and war and defeat and Fascism, General de Gaulle seemed to stand out in enhanced purity of motive as he denounced Vichy and all its works and preached resistance. It is hardly surprising that he came to be regarded as the voice of disarmed but unbeaten French nationalism and an augur of French liberation and rebirth. It was this nationalism that led him to insist, almost to the point of absurdity, upon the inviolability of French sovereignty by opposing Allied control of ports and communications in North Africa — even as General Giraud had insisted upon the same principle in agreeing to join the American forces and later in proposing revision of the Clark-Darlan accord fixing those military conditions.

But it was a nationalism that was tinged with social implications, particularly in the time and circumstances in which it was asserted. De Gaulle seemed to his followers and sympathizers to represent and to promise a France which should not only be free and independent but socialized.[3] It would

[3] De Gaullists in London objected that Giraud's proposal of April 1, 1943, that the resistance movement in France be divorced from partisan politics came too late; for, they said, the largest and best organized underground movements in France were those of the Socialist Committee of Action, the French Communist Party and the French Workers' Movement. (Dispatch to *New York Times* from London published April 16, 1943.)

not be dominated by the older army officers or the clergy or the capitalists who had so long resisted and were still resisting the Revolution, and who were to a large extent clustered around Vichy and the projection of Vichy in North Africa. These groups and classes had never accepted the French Revolution of 1789, which had continued to be the basic issue in French politics — a real ideological issue stirring passionate emotions — down to the war. So far as those terms may be used today, de Gaulle is now Left in the sense that he believes he speaks for the majority of Frenchmen who have been Left hitherto, and in the sense that he proposes a "Fourth Republic" whose "new road" would be that of what he calls "pure democracy" which would abolish "interest and privilege" and would see to it that natural resources, labor, and organizing skill should not contribute only to the benefit of the few.[9]

Whatever this may mean specifically in terms of social legislation, whatever may be the means by which de Gaulle proposes to establish "pure democracy" along with state control over economic life, his words indicate at any rate something different from the divided, lobby-ridden, inefficient Third Republic which was dying of hardened arteries long before the German tanks rolled into France. That Republic commends itself to few Frenchmen today, whether they were Left or Right before the war; and the traditional term "republican," which once meant so much to the French, requires re-definition now that the Third Republic is associated with the defeat and the suffering brought on by its failure to defend France.

This nationalism is intense and emotional and revolutionary. Like the great French Revolution, it is accompanied by more than a trace of the ruthlessness of fanaticism. It called for purges in North Africa and calls for them in France. De Gaulle, in the speech quoted above, said: "There are still Bastilles, and it would be a good idea for them to open their doors, for in the battle between the people and the Bastille it

[9] Speech delivered at Algiers July 14, 1943; quotation from *New York Times* of July 15, 1943.

is always the Bastille that falls." These words were a sign of the political war that has mingled with the military war in Africa and must — in one form or another — follow that war in France.

This political war has already collided with the military war, and it seems inevitable that it should do so as long as the military war lasts. An indication that de Gaulle realized this was found in the speech just mentioned, where he said that "Certain people think it is possible to consider the action of the French armies independently from the sentiment and wishes of the great mass of our people." Some thought this suggested a political army; or it may have been an allusion to the insistence of General Eisenhower upon the retention by the Allies of the power to determine the commander of the French forces in North Africa and the manner of their cooperation with the Allies, an insistence which de Gaulle thought infringed upon French sovereignty.

Here two points of view were in conflict. General Eisenhower doubtless regarded the French Army primarily if not exclusively as a part of an Allied force which has a definite task to perform in beating the Axis and in occupying liberated regions. General de Gaulle regarded it as an instrument and emblem of French independence or of the "Fourth Republic" which would continue after the war of Allies against Axis was finished. To the Allies the French Army was a minor fraction of a larger whole; to de Gaulle it is an intrinsic part of the France of the future. Our minds, at least our military minds, were concentrated on the war, while de Gaulle — possibly recalling the defection of France's allies after the last war — must think, in both the military and the political sense, of a much longer period during which the relations of states and peoples may become very different from what they are today.

A hint of the possibility that French nationalism might turn against France's present allies was visible in the insistence, not only by de Gaulle but by Giraud and his associates, upon French sovereignty; and in the complaints of Frenchmen that the Allies were treating France inconsiderately in not recognizing the French Committee of National Liberation more completely.

That committee, formed by a formal union of the de Gaulle and Giraud forces in June 1943, was not recognized by the great Allies until August 26, 1943, and then by the United States and Britain only in a limited sense. It was recognized as the administrative authority which would be acceptable to the French territories overseas, but not as a provisional government of either the French Empire or France. Russia, on the other hand, recognized it as representing the interests of the French state, a more generous and inclusive form of recognition — the form the committee had sought to have adopted by the United States and Britain.

The form adopted by those two governments — which was more sharply defined by President Roosevelt who, unlike the British, explicitly stated that the committee was not recognized as a government — reflected the President's insistence all along that the only governmental authority that could be considered to represent the French people was one they should choose when liberated. He did not admit that any Frenchman outside France could speak for France. He was, moreover, further convinced of this view because of the difficulty of the French in North Africa in attaining even formal unity. In deferring full recognition of any régime until the French should be liberated, the President felt he was following both American and French principles. Yet he was, in a sense, assuming the responsibility of seeing that the French retained their liberty of choice, and possibly also the responsibility of an Allied supervision of France during any period of Allied military occupation which might precede that choice. It was thought in our government that the French in France would be more fully in accord with this policy than the French in the committee at Algiers, who desired to be regarded as trustees for France.

The antagonism which developed between the United States Government and the French Committee should not obscure the fact that the animating motive among Frenchmen was the recovery of their country's liberty and of its place among the great nations. As one of my French friends put it, France was a great power in May 1940, but a month later she had ceased to be a power at all. The moral shock as well as the physical suffering which this caused must always be kept in mind in considering the divisions and bickering among Frenchmen and their criticism of American policy.

The French tend to be extremely sensitive about their sovereignty because during the war there was only a remnant of it left. France has been crushed and humiliated, and new divisions have been created between Frenchmen who feel very bitter about this tragedy and other Frenchmen who have been suspected of accepting it too readily and collaborating with the Germans too eagerly. The two great American and British leaders believed that Frenchmen should look to the future rather than to the past and take a tolerant view of those in France who in many cases were compelled to collaborate, at least formally. The French in Algiers say they will know how to distinguish between Pétain and his government, whom they hold guilty and desire to place on trial, and the Frenchmen who obeyed that government because they must or because they could in that way serve their people. But the process of retribution, and of drawing such lines, seems likely to be difficult and disturbing in a time when France will require above all national unity in the task of rebuilding a nation.

Assuming that the United States adopts a broader foreign policy and takes a more specific interest in the re-creation of a free Europe, she will require close relations with the revived France who will play a leading rôle in that continent and may indeed determine whether its orientation is westward towards collaboration with Britain and the United States or eastward towards a strictly European constellation of power in which Russia may be the moving influence. Some have feared that the ill feeling that grew up between Algiers and Washington might be transferred to post-war Paris and tend to stimulate a continental policy which would turn France away from the Western Allies who will have assisted France's liberation. It will depend upon the forces within France that rise to power after the war and upon the policies of Britain and the United States towards France and Europe. In much of the discussion of the immediate future too much stress has been placed upon our relations with Russia as the only great continental power left for the time being, and too little consideration has been given to the fact that Europe remains a populous continent where powerful states will rise again. Among them, perhaps chief among them, will be France.

VI

OUR BRITISH ALLIES

Parting of the Ways

IN North Africa the Americans alone were responsible for dealing with Darlan and Giraud, since the Allied Commander-in-Chief was an American and the major decisions were those of the United States authorities. In London and in the Free French colonies the British were chiefly responsible for the position of General de Gaulle. He had been the only French leader to remain actively loyal to the Anglo-French alliance by going to England, by opposing the armistice, by rallying there and in France such French forces as he could for continued resistance to the invader. To do this he had used the British radio as a means of communication with France, and he had been financed by the British Treasury.

Consequently the Americans were closely associated with one French group, and the British with another; and the conflict among the French was to some extent a conflict between the policies of the American and the British governments. There was not only French unity to be attained, but also Anglo-American unity in dealing with the French, since the policies of Washington and London towards France had differed for more than two years.

This divergence of policies began in 1940 when Britain, fighting desperately for survival, took one attitude towards defeated France while the United States Government, not yet authorized to fight our enemies, took another attitude. Both those attitudes were logical and justifiable in the circumstances of the two governments at that time, but the result was to set the two governments upon different paths. This made it difficult for either to change its course so as to achieve a common policy after the United States did begin to fight.

This difficulty was accentuated by a whole heritage of misunderstanding and distrust and rivalry which magnifies and complicates every difference of view or of interest between Britain and America, and which may well prove to be one of the principal obstacles to the collaboration between those two powers upon which the peace of the world will depend in the immediate future.

Britain, then fighting alone against Germany and Italy and uncertain of active American aid, could not afford to take chances with the French Fleet when France surrendered to Germany. The Franco-German Armistice provided that France was to keep a part — undefined — of her Fleet to protect "her interests and her colonial Empire," while the rest of her warships were to return to their accustomed ports to be demobilized and disarmed under German and Italian supervision. Germany promised not to use these ships for purposes of war, except those that might be assigned to patrol the coasts and sweep up mines, and not to demand the French Fleet in the final peace.

Darlan, in an address to the Fleet by radio, interpreted these terms to mean, "We keep all our warships and naval planes." He added: "What more can we expect, being defeated?" He urged the naval crews to pay no attention to the armistice terms they might read in the press or to what the British might say, but to await his (Darlan's) explanations and to carry out "loyally" the terms signed by the French Government.[1]

This was not good enough for the British, and there is not an American naval officer who would suggest that it should have been good enough. Even if the armistice agreement had been more specific and had been signed by a conqueror who was noted for keeping his word, it still would not have been good enough for a nation depending largely upon sea power in a battle for its life. The French Fleet was too vital to be left in an equivocal position.

At Mers-el-Kebir, Algeria, a British squadron under Vice-Admiral Somerville gave an ultimatum to Vice-Admiral Gen-

---

[1] Pertinax: *Les Fossoyeurs. Op. cit.*, pp. 175–6.

soul, commander of the French warships anchored there — the battleships *Dunkerque* and *Strasbourg*, an aeroplane carrier, several cruisers, and smaller craft. The ships were to go to British ports, to join the British Fleet, to be interned in American harbors, to put in at the French West Indies and be disarmed, or to be scuttled. Gensoul insisted on consulting Vichy. The ultimatum was refused. At 6 p.m. on July 3 the British opened fire, sinking a cruiser and a destroyer and damaging the *Dunkerque* and seven light cruisers. The *Strasbourg* got away. Confronted by the same ultimatum at Alexandria, Vice-Admiral Godfroy agreed to intern the French warships which lay in that harbor, ships which nearly three years later were to join the Allied forces when North Africa came into the war and placed the French flag alongside those of the Allies. Meanwhile the British seized in English harbors two French battleships, two light cruisers, eight destroyers, and many smaller ships. Thus a large proportion of the French fleet fell into British hands or was put out of action. Vichy then severed diplomatic relations with Britain.

The clash at Mers-el-Kebir delighted the Germans. French sailors had been killed by British gunfire, and the always latent anti-British feelings in the French Navy and among Frenchmen generally flared forth under the stimulus of German and Vichy propaganda. The Germans now began to believe that the French Fleet might protect French bases against British seizure.

Washington and Vichy

IN WASHINGTON the apparently generous armistice terms and the German pledges were taken no more seriously than in London. But we were not at war and could not do what the British had done at Mers-el-Kebir, Alexandria, Portsmouth, and Plymouth. We could only exhort, and in order to do that our government retained its Embassy in France and instructed its Ambassador to follow the government of Pétain to Vichy.

"All that the Americans see in the tragedy of France is the French Fleet," said M. Baudoin, French Foreign Minister, at the moment of the Armistice when our representative, Anthony Drexel Biddle, on June 18, 1940, at Bordeaux, exacted from Darlan a pledge on behalf of the French Government that the French Fleet would never be surrendered to the enemy. It was hinted that the ships might be sent overseas or sunk.

M. Baudoin hardly exaggerated. The Fleet was not the only question, but it was the most urgent question in the minds of the President and Mr. Hull, as well as in the minds of the British Admiralty. It was the main task of our representatives who stayed in France to keep their eyes on the Fleet and, on instructions from Washington, periodically to remind Pétain that we trusted nobody with regard to that Fleet and insisted upon renewed assurances about it from time to time. One might have thought it was our Fleet which we had lent to the French and wanted back in perfect condition.

Despite Darlan's assurances, the fear persisted on the part of the President and Mr. Hull that Germany would somehow get the French warships and use them against the British. On October 25, 1940, Mr. Roosevelt against sent a message to Pétain, saying that although the French Government "alleges it is under duress," this did not justify it in serving France's conquerors in operations against her former ally. Pétain, as if weary of these proddings, replied with some asperity that "the French Government has declared that the Fleet would never be surrendered and nothing can justify questioning today that solemn undertaking."

Yet suspicion remained, precisely because, as Vichy had expressed it, Pétain's régime was under duress and for that reason alone Washington was never sure, during the more than two-year interlude between the fall of France and our landing in Africa, that Vichy's word had any great value. On November 11, 1940, in a talk with the Vichy Ambassador in Washington, M. Henry-Haye, Mr. Hull complained that Vichy, like Berlin, Rome, and Tokyo, "lacked frankness," and noted that there were reports that Vichy might take an attitude contrary to the interests of the United States.

Vichy, said Mr. Hull, must not imagine we were ignorant

of the purposes of M. Laval, an "extreme partisan of Hitler and Mussolini." We proposed, he told the Vichy Ambassador, "to be on guard with respect to the acts of the Vichy Government inspired by Laval that are intended to aid by French connivance the military activities of Hitler." Those words — not published at the time — should have been strong enough to suit the most ardent de Gaullist.[2]

[2] It was likewise not deemed appropriate to publish at the time the instructions of the President to Admiral Leahy whom he sent as Ambassador to Vichy. They were contained in a letter dated December 20, 1940, which made the following seven points:

(1.) "Marshal Pétain occupies a unique position both in the hearts of the French people and in the government," wrote the President. "Under the existing constitution his word is law and nothing can be done against his opposition unless it is accomplished without his knowledge. In his decrees he uses the royal 'we' and I have gathered that he intends to rule. Accordingly I desire that you endeavor to cultivate as close relations with Marshal Pétain as may be possible. You should outline to him the position of the United States . . . that only by the defeat of the powers now controlling the destinies of Germany and Italy can the world live in liberty, peace, and prosperity; that civilization cannot progress with a return to totalitarianism. I had reason to believe that Marshal Pétain was not cognizant of all the acts of his Vice-Premier and Minister for Foreign Affairs, M. Laval, in his relations with the Germans. . . . You should endeavor to bring to Marshal Pétain's attention such acts done or contemplated in the name of France which you deem to be inimical to the interests of the United States.

(2.) "I have made it abundantly clear that the policy of this administration is to support in every practicable way those countries which are defending themselves against aggression. In harmony with this principle this government is affording and will continue to afford to the government of Great Britain all possible assistance short of war. You may wish from time to time to bring to the attention of Marshal Pétain and members of the government concrete information regarding the American program to this end.

(3.) ". . . I have reason to believe that, aside from the selfish interests of individuals, there is unrequired governmental co-operation with Germany, motivated by a belief in the inevitableness of a German victory. . . . You should endeavor to persuade Marshal Pétain, the members of his government, and high ranking officers in the military forces . . . of the conviction of this government that a German victory would inevitably result in the dismemberment of the French Empire and the maintenance at most of France as a vassal state.

The assumption that France's Fleet was an American interest, which we had a right to insist that the French should protect, was implicit in all these admonitions. It became more than implicit when Secretary Hull, on May 29, 1941, denouncing to the French Ambassador the German use of French air bases in Syria against the British, blurted out that French military aid to Germany beyond the armistice terms was "an attempt indirectly to slit the throat of the United States."

We were now practically accusing Vichy of attacking the United States — and in Syria! Yet the United States was not protecting her threatened throat save in a cautiously nonbelligerent manner. Our protests sounded a bit fantastic. But

---

(4.) "I believe that the maintenance of the French Fleet free of German control is not only of prime importance to the defence of this hemisphere but also vital to the preservation of the French Empire and the eventual restoration of French independence and autonomy." (The President then recalled that it had been "a cardinal principle of this administration to assure that the French Fleet did not fall into German hands," cited the promises given to that effect by Baudoin, President LeBrun, Laval, and Pétain, and concluded that if after those assurances the French Government permitted the use of the fleet against the British, it would be "a flagrant and deliberate breach of faith to the Government of the United States." Admiral Leahy was asked to try to convince the officers of the French Navy that "to permit the use of the French Fleet or naval bases by Germany or to attain German aims would most certainly forfeit the friendship and good will of the United States." The President thus appealed over the heads of Pétain and his cabinet to the naval officers themselves.)

(5.) The President told Admiral Leahy that before trying to induce the British to permit food to be shipped to France, we must be sure it would not assist Germany "in the slightest."

(6.) In the French West Indies, said the President, our "sole desire is to maintain the *status quo*," and to be sure that those islands would not be used to the detriment of the United States or the American Republics. To this end naval vessels there should be immobilized and there should be guarantees that the gold at Martinique would not be used for the benefit of Germany.

(7.) The United States, the President said, was prepared to assist France to maintain her authority in North Africa and to improve the economic status of those territories.

they were quite logical, for the French Fleet *was* an American interest, and so were the bases in Syria.

As we have seen in the preceding chapters, our official suspicion towards Vichy, especially towards Laval and Darlan but also towards the entire régime, continued throughout the years 1940, 1941, and 1942, when we were seeking by the limited diplomatic means at the disposal of the government to keep both the French Fleet and French Africa out of German clutches, to retain our official contacts with the captive French nation, to encourage the French people so far as possible, and to limit the collaboration that they and their government gave to their conquerors.

As regards the French Fleet our aims were identical with those of the British but were pursued by different methods because we were not at war while they were. The justification of this policy, in the opinion of our officials, is that if we had broken relations with Vichy France we could not have brought to bear the influence we did bring, and that both the French Fleet and French Africa were in fact kept out of German hands and the way was paved for our military entry into those French territories.

Washington and de Gaulle

YET THE official British and American paths continued to diverge. Though the British Government at times admitted that our diplomatic relations with Vichy might be useful and, as shown in Chapter IV above, sought in March 1941 to induce us to negotiate with Vichy on behalf of Britain to prevent a further clash between British and French naval forces, many individuals both in Britain and in the United States thought our relations with Vichy somehow dishonored the democratic cause and betrayed a lurking sympathy with Fascism. General de Gaulle naturally was displeased, for to him Vichy represented treason and cowardice. Moreover, so long as we regarded Vichy as a legitimate or at least recognizable French Government, we were thrown into conflict with de Gaulle's desires.

Yet in November 1941, President Roosevelt was sufficiently respectful of de Gaulle to extend Lend-Lease assistance to the Free French "authorities" — as the State Department's publication "Peace and War" rather oddly called them in view of our lack of recognition. But the following month the de Gaullists angered the American Government by seizing St. Pierre and Miquelon, small French islands off the Canadian coast. The effect was not to encourage Washington to drop Vichy in favor of de Gaulle.

Mr. Churchill was then in Washington to shape the beginnings of Anglo-American strategy in a world-wide war. The British, without excessive tact, only two days after the seizure of the islands suggested that a representative of the Free French be included when the Prime Minister and the President met on December 27, 1941, with envoys of the refugee governments.

The suggestion was promptly rejected. It was pointed out to the British that while they had granted a measure of recognition to the de Gaulle movement, the United States had not done so. We were doing our utmost to bring our influence to bear at Vichy to keep the French Fleet and French Africa out of German hands. If a Free French representative were to be received at the White House, the Germans would persuade Vichy that we were playing a double game and this would impair our influence with Pétain, the British were told.

To this government, it was explained, it still seemed wise to keep our contacts with Vichy so long as Vichy was not completely subservient to the Germans. If that situation changed, we could consider a different policy towards the de Gaullists, but practical reasons were against doing so at that time. The President's advisers believed that neither de Gaulle nor those associated with him — particularly those associated with him — provided the leadership that might rally the free men in France and the Empire in a movement against Germany.

De Gaulle was carrying on a kind of civil war against Vichy and was not averse to seizing territories from it, while the United States Government — though with many misgivings and mental reservations — was dealing officially with

Vichy as the Government of France. Between those two attitudes there was no ready reconciliation. De Gaulle was unwise in taking St. Pierre and Miquelon just after being placed on our Lend-Lease list; while the President's advisers, I think, erred in underestimating de Gaulle's influence among Frenchmen in the Empire and in France. Each had taken up a position from which it was difficult to recede, and feelings on both sides grew sharper as the months passed, particularly when the uncompromising nationalism of de Gaulle collided head-on with the uncompromising views of the American authorities regarding military necessities in North Africa in relation to French politics there.

Washington and London

ARTIFICIAL though the relationship was, our official link with France was through Vichy until the Allied landing in North Africa, while Britain's link with France was through de Gaulle; and this continuing divergence of policies affected our relations with Britain even after we entered the war at her side, even after we entered North Africa at her side.

This was manifested in Washington in a certain distrust of the pro-de-Gaulle British policy, and in Britain in an outspoken and often bitter distrust of the American relations with Darlan and Giraud. The American critics of our official policy, the American de Gaullists, took the British side in the affair — unusual as that was for many of them, who previously had been anything but pro-British.

British policy was strongly, even bitterly, resented by American officials, who sometimes described de Gaulle as a creature of the British. They seemed to believe he represented the British Government more than he represented the French people. They believed that the Frenchmen who escaped from France through the underground channels, which they were convinced de Gaulle controlled, were carefully selected by the de Gaullists and hence were not typical of French opinion, though they agreed that de Gaulle deserved all praise for having taken his stand early in the war and that he was at least a symbol of resistance to the subjugated French people. The fact that de Gaulle, while financed by the British Treasury, criticized American policy, often severely, both before and after American participation in the war and before and after our landing in North Africa, was a source of Anglo-American contention, and the suspicion was voiced in Washington that Britain's support of de Gaulle might represent desires extending beyond the war itself. Meanwhile the British themselves were having trouble with de Gaulle about the administration of Syria,[3] and in the summer of 1943 a high British official described de Gaulle as an Anglophobe. De Gaulle in fact was the creature, not of the British, but of his own patriotism, which may be called an ambitious patriotism.

These American suspicions did less than due justice to Britain's geographic right, so to speak, to take the kind of special interest in France and French North Africa that we take in the Caribbean Sea and in Latin America. They may have derived less from any current evidence than from that vast and long-accumulating heritage of Anglo-American distrust, especially where trade is concerned. But they existed, and they are mentioned here because they formed a part of the background of our relations with the French, and because it is only by facing and dispelling such suspicions that Britons and Americans may achieve the common policies that will be so necessary in the immediate future.

The gaps in the mental and emotional accord between the British and American governments were not diminished by the attacks on American policy in the British press and by

[3] Mr. Wendell Willkie tells of the conversation he had with General de Gaulle in Syria. Discussing his quarrel with the British as to whether he or they should run Syria, de Gaulle said, "I cannot sacrifice or compromise my principles," and his aide added, "Like Joan of Arc." When Mr. Willkie referred to the Fighting French (Free French) movement, de Gaulle corrected him sharply, writes Mr. Willkie, by saying: "The Fighting French are not a movement; the Fighting French are France itself. We are the residual legatees of all of France and its possessions." (Wendell Willkie: *One World;* New York, Simon & Schuster, 1943.)

certain British officials. In the spring of 1942, when the British were hard pressed in Libya and Marshal Rommel was getting oil from French North Africa, the story was circulated that this was some of the oil we had sent to North Africa in consequence of the trade arrangements described in Chapter IV. Some Britons probably believed it; at least they repeated it in this country, and American officials felt it necessary to make to the British Ambassador an emphatic denial of the truth of the story. They contended that the supervision of railways and ships in North Africa by American observers convinced them that none of our oil could have reached Rommel, though it was known that oil from French territory had reached him.

British criticism of American policy became sharper and more voluminous when we went into North Africa and accepted the aid of Darlan and Giraud. The Prime Minister and Mr. Stalin reluctantly agreed to our deal with Darlan, but writers in the British press protested vehemently. Their criticism continued through November and December 1942 (in spite of the fact that a censorship in North Africa made it impossible for them to know precisely what had happened or why) and into January 1943 and afterward. A notable instance was an article in the *News-Chronicle* of London [*] placing upon General Eisenhower the responsibility for "the confusion" of the French political situation in North Africa. This was regarded by military officials in Washington as exceedingly unfair because, they said, the decisions of General Eisenhower regarding political affairs (such as his approval of the appointment of Marcel B. Peyrouton as Governor of Algeria by General Giraud) had the full agreement of the British commanders in that theater, even though they appeared to lack the approval of all quarters in London. British protestations that their government was not responsible for what their press said provoked in Washington smiles which reflected the American belief that, without being controlled, the British press in general responds to official wishes even in peacetime.

But the British Government was resolved not to quarrel

[*] Quoted in *New York Times*, January 14, 1943.

with the American authorities about North Africa, and not to allow such differences of policy as those which arose regarding France to recur in relation to other regions in which British and American forces might operate. On January 7, 1943, a British *aide-mémoire* suggested that the single French authority which it was hoped Giraud and de Gaulle could establish at Algiers should be recognized by the Allies as a *de facto* authority provisionally exercising French sovereignty over certain parts of France (meaning Algeria, which is constitutionally an integral part of France, not a colony) and over the whole French Empire pending the selection by the French people of a government which could be recognized as a provisional government for France. This was approximately the American point of view, which opposed the recognition of a French provisional government, and this form of recognition was accorded on August 26, 1943. (The impression had existed earlier that the British desired to place de Gaulle at the head of a provisional government.)

The meeting of the President and the Prime Minister in January 1943 at Casablanca, Mr. Eden's visit to Washington in March 1943, and Mr. Churchill's visit in May served to clarify and unify British and American policies towards the French. Immediately after Mr. Eden's discussions in Washington, General de Gaulle was requested not to go to North Africa for his political negotiations with General Giraud until the Tunisian campaign should be finished, although the delay had already incensed him and caused him at one point to threaten to disband his committee and break with the British. De Gaulle's use of the British radio to speak to the French was now made subject to Mr. Churchill's personal approval of each of his speeches in advance. These actions were regarded by de Gaulle as undue interference in French affairs, a charge he was to repeat after he went to Algiers and found that General Eisenhower insisted that Giraud remain in command of the French forces. De Gaulle's indignation at the British and American authorities is comprehensible in view of his statement to Mr. Willkie that the Fighting French were

"France itself," which implied that de Gaulle, being the leader of the Fighting French, was the leader of France.

To whatever extent this may have been true at the time or may become true in the future — and there seems no doubt that de Gaulle was accepted as the leader of a large bloc of Frenchmen inside and outside continental France — at the time of Mr. Churchill's visit to Algiers in June 1943 the tension between the French groups was noted by that observant statesman, who regarded de Gaulle as an obstacle to good relations between Washington and London. The British Prime Minister resolved that whatever tension might exist among Frenchmen must not again be permitted to extend into Anglo-American relations. If the British had to choose between the United States and de Gaulle, there was no doubt what their choice would be. French nationalism, whether led by de Gaulle or another, would not again become a barrier between London and Washington — at least not during the war.

The paths of Britain and America, which had diverged when France fell, had joined at last. Our Vichy policy was liquidated and Britain's de Gaulle policy of the Vichy period had likewise lapsed with changing circumstances, Britain now transferring to the French National Committee at Algiers the funds she had for nearly three years made available to de Gaulle's group in London (£1,200,000 a month).

Frenchmen of both groups, or all groups, are inclined to resent the necessarily secondary rôle that they are now compelled to play in relation to Britain and America, just as representatives of smaller states resent it. The French tend to be hypersensitive about their sovereignty, even towards Allies who use French territory for the liberation of France. They are critical and perhaps a trifle apprehensive of the massive power represented by the combined resources, efforts, and policies of the United States and Great Britain — just as you and I doubtless should be if we were Frenchmen.

Yet that power alone can liberate France and Europe and keep them liberated; and though it would be unreasonable to expect unalloyed gratitude from the French towards nations who after all were acting primarily in their own interests, it would perhaps not be unreasonable to hope that as she rises from oppression and humiliation France will recognize (especially if we ourselves recognize) how important it will be to civilized humanity that the paths of Britain and America, divergent so long, even after they became active allies, should henceforth remain joined.

VII

FRENCH *VERSUS* FRENCH

Allies and French Unity

THE *rapprochement* of the British and American policies towards the French, described in the preceding chapter, was an indispensable wartime achievement. But it did not insure that unity of the French which was the professed desire of all sides — and there were really four sides: the two French groups and the two great powers. I am not sure that it greatly contributed to that unity save in a formal sense.

The first effect was to postpone the negotiations between Girard and de Gaulle until after the Battle of Tunisia was won, which angered de Gaulle and thus did not serve to create the most propitious atmosphere. When the question of the command of the French forces arose and General Eisenhower, on behalf of the Allies, insisted upon the retention of General Giraud, this was widely regarded by Frenchmen — and not de Gaullists alone — as undue interference in French affairs. Under the stimulus of the controversy and the presence in North Africa of the dynamic and magnetic de Gaulle, whose oratorical and conversational influence spread potently among some Giraudists as well as de Gaullists, there was a kind of outburst of French nationalism which was directed against the Allies. This inevitably increased Allied distrust of de Gaulle and reinforced the view of those who had objected all along to his introduction of the political issue at the time and in the form on which he introduced it.

Therefore it seems certain that while the Anglo-American understanding put an end to an equivocal situation in which Britain and America were in effect supporting rival French candidates for leadership, it created a new situation in which de Gaulle was on one side and the two great Allies were on the other, with French sentiment tending to rally to de Gaulle on issues that touched or seemed to touch ever so slightly the sensitive Frenchmen's jealousy of their sovereignty and independence.

This may have been inevitable in the circumstances, the Allies being responsible for the defence of French territory and therefore insisting upon certain measures of protection like control of ports and communications, and the French, perhaps not unnaturally, protesting that in their own domain they should be the unqualified masters. The only alternatives were that we should occupy the French territories outright and set up an Allied military government there, which would have incensed the French still more; or that we should leave to the French full control of their territory and their army, which might have led to a bitter struggle between French factions behind the Allied lines — a struggle which, in the opinion of both Americans and British, might not have been merely political. Thus neither alternative seemed to offer a more satisfactory arrangement for carrying on the war or for attaining French unity in the war than the admittedly imperfect plan which was adopted.

Consequently the question of Allied intervention or nonintervention in French affairs was not so simple as some seemed to imagine. Our forces were in French territory and their presence there was in itself a form of intervention. We regarded ourselves as friends, allies, guests of the French, although we had in fact been invited by only a handful of Frenchmen and were violently resisted by others. We were sure that our invasion was in the interest of France as well as of the Allies, whatever some Frenchmen on the ground might say or believe to the contrary. We were ready to protect our lines in French territory by force if necessary; and that action would have been as much in the ultimate interest of France as was the British action in sinking a part of the French Fleet to make sure it would not join the Germans. Thus does war complicate life.

Meanwhile we hoped the two French groups, or whatever number there were, would recognize this less than ideal situation and would resolve at least to help us fight the Germans without too many preliminary arguments. Such a course seemed compelled by the obvious logic of the position. Frenchmen wanted to help liberate France; then why should they not do so at once and directly by getting together as a fighting force? Such was the attitude of some officials in Washington.

But French logic went further. The French should unite, certainly, in the military sphere and use Allied arms and supplies to help win the war. But if the French were to do this, why should not their flag fly along with those of the other United Nations, and why should they not have a recognized government like those of the Poles and Yugoslavs and Czechoslovaks? If the French were to fight with the United Nations, why should they not be regarded as forming one of those nations, especially since both major groups in the French Empire agreed in repudiating the armistice signed by Pétain and with it all the subsequent acts of submission, collaboration, and imitation? And why should they not have their own army and themselves choose its commander? France was not Luxembourg. She was, or again would be, a great power. Let her be treated as such by being admitted to the United Nations as a full equal. Such was the plea of de Gaulle, and there was no Frenchman in any faction who would oppose it.[1]

Moreover, the French were thinking not only of winning the war but of what was to follow in France, how a new government was to be established, how the eternal political war was to be fought out — and, inevitably, who might lead the

[1] When visiting Canada in July 1943, General Giraud made a similar plea in the form of "a reminder that the countries that have been defeated and overrun are just as much entitled to respect and to their independence of thought and action within the limits of war conditions as are those which for geographical reasons escaped invasion and had time to carry the war against the enemy," as Mr. Percy Philip described it in a dispatch to the *New York Times* (July 18, 1943). Mr. Philip added that the General indicated he thought the French were "free partners with the other United Nations and not in any sense to be treated as subordinates." This view is the essence of the French nationalism mentioned above.

French army that would march into Paris to the strains of the *Marseillaise*, and who might shape the new régime that would arise from defeat and misery.

Hence it was that political questions at once arose in connection with the wartime unity of the French which to some in Washington seemed such a simple affair. Those questions revealed the new sense of unity and a now more hopeful nationalism, but they reflected also the heritage of disunity from the past and carried a hint of equally marked disunity in the future among Frenchmen who would be obliged to re-create a state. Those who ask why the French do not get together expeditiously might recall the disunity that has beset Americans from the Constitutional Convention of 1787 to the period of the New Deal. In the nineteen-thirties factionalism in this country closely resembled in character that which split and weakened France in the same years.

Some in Washington thought of these French political issues in the somewhat negative sense of problems that should be postponed until the war was finished and that should then be left, without prejudice, to the French people. Adherence to this principle on the part of the Allies — whose military power and whose largesse in the form of relief were potential instruments of enormous political influence in Europe which might prove tempting in the disordered times that would follow the armistice — involved much more than France. It involved a good part of the world which would be at the mercy of the Allies. We knew from the experience of both the last war and this one that many factions in many countries would appeal to us to support them against their domestic rivals, and the desire was to discourage all such attempts at the outset by taking the position that the choice of a government for each country was the right of the people living there — with qualifications as regards Germany and Italy whose Nazi and Fascist régimes had been responsible for the war. The exiled governments in London were not regarded as representative of their countries save in a formal and provisional sense. This was true also of the French committee in North Africa.

Frenchmen Try to Unite

GENERAL DE GAULLE first suggested that French unity be achieved simply by enlarging his own French National Committee in London to take in North Africa "in accordance with the new conditions." But that proposal was unwelcome to Giraud and was soon dropped. De Gaulle's principal demand then was that the armistice signed with Germany in 1940 by the "pseudo-government" of France should be repudiated and declared null and void as regards not only North Africa but the French nation. The next step was to agree upon the "political and moral impossibility of leaving in the principal posts of direction men who have assumed a large personal responsibility in capitulation and in collaboration with the enemy."[2] This referred, among others, to the Governor of Algeria, M. Marcel Peyrouton, who had served in a Vichy cabinet; to the "Resident" or Governor of Morocco, General Noguès, who had resisted the Allied landing; to Governor of West Africa, M. Boisson, although he had assisted the Allies to obtain access to Dakar and had not aided the Germans in previous use of that harbor, as our naval officials had at one time believed.[3]

It was a logical consequence of the repudiation of the armistice and of the Vichy régime that de Gaulle should insist upon re-establishment of "republican legality," which meant the abolition of the changes made by the "national revolution" in North Africa, which had been carried through under the Nazi conquerors with whom the Vichy leaders had decided France must co-operate. De Gaulle also suggested the formation, in addition to a central authority, of "a consultative council of French resistance" in which would be represented the resistance movements within France, elected bodies in the Empire, "economic, trade-unionist and univer-

[2] Memorandum to General Giraud, February 23, 1943.
[3] This is the testimony of Mr. Thomas C. Wasson, American Consul at Dakar from August 1940 to February 1942. (See his article in *American Foreign Service Journal* of April, 1943.)

sity groups" in the Empire, and associations of Frenchmen abroad.[4]

De Gaulle thought there must be a sharp line between the control authority and the governors, who would be subordinate to it and act on its instructions, and that the commander-in-chief of the armed forces likewise must be under the central authority.[5]

Immediately upon the liberation of France "free expression of the popular will by election with universal suffrage of national representation" to establish a constitution would supplant whatever *ad interim* authority should act on behalf of France during the war.[6]

General Giraud agreed that the armistice should be repudiated, the Vichy laws annulled, and totalitarian groups like the *Légion des Combattants* dissolved, and as civil and military commander he himself took those actions. As for the desired "purge" of officials who had obeyed Vichy, he thought this should be considered by the executive committee which he proposed to set up jointly with de Gaulle. He gave his own definition of "collaborators" as those who by action or attitude had helped the enemy, but declined to apply that term to those who had resisted the enemy by remaining at their posts "and whose task has often been more difficult than that of those who have left France and served her abroad" (as de Gaulle and his group had done).[7]

General Giraud proposed to include in the central council the governors and secretaries of administration as well as other "qualified individuals," and suggested that an executive committee of the council should meet periodically and be responsible for the "general direction of affairs." General Giraud agreed to the consultative council or, as he called it, advisory committee, which he suggested be composed of sixty to eighty members divided into sections dealing with finance, agriculture, etc. He thought that when the Allied armies en-

[4] Memorandum to General Giraud, February 23, 1943.
[5] Letter to Giraud, May 10, 1943.
[6] Memorandum to Giraud, February 23, 1943.
[7] Speech of March 14 and memorandum of April 27, 1943.

tered France the French commander-in-chief should be responsible to the Allied High Command for maintenance of order, while the central council would appoint the prefects (local civil authorities). For the restoration of government in France he proposed applying the Treveneuc Law of 1872 providing that in the absence of a regular government the *Conseils Généraux* or departmental councils should choose delegates to an assembly which in turn would create a provisional government.[8]

Giraud insisted upon the "political disinterestedness" of the new council and objected to having the resistance of the French "linked to any political formula or purposes." He wanted France to take her place at the peace table alongside Britain, the United States, Russia, and China and on an equal footing with them, and for this eventuality as well as for postwar co-operation between France and the other United Nations the proposed council should prepare the way, he said.[9]

From negotiations through General Catroux, who went to Algiers from London, and exchanges of notes and memoranda extending over four months, there finally emerged in June 1943 the French Committee of National Liberation, of which General de Gaulle and General Giraud were joint chairmen and in which they were supposed to be equally represented. The committee aspired to govern Algeria and the free parts of the French Empire, to represent France in Allied councils, and to act as trustee for French interests of all kinds until the liberation of France and the re-constitution of a French state.

But the equality of the two groups seemed in the early weeks hardly more than nominal. The dominant personality was that of de Gaulle, whose voice charmed many in public halls in Algiers and in his private office. With his doctrinaire rigidity was mingled an ingratiating manner which enhanced

[8] Memoranda of April 1 and April 27, 1943. Regarding the Treveneuc Law, General de Gaulle's party objected that it would revive the pre-war councils, made up of "men living in the past" and therefore not representative of the underground resistance groups (which de Gaullists said were largely de Gaullist) that had sprung up during the war and represented present-day France, at least in its will to resist.

[9] Memorandum of April 1, 1943.

his influence in that region long dominated by Vichy. His fervent nationalism and his allusions to a Fourth Republic, which was to be democratic and economically egalitarian, appealed to many of the younger Frenchmen especially.

The "purge" of governors, which de Gaulle had advocated again upon his arrival in North Africa, began immediately with the voluntary resignation of M. Peyrouton — a dramatic victory for de Gaulle. The other two governors soon followed, and it appeared that de Gaulle dominated the committee and the political situation until, a fortnight after his arrival, General Eisenhower made it plain that his domination must not extend to changes in the command of the army. This resulted in a division of military powers, General Giraud retaining command of the French forces in North and West Africa while General de Gaulle retained command of those in other territories. Thus division was a sign of the basic division between the two generals and within North Africa, a division not overcome when later the whole of the armed forces were placed under Giraud.

It had been widely agreed that the two governors, M. Peyrouton and General Noguès, though one was a skilled administrator and the other an apparently capable soldier, had been too closely linked with Vichy to fit into the picture of liberated North Africa, now fighting with the Allies. M. Boisson, Governor of West Africa, was in a different category, for General Giraud particularly defended him and Washington officials did not regard him as having collaborated with the Germans, as he had collaborated with the Allies in making Dakar available to them. It therefore would have seemed logical to keep Boisson and dispense with Peyrouton and Noguès without waiting for de Gaulle to force the dismissal of all three. For by so doing de Gaulle not only gained a tactical success in political maneuvers but reinforced the impression that Giraud was very tolerant towards the Vichy office-holders while de Gaulle was the only real republican. General Giraud apparently thought he might win on this issue, but de Gaulle, and indeed Peyrouton himself, proved too quick. Consequently de Gaulle was enabled to make a dramatic début by appearing to sweep away relics of Vichy which without him would have remained.

Meanwhile the originally proposed joint committee of nine (three de Gaulle appointees, three Giraud appointees, three chosen by the first six) became a committee of seven and later a committee of fourteen in which de Gaulle steadily consolidated his advantage. De Gaulle showed himself quick and adept at political maneuvers within the committee, where he had astute aides; while Giraud seemed easy-going and pliable as though he could not take the committee too seriously but had his mind mainly upon the army which was to expand to some 300,000 with modern American equipment, for which he arranged on his visit to Washington in July 1943.

When General Giraud resigned as co-chairman of the committee on November 9, 1943 and three of his nominees in the committee were dropped, de Gaulle's control appeared complete.

The de Gaullists spoke of Giraud as an "American puppet," and his invitation to Washington did not dispel that impression. Giraudists accused de Gaulle of dictatorial aspirations and methods. Both sides professed the desire that the French people choose freely what form of government they would have after the war.

Meanwhile the political conflict in North Africa indicated some of the complications of such a choice and some of the forces and groups that would seek to influence it. North Africa was not France or a microcosm of France. Yet into that Oriental environment was projected a reflection of some of France's problems of the past and the future — above all, the divisions among Frenchmen which will not soon be removed. For years to come Frenchmen who were inside and outside France are likely to be judged largely by what they did in the years of France's eclipse and agony, and it would be surprising if the same test were not applied by Frenchmen to those who are now France's allies.

VIII

ITALY'S SURRENDER

The Classic Diplomatic Dilemma

WHEN we stepped across the Mediterranean from Africa and touched European soil, first in Sicily, then on the mainland of Italy, we faced what may be called our second major European political problem in the war. The first arose in North Africa, where we came into perplexed contact with a bit of France — a France we little understood.

In Italy the problem was different in the sense that it involved an enemy country that was about to give in — an old and civilized European nation which had oddly and paradoxically got on the side of barbarians who were as alien and unwelcome to Italians as they were to us. The problem was to right this historical error by getting Italy out of the tragic mess into which she had been led by Mussolini and the Fascists and the years of democratic failure described in Part III of this book.

Its solution required both military force and diplomacy, deftly mixed. It called for the first application on the Continent of Europe of policies and methods which were to meet far greater tests as the war advanced and as larger sections of Europe came within our power. It was a test of our ability to comprehend as well as to liberate Europe. And the comprehension might prove almost as important as the liberation. War-weary Italy thus posed in a still more acute form just such a European riddle as that posed by our invasion of North Africa. It presented, as in North Africa, both an immediate military problem and a far-reaching political problem.

Any comparison between that colonial French region and Italy must be somewhat arbitrary, yet from the point of view of the invading Allies there were similarities. Both had been under German influence since 1940. Both had taken on a superficial Fascist character. Both resisted the Allies; and it is an ironical fact that, while in Italy the resistance was mainly German, in North Africa it was French. Italians were eager to get out of the war and hence to welcome the Allied forces, while North Africa had not been in the war but in its curious isolation had been contaminated by Axis and Vichy propaganda and the French bitterness towards Britain that had been deepened by the collapse and division of France.

North Africa was a more difficult problem in that it was regarded as friendly territory where we must act with caution, while Italy was officially hostile and we were free to set our own terms. But this was qualified by the need to consider the future, in Italy as in North Africa, and to weigh the possible political implications of every military act, from the bombing of Rome to the armistice and the subsequent relations with an Italian régime. Moreover, everything we did in Italy affected our still unsatisfactory and undefined relations with the French, who had no recognized government and no great army and hence were somewhat in the position of minor partners, even though they had been — and we hoped they soon again would be — one of the great powers of Europe.

As our forces moved across the Mediterranean our government was still smarting under — or at least was still keenly conscious of — the severe criticism that had come from Britons, Americans, and de Gaullists when our army dealt with Admiral Darlan, when we permitted the summoning of M. Peyrouton, when we resisted what many thought were the legitimate claims of General de Gaulle to French leadership. The moment Mussolini fell, on July 25, 1943, the same critical voices were quickly raised to inquire suspiciously whether the Darlan episode would be repeated in Italy — whether our officials would find a Fascist or ex-Fascist to treat with, or would deal with the King, or would manage to make contact with and to sustain some more acceptable and more democratic authority. The Darlan affair, however justified, had deepened the fear in some quarters that officials of the United

States, forgetting the Atlantic Charter and the Declaration of Independence, would seize any opportunity to set up in Europe monarchist or reactionary forces in the Metternichian manner on the pretense of saving Europe from anarchy or revolution.

Here was what may be called the classic dilemma of diplomacy, the dilemma we had met in North Africa, the dilemma we had met in Latin America, the dilemma we shall meet pretty much everywhere. It consists in the fundamental and perhaps irreconcilable opposition between the normal and natural desire of a government, particularly in wartime, to deal with an orderly country where authority is respected, and the desire of the liberal or democrat that popular and liberating forces should be released even if they are disorderly and revolutionary.

President or Prime Minister or General is inclined to say: "Let us have order above all, so we can get on with the war; and let us deal with whatever authorities can maintain order" — an attitude perfectly comprehensible in those responsible for the war. This is precisely what Mr. Roosevelt and Mr. Churchill did say as Italy began falling into our arms. But the suspicious democrat, whose eye is fixed upon the political future rather than the military present, is disposed to say: "When dictators fall, let us above all use our military power to support — or at least to open the way for — those liberal forces within the dictator's country which have aims similar to ours; if this is not our purpose, for what are we fighting the war?"

Exit from the Dilemma

THERE IS logic in both these arguments. Obviously the military man taking over a hitherto hostile and disorganized land must have order if he is to stay there and fight there, or to fight from a base there. He cannot pause to examine too minutely the political emotions or the political records of those who prove ready and able to help him keep order. He must assume that his task is to win the war, not to make the peace or to carry out a revolution in a foreign land. He must assume that his country's victory is assurance enough regarding what will follow the armistice. He must take his orders from the government at home, not from the critics of the government. But the critics, having no military responsibility, are free to question the political intentions that might be expressed in military acts, and to remind us that there are the two problems which above I have called the military and political.

These problems inevitably overlap and intermingle. It is impossible to separate them altogether, since military measures taken in an emergency cannot be dissociated from political implications which few commanders in the field are in a position to understand or in a mood to weigh. Yet the heads of Allied governments, who are civilians bearing both military and political responsibilities, must strive to give due weight to both problems while giving priority to the military problem. They might permit the commander in the field the fullest freedom to treat with any authority, even a Darlan or a Badoglio, for strictly *military* purposes, while making it plain that these military acts involved no political commitments of any sort for the future. The military policy of pure expediency could thus be sharply distinguished from political policies, especially if the Allied governments *had* political policies which they could enunciate in general terms at the same time or soon afterward, so as to remove all doubts regarding their intentions.

Political policies, even in war-time, may be as important as military measures, while after the armistice they become immeasurably more important. It is not the business of a general, when he lands on a hostile beach, to hunt out the local equivalent of Thomas Jefferson, if there is one, and to establish him as head of a government in the invaded territory. The general has quite a lot of other things to do with a good deal of urgency. But it is the duty of the State Department in Washington and of the Foreign Office in London to consider from the first the political aspects of what the general may do. They cannot dodge those questions on the ground that military operations are in progress; for it is precisely then that these officials, who are not involved in those operations, should be preparing intensely for what may follow.

The political consequences of military operations were under-rated and misjudged during our campaign in North Africa. Mere mention of North African politics in Washington in the winter and spring of 1943 brought the impatient retort that it was no time for politics but only for fighting. Why did not General de Gaulle stop arguing and go out and fight? But the political problem could not be postponed, and officials who had turned their backs upon it eventually had to sit down and try to solve it. The problem had meanwhile grown more acute; the gulf between de Gaulle and the American Administration had widened. It would have been better to have faced that problem sooner and more graciously — that is, more realistically.

Twenty-four hours after the fall of Mussolini, the Office of War Information broadcast the view that Marshal Badoglio, who had succeeded Mussolini, was "a high-ranking Fascist." It quoted Mr. Samuel Grafton to the effect that Fascism was still in power and that nothing had happened but that the "moronic little King" had moved forward. President Roosevelt a day later repudiated the broadcast, saying that it should not have been made and that it had been made without the authorization of himself, the Secretary of State or Mr. Robert E. Sherwood, chief of the overseas branch of the Office of War Information. The result was to create an impression of confusion and of absence of agreement in official quarters regarding what our program was in the event, soon to take place, of Italy's surrender. The President a few days later explained that we intended to treat with the King or Badoglio or such other Italian officials, national or local, as could maintain order and carry out an armistice.

Subsequently, on September 21, 1943, Mr. Churchill called upon Italian liberals and "Left-wing elements" to rally around the King and Badoglio to liberate Italy from the Germans. He added that his appeal was made "without the slightest prejudice to the untrammeled right of the Italian nation to make what arrangements it chooses for the future government of the country on democratic lines when peace and tranquillity are restored."

Dangers of Military Government

Mr. Churchill seemed to regard the Badoglio régime, supported by the Allies, as a war-time régime which would leave Italy free to choose her government when the war was over. He thus tried to draw the line suggested above between military and political measures and régimes; although he doubtless was aware that the acts of that régime itself might prejudice the future Italian freedom of choice and that the Allies, by supporting the régime, might be considered to have assumed some responsibility for the freedom of Italy in deciding its subsequent course. If the Allied-sponsored régime were to become so strong that only revolution would give Italians their freedom, then the action of the Allies would have prejudiced that freedom. Such are the political dangers that may flow from any military decision which, like this one, imposes a government upon a people, however temporary it is intended to be.

Similar dangers exist wherever military governments are placed in charge of conquered nations. Those governments are primarily interested in security and order and are tempted to sustain in power such local officials as best serve those immediate ends. Such a course is understandable, if not justifiable, from the strictly military point of view, which must take precedence in the beginning of an occupation. Yet very soon the favored local officials obtain, by virtue of the alien military authorities, a political power that may continue after the military régime has gone and may control the machinery by which the people eventually seek to express their desires. Any government that is in power may, in most countries, exert a tremendous influence upon elections if it so desires. This is doubly true of countries which, like Italy and Germany, are not accustomed to elections.

For this reason military governments, with the aid of civilian advisers acquainted with the internal affairs of the occupied country, should strive from the beginning not to load the dice, so to speak, in favor of any one group or class or faction. They should choose native collaborators, so far as possible, on a non-political basis. And the military governments should be succeeded very soon by Allied civilian governments better suited to make good the pledge of freedom of choice that we have made to the nations temporarily in our power.

The moment the Allies take over a country, either by military government or by co-operation with an existing régime, they exert an influence upon that country's political future whether they so intend or not. The longer the Allied authority continues, the greater becomes the influence. Even if the Allies withdraw and leave entire control in the hands of local authorities, they may endow the local government with enormous power by entrusting it with the administration of the relief of the population in the form of food and other goods sent by the Allies.

This Allied influence is unavoidable, and even though Mr. Churchill hoped it could be exerted "without the slightest prejudice" to the freedom of the occupied country, such prejudice, in one direction or another, seems inevitable. The restoration of liberty to a Fascist-governed land is not a simple process. Nor can a conqueror bestow that liberty, save in the negative sense of destroying the tyranny. Each nation must work out its own salvation and its own form of liberty; and the best contribution the Allies could make would be to reduce their political influence to a minimum and so to insure that an occupied country may exercise, as freely as circumstances permit, the "untrammeled right" of which Mr. Churchill spoke.

Mr. Churchill Gave Us the News

OUR GOVERNMENT would be fairer to itself as well as fairer to the American people if it were more candid about its foreign policy, so far as it had a policy. Much of the criticism of recent years has thriven upon the obscurity that has been permitted or created regarding our relations with foreign nations.

It is not primarily a matter of military secrecy. For during this war our real Office of War Information has not been that which has spread lavishly over a large building in Washington; it has been the office of the Prime Minister of the United Kingdom. It has been Mr. Churchill who has told us more important war news than any other individual or agency — Mr. Churchill speaking in the House of Commons, or in Congress, or over the microphone, or less publicly at luncheon tables. Mr. Churchill has often told us something important about the war that our people and his are fighting and paying for — something that our own officials had forgotten or been unwilling to tell us. He has informed us not only about British policy but about our policy, not only about British losses and gains but about ours.

For instance, it was he (in his speech of September 21, 1943, to the House of Commons) who first told us how the armistice with Italy had been negotiated, how the German submarines had suspended their operations for four months, how the Russians had suggested a Mediterranean Commission, how Mussolini had escaped capture, how the Germans were using and planning new weapons. No American official had vouchsafed this information to the American public. American readers had to turn to Mr. Churchill for the news.

Mr. Churchill is an accurate and gifted reporter of events — in fact, a genius. Yet our officials, even if they could not hope to equal his lucidity or diction, could have contributed to us as much enlightenment about the progress of our war as Mr. Churchill contributed via the House of Commons.

In August 1943, in Washington I sat near Mr. Churchill at a luncheon lasting until four o'clock in the afternoon and, with other correspondents, was able to ask him questions and to get generous and candid answers. Looking ten years younger than he was, toying with a large cigar, tossing off witty and picturesque phrases with almost every sentence, ready and eager to answer all questions but naturally without revealing any military secrets, he completely captivated that group of not highly emotional and not uncritical newspaper writers. "If he could run for President, he would carry a lot of states," said a political writer, and there was no doubt that Mr. Churchill's visits to this country and his speeches heard by radio had made him an almost familiar hero to Americans.

Mr. Churchill is unique, being a product of an old English family, of aristocratic associations, of Sandhurst and the army, of the House of Commons. He has distinguished himself as a soldier, a war correspondent, a historian, a statesman. His perfection of style in speech and writing is the expression of a clear and luminous mind. He can describe a military operation or a political policy as none but an exceptional writer can. He is one of the greatest assets of the Allied cause, the giant of our time, and in this sense he belongs to us as well as to the British.

Yet I wished — and not I alone — that it had been possible for an American official to give, in public speeches and at meetings like that luncheon, half as much information to Americans about the war and Allied policy and aims as Mr. Churchill habitually gave to his people and to ours.

Information, Please

MR. CHURCHILL's method — perhaps the result of the give-and-take of House of Commons debates, where Ministers must answer questions — is to face criticism and overwhelm it by fact and logic. Our officials, unaccustomed to debate, too often ignore criticism or denounce it in public while fretting about it in private. The criticism of their policy in North Africa worried them, but they did little to dispel it or to explain their policy. It is not easy for the President or a member of his cabinet to answer criticism in Congress, while British Ministers have to answer it face to face with their Parliamentary critics or opponents; beyond a certain point, reticence becomes self-accusation. It is a healthy system of public enlightenment; and, though it is not an American practice, it ought to be. It is only custom, not the Constitution, which prevents the President or his cabinet members from appearing before Congress to be questioned — a practice that would do them and us much good.

If after the war we are to have an intelligent foreign policy, it must be approved by the American people; and if they are to approve, they must understand what is done and why. They must be told far more than they have been told during the war about their own affairs in relation to those of other countries. Our government is not a private enterprise. Military secrecy does not apply to political policy. The exigencies of war-time need have restrained Washington officials no more than they restrained Mr. Churchill when he rose in the House of Commons.

Critics sitting at typewriters or microphones have no proper business telling the general in the field whom to treat with in conquering a country or in receiving its submission; but they and the American people have a right to know whom we are treating with and why, and what plans we have for the future of the conquered country — and, if we have no plans, why we have not got them. If we have plans and keep them secret for fear of criticism in Congress or elsewhere, then we need a more democratic system of managing foreign affairs — as democratic as that of Britain.

Our experience in North Africa and in Italy compels the conclusion that we were politically unprepared for those phases of the war — as for earlier phases — partly because we had not fully anticipated the problems that would arise in those European zones, and partly because neither before nor after they arose was the American public adequately informed regarding what we were doing. The Atlantic Charter was an admirable document which meant little, if anything, that was precise to Americans and in some respects implied policies (such as free trade) which probably are not practicable. The doctrine of unconditional surrender, enunciated at the Casablanca conference in January 1943, seemed to close the door to negotiations which might conceivably be to our advantage and might shorten the war by permitting us to offer terms to induce capitulation. The President and Mr. Churchill therefore qualified the doctrine by telling the Italians that we meant to restore Italy to a respectable place among civilized nations. Their surrender thus became, to some extent, conditioned by our reassurances, even though technically it was unconditional.

This doctrine, as the basis for dealing with Germany, was finally accepted by the Soviet Government in October 1943, though Russia had until then appeared to sponsor a quite different policy, as described in Chapter XIV.

The great problem then seemed to be the rebuilding of Europe, politically and economically, under the leadership of Russia, Great Britain and the United States. This would involve agreement among the three regarding the treatment of Germany, regarding the future frontiers of Central and Eastern Europe, regarding the economic relations among the European states and the extra-European powers.

Though wide differences of view not only between nations but between groups and individuals within each nation make this difficult, and the disorganization of the liberated Continent may produce a revolutionary situation which will add to the difficulty, such an agreement is possible. Through their governments, their armies and their officials, the Allied nations outside Europe will resume acquaintance with a Continent greatly changed by its ordeal; and the greatest danger may be a tendency to under-estimate the change and to seek to restore what had been instead of building anew politically. Against this danger our experience with the French in North Africa and with the Italians should have armed us, just as memories of the last great peace should warn against neglect of economic relations within Europe.

PART THREE:
Democratic Failure

IX

SPAIN DIVIDES AMERICANS

Franco, Pétain, Darlan

THE sharp and dangerous division of American opinion regarding the motives of our diplomacy, which was marked by the controversy over our policy in North Africa and will not soon be overcome, is traceable chiefly to one of the most amazing of Hitler's exploits in the days when he relied more upon effrontery than upon military power — the conquest of Spain by Germans and Italians on behalf of a Spanish Fascist group, and the unanimous, collective, and organized tolerance with which the democracies met that challenge. Then for the first time the Axis powers invaded a European country to establish there a régime favorable to themselves; and the democracies, unwilling to counter that Axis move because of what they thought was the risk of war in so doing, adopted a policy of non-intervention which the Axis went through the farce of accepting even while German and Italian troops and war materials poured into Spain.

Non-intervention was defended on the ground that the Spanish conflict was a civil war, though from its inception onward it was actually an international war, the boldest step up to that time in the Axis progress towards the conquest of Europe. The response of the democracies was such as to encourage further steps along the same path, which Hitler took when he thought the time was ripe.

American policy towards this conflict, which was that of the European democracies — non-intervention with the purpose of avoiding a larger war — aroused passionate criticism within this country. That criticism has continued ever since. The American recognition of the Vichy Government in France in 1940 and the American use of Admiral Darlan in North Africa in 1942 seemed to these critics to confirm their charge that in Spain and elsewhere we were pursuing, even after Britain had abandoned it, a policy of appeasement towards the Axis; and that certain officials in Washington and in our Foreign Service were inclined to seize every opportunity to ally themselves with Fascists rather than with the liberal and democratic groups abroad who were our natural allies because they believed in our cause.

The intense feeling excited in this country by the American policy in North Africa and the American difficulties with General de Gaulle — a feeling which in many cases represented a refusal to believe that anything our State Department did could be right — derived largely from the resentment left in many liberal and Leftist minds by our decision to deny arms to the recognized government in Spain in 1936 when it was attacked by a monarchist-reactionary-Fascist rebellion. To many Americans that action seemed utterly inexcusable, so pro-Fascist in its effect as to imply pro-Fascist motivation, so flagrant a departure from the democratic principles which they thought should determine our every action in foreign affairs that they could only imagine that in high places in the State Department were men who did not believe in democracy and aspired to be modern Metternichs who would recast Europe after the war to make it immune to revolution and safe for reaction.

It was not only our Vichy policy, or our North African policy, but the fact that these were apparently repeating our policy towards embattled Spain in 1936, which caused many in this country to question the entire motive and purpose of our diplomacy in the Second World War — some professing to fear that on our part this might turn out to have been an imperialistic war for territory or power or a war against democracy instead of for democracy.[1]

This suspicion of the aims of the makers or practitioners of our foreign policy results from emotions that have continued undiminished for more than seven years and have lately been intensified by our wartime policies. It has created a new division within the United States regarding foreign policy — a division not between isolationists and supporters of inter-

[1] Typical of these criticisms and imputations are the following:

"At the very moment when the State Department heads seek to reassure us as to their intentions, new enigmas continue to arise which cast doubt upon whether the State Department is seeking to create a democratic and militantly anti-Fascist post-war Europe or is shaping a new world in the image of its fears of democratic regimes." (*New Republic*, April 26, 1943.)

"There are persons, well informed with regard to France in general, who charge that the United States is handicapped in its North African policy by agreements, still in force, which were made many months before we landed in that area, between Robert Murphy of our State Department and representatives of a group of Frenchmen. The bargain, these men say, tied the United States to a policy of working with Vichyites in North Africa who represent ultra-conservatism, Roman Catholicism and big business interests, notably three important French banks, the Banque de Worms, the Banque de Paris et des Pays Bas and the Banque de l'Indo-Chine. . . . These charges . . . do not reflect upon Mr. Murphy personally. They perhaps do reflect upon his superiors in the State Department who chose an ultra-conservative, devoted Roman Catholic as their agent to deal with a subjugated country — France — which is on the whole liberal and anti-clerical. . . . We do not know what truth there is in this story, any more than we know what lies behind the charges made by Edgar Ansel Mowrer, one of America's most reliable and responsible journalists. Mowrer says that the United States and Great Britain are thinking seriously of taking away from France important points in her colonial empire. These would include Dakar, to be ruled by this country; Bizerte, to be ruled by the British; and French Indo-China, to be governed by an international committee on which China would play a prominent part." (*New Republic*, May 3, 1943.)

"The continued presence of Ambassador Hayes in Madrid is a symbol of our futile policy of appeasement. Much worse, it is a symbol of our willingness to trade ideologically with the enemy." (Editorial in *PM*, New York, June 11, 1943.)

national co-operation, but between Left and Right, or between old-fashioned liberals like the Secretary of State, Mr. Cordell Hull, and the new-fashioned liberals who sometimes regard our attitude towards Russia or towards Communism as the "acid test of our good will," as Woodrow Wilson said of our attitude towards revolutionary Russia in 1918. While some accuse our government and our State Department of being too liberal-minded towards the foreign world in the sense of being willing to assume too generous commitments of aid and protection, others accuse them of being too narrow-minded in the sense that they share the fears of democracy entertained by reactionaries abroad and are disposed to use our power to check it.

The liberal or Left critics do not desire a return to isolation but urge more active support by the United States of democratic elements abroad against the Fascists and monarchists and reactionaries who logically ought to be our ideological enemies. The policy towards Spain which they so vehemently denounced was a policy of isolation. Yet the effect of their attacks might be to play into the hands of the isolationists by serving to discredit a government which, for all its errors, has represented the most enlightened attitude towards foreign affairs that has been displayed by any government since Woodrow Wilson's. The liberal critics would not favor exchanging the Roosevelt foreign policy for a Harding policy; yet this danger might exist, and in that case whatever weakened the Roosevelt policy would strengthen the trend towards the isolationist obscurantism which the liberals would be the first to condemn.

If one were convinced that our foreign policy sought to create a kind of Holy Alliance of Fascist or reactionary powers to rule Europe or the world, one might prefer isolation on the theory that, if we cannot help the democratic and progressive elements abroad, we might at least refuse to conspire against them or to "gang up" on them. The liberals who suspect such a reactionary plot in Washington might therefore be driven into the isolationist camp, along with the conservatives who fear that our association with foreigners may infect us with too much democracy of the economic kind which British Conservatives have enacted into law.

Spain and the Democracies

SINCE IT WAS our policy towards Spain which most shook confidence in the intentions of our officials, or at least evoked the most passionate opposition, it is well to recall what the position of Spain and of Europe was at that time and why our policy took the form it did, according to those who made it.

In the summer of 1936 the German press went into one of the fits of co-ordinated indignation and alarm which were becoming such revealing instruments of Nazi foreign policy. The alarm was this time caused by the discovery that, as that press put it, Spain was being overrun by Bolshevism. Spain was a long way from Germany, yet the Nazis felt called upon to save it from Bolshevism. The cynical suggested that Hitler desired a pro-Nazi régime on the other side of France; that he coveted the strategic raw materials of Spain; that he longed to experiment upon Spanish workers and peasants to advance the art of precision-bombing which might prove useful elsewhere — especially since he had just marched into the Rhineland while holding his breath to learn whether the "decadent" democracies would push him out again, as they could easily have done.

At any rate Hitler grew concerned about Spain and, oddly enough, Mussolini felt exactly the same concern at exactly the same moment, while General Franco and his indigenous collaborators were opportunely moved by the same emotion — possibly for slightly different reasons. On July 30, 1936, three Italian military planes made a forced landing in Algeria and from them emerged Italian crews who wore Spanish uniforms and were on their way to Spain to help save it from Bolshevism. Franco's uprising had just begun, and it seems certain that the Axis planes and uniforms and war supplies had been arranged well before that uprising. The Germans were more skillful than the Italians. They made no forced landings in unsympathetic countries, but they too reached Spain in July; and when I was there in 1938 not only was their air force advancing the Franco cause by block-busting Barcelona and gayly machine-gunning peasants and villagers, but German technicians controlled communications and trade in Franco territory and readily explained to me how they did it.

On August 1, 1936, when Germans and Italians were already in Spain, having entered almost simultaneously with Franco, the French Government proposed that the conflict be localized by non-intervention. The French invited Britain and Italy to adopt this policy. But the British suggested extending it and, by the end of August, Germany, Russia, and Portugal, as well as France and Britain, all blandly agreed that they heartily opposed intervention — which was then being practiced by three of them: Germany, Italy and Russia. A joint committee representing these governments and twenty-one others sat in London to see that nobody intervened, or that if anyone did he should not do it any more than could be helped. Meanwhile the Italian press praised the heroic Italian troops fighting in Spain and claimed the capture of Malaga as an Italian victory. The Germans were less vocal but more efficient and therefore not unpopular, as the Italians were, in Franco Spain. German and Italian troops and armaments gave Franco superiority over the Republicans and insured the success of the Spanish counter-revolution.

The Case for American Policy

THE AMERICAN decision was quickly made in favor of complete abstention, even to the point of refusing to sanction the sale of arms from this country to the recognized government of Spain, which would have been in conformity with international custom and with the Treaty of Havana of 1928. That decision was first officially formulated on August 7 in instructions sent to American representatives in Spain by Mr. William Phillips, Under-Secretary of State. It was made public on August 11 in a statement to the press, and again on August

SPAIN DIVIDES AMERICANS 119

22 in a letter from Mr. Phillips to an American manufacturer who had inquired about selling airplanes to Spain.

The reasons then given for that policy were that it was our practice not to intervene in the internal affairs of other countries and that, though the Neutrality Act did not apply to a civil war (which was what we called the conflict in Spain in spite of its international character), nevertheless our government thought that the logic of our non-interventionist attitude implied that private sales of munitions, though legal, would not conform to "the spirit of the government's policy."

This policy, created by executive decision, was confirmed by Congress five months later in a joint resolution extending the embargo on munitions to both "the opposing forces" in Spain.[2]

While preparing this chapter I asked Mr. Hull, who had been Secretary of State in 1936 and since, what he now thought of the policy towards Spain adopted at that time.

"The opposing groups in Spain had sympathizers outside Spain," he said. "The European powers had agreed to segregate the Spanish war to prevent its spread. The initiative in non-intervention had come from France and Britain. In these circumstances we were determined to stay away from it, quite apart from the merits of the war. Before reaching that decision I consulted my associates in the State Department and listened to all their views, which were not all the same.

"One reason for our policy was that we had been preaching non-intervention in Latin America and it seemed logical to apply it to Spain in the form we did, even though we had the technical right to sanction the sale of arms. Another reason was that the chances seemed more than even that, if we exercised our right to sell arms, our navy would soon be following. We were in no condition to be drawn into war in view of the aggressive intentions and preparations of Germany and Japan.

[2] The official texts of Mr. Phillips's instructions, his letter to a manufacturer, and the resolution of Congress are included in Appendix B at the end of this volume.

"Our policy towards Spain yielded the results we hoped for. It kept us out of war when we were not ready for war. It kept Spain neutral when we went into North Africa with a long supply line passing along the Mediterranean and the Atlantic close to Spain. Both this policy and our Vichy policy have been vindicated by events, in spite of the attacks made upon them. When Mr. Churchill was here in May I asked him whether he did not think our Vichy policy had justified itself 100 per cent, and he said, 'No — 140 per cent.'"[3]

Another argument put forward in official circles in Washington is that the Spanish navy was mainly in Franco's hands and might have stopped shipments of arms from this country to the Republic; this would have obliged us to protect our ships with our Navy; there was thus the risk that the result might be to turn the Spanish war into a European war and to render the United States liable to the charge of having precipitated that transformation. Moreover, it is contended in these same quarters, it was a European affair and, though the existing Neutrality Act might not apply to the case, that Act was a mandate from Congress to the Government to keep out of European wars.

Exaggerated Risk of War

ONE AMERICAN official with whom I discussed the subject thought that if we had exercised our right to sell arms to the Spanish Republic, Britain and France might have been encouraged to do the same and the Republic might then have been able to hold out. As against this, some students of contemporary history believe that the non-intervention committee, farce though it was, did succeed in preventing the growth of the Spanish conflict into a European War.[4] If so, it must be agreed that our policy helped towards that end.

This raises the larger question whether a European war in

[3] Conversation on July 20, 1943.
[4] *This Age of Conflict*, by Frank P. Chambers, Christina Phelps Grant, and Charles C. Bayley (New York, Harcourt, Brace & Co., 1943).

July 1936 would have been preferable to one in September 1939. From the purely military point of view it might have been. Though the democracies were not fully prepared for war, neither was Hitler. In 1936 the French Army could have annihilated the German Army without great effort, for conscription had been in operation in Germany for only a year and there had not yet been time to train either the massive forces that were to come or the officers to direct them. The British Navy could have disposed of the German fleet with equal ease. The German air force also was then small, but, whatever its size, it could not have beaten the democracies alone. Yet the decisive point perhaps is that, though superior to Germany in fighting power, France and Britain were in no mood for war, as was demonstrated by their inaction when Hitler, with a small force, marched into the Rhineland in March 1936, and by their subsequent inaction in Spain. Hitler's half-surreptitious aggression in Spain, like Italy's aggression the previous year in Ethiopia, was insufficient to create a different mood in those pacific, and also short-sighted, democracies.

As for the United States, the nearest approach to a foreign policy that we had was a determination to keep out of war. That was unmistakably the intention of Congress, and few doubt that it was the desire of the country. The President and the Secretary of State, compelled to shape their policies according to the will, however mistaken, of the country, had to decide not whether they preferred the Spanish Republic or Franco but what policy would accord best with American desires and with American interests. Both seemed to dictate avoiding war and the risk of war, whatever the effect upon Spain or Europe or, indeed, upon America. There was little if any doubt about the overwhelming American desire to keep out of war, and it would have been difficult then to argue that American interests demanded any other course. American interests in Spain were negligible in any case, save to the extent that Spain's destiny was bound up with Europe's and that Spain was a battleground of forces doomed to involve us — which few at that time would have conceded.

Had the United States insisted upon the right of its citizens to sell arms to the Republic and backed it up with the Navy to see that the arms arrived, the shipments would have had to be on a huge scale to offset the Axis shipments, which could be delivered more rapidly because they came from nearer ports. Italy sent to Franco, besides 100,000 men who were not too eager to fight in Spain, some 4,300 motor vehicles, 750 guns and 40,000 tons of war material; while Germany sent equal or greater quantities in addition to a large contingent of her own air force with its own pilots and ground crews.

But if we had thus given the lead to European powers in a European conflict — which would have been a distinct departure from our customary practice — and if Britain and France had followed suit, the democratic arsenals might have been able to outbid the Axis and the Spanish Republic might have been so well armed that it would have won. My opinion is that a European war would not have resulted, chiefly for the reason mentioned above — that Hitler was not at all ready for a major conflict and wanted it as little as anyone. He was bluffing in Spain, as he had done four months earlier in occupying the Rhineland, and if his bluff had been called in either case he would have had to withdraw. But the democracies were in no position to bluff back — neither ours nor Europe's — simply because they were democracies; that is, countries in which public opinion counted. Their governments were not authorized to play Hitler's game.

The Evidence of Events

Mr. Hull's best argument is neither that based upon our non-intervention policy towards Latin America nor that based upon the risk of war. As for our non-intervention policy as it related to private sales of arms and munitions, it was embodied in the Havana Treaty of 1928, which committed us to permit sales of arms to recognized governments in Latin America but not to rebellious forces seeking to overthrow those governments. If the same doctrine had been applied in the case of Spain, we should have permitted Americans to sell arms to the Madrid Government, which we recognized, but not to Franco, who was in rebellion against it.

On the other hand our generalized policy regarding sales of arms, which had not been uniform before, had been defined in the Neutrality Act of 1935 as one of refusing permission of such sales to non-American states engaged in war. Consequently if Mr. Hull, instead of deciding that the Spanish war as a civil war was not covered by the Neutrality Act, had described it as an international war (which it was) and therefore covered by the Neutrality Act, the result would have been the policy of opposing sales of arms to either side, which was the policy he in fact adopted.

As for the risk of European war, or of our being involved in war as a result of adopting towards Spain the same non-intervention policy we had adopted towards Latin America, I am convinced that the risk was negligible because of Hitler's unreadiness for war.

Mr. Hull's last argument is the best: the evidence of subsequent events. This argument disposes of most of the criticism of his policy towards Spain that has been made in the last two years — criticism based upon the assumption that Spain would aid the Axis in its military conflict with the democracies, that Franco would permit or assist Germany to move through Spain to strike at Gibraltar or at our communication lines in North Africa. This danger was the theme of many an editorial. It was in the minds of our military men down to the fall of Tunisia. It was even — incredible though this may seem to some — in the minds of those in our State Department. There were many impressive reasons to fear that Franco might lend the Axis more than his verbal support and his sympathy. It might have happened. But it did not.

We might possibly have avoided all that worry if we had had a friendly government in Spain during that time instead of an obviously unfriendly one, snarling and sneering at democracy and, now and then, at us. But the fact remains that this unfriendly, pro-Axis government did us no great harm and the Axis no great good; and the final test of a foreign policy is its service to American interests.

The Forces behind Franco

HAVING SPENT two months in Franco territory during the Spanish war and conversed at length with most of Franco's principal advisers, the leaders of the Fascist Falange, and the chief representatives of Hitler in Spain, I had some opportunity to observe the character of the Franco movement. My impressions, sent uncensored from Gibraltar, are on record,[5] and I believe they include no illusions about Franco or his followers. For this I shall always be exceedingly grateful to the young, enthusiastic, and naïve members of the Falange from Bilbao to Sevilla; to the very different yet equally young, enthusiastic, and naïve Requetés; to the often young, always enthusiastic, never naïve Germans who — as diplomats, engineers, exporters, soldiers, and propagandists — were quietly, efficiently, and quite undisguisedly appropriating Spain for the larger purposes of the "master race" and did not in the least mind explaining to me in some detail both their aims and their methods. From the point of view of a correspondent whose main purpose was to try to understand what was going on, I found Falangistas, Requetés, and Germans all quite delightful people.

Probably the most memorable thing about them — though there are to this day people in the United States and in Latin America who will not believe it — was that their ways of justifying the Franco revolt were so different from those of its many ardent defenders in England and the United States. Almost the only thing common to the Anglo-American Franquistas and the Spanish-German ones was that they called all the republicans "reds" and seemed at times to consider republican doctrines to be a Russian invention. It is difficult to recall much further common ground.

The Requetés or Carlists seemed to desire to set the clock

[5] In the columns of the *New York Times* in May, June, and subsequent months of 1938.

back to the time of Ferdinand and Isabella and absolute monarchy and to wash out all that had happened in Europe since the birth of Martin Luther. I say "seemed" because the Requetés represented not so much a program as a tradition which was very vigorous but lacked very clear definition in modern language, apart from their conviction that a king, good or bad, was indispensable.

The Falangistas cared little about the monarchy or about the Church or about religion, although they wore on the sleeves of their dark blue shirts the emblem of the Catholic sovereigns, Ferdinand and Isabella, and admitted with a shrug of the shoulders that Spain was a Catholic country. Their inspiration was more modern, since it came from Fascist Italy and Germany, and their creed and uniforms and salutes and vocabulary may as accurately be called importations as if they had been manufactured goods shipped in from Rome or Berlin (as in one sense they were). Though they were fighting the republican "reds," the Falangistas boasted that many Communists had joined their ranks and that their blue shirts were, so to speak, lined with red. By this they meant that they too were out to overthrow the rule of capitalists, aristocracy, and Church and to create a proletarian state, which they called national syndicalism.

The German attitude — as explained to me at length and with great frankness in Salamanca in May 1938 by the German Ambassador, Herr von Stohrer, an experienced diplomat of the old school who had served in Cairo and emphasized the half-oriental character of Spain — was that after the war Spain would be ruled not by the Church or the aristocracy but by the Falange, whose aims would largely coincide with those of Nazi Germany. He was too much of a diplomat to put into words the implication, which was plain enough without it, that this Fascist state, not the defeat of Communism, was the purpose of the military, economic, and political intervention in Spain by the Nazi Reich.

American Misconceptions

NEITHER OF these attitudes — neither the essentially medieval one of the Requetés nor the frankly non-Catholic and Fascist one of the Falangistas and their German models and allies — seemed to be understood by the disciples and apologists of Franco in the United States, in England, and in Latin America. Neither was, at any rate, expounded.

When I made a tour of South America in 1941, I found that even distinguished and scholarly Catholics there, as in the United States, still refused to believe that the major factor in the Franco revolt was neither religious faith nor the "Christian corporate state" of which Catholics speak, but Axis inspiration and material support. When I mentioned to them the views of the Church that had been expressed to me by leaders and members of the Falange, they were astonished and, I think, incredulous. They regarded the Franço-Falange régime as essentially religious in its motivation and aims, largely because it seemed to oppose Communism. No distinction was drawn between those on the one hand who opposed Communism because they were Catholics or because they were democrats or because they were capitalists or capitalistic-minded, and those on the other hand who opposed it because they were Fascists and therefore equally opposed to the Church, democracy, and capitalism.

The Spanish Fascists had been branded as religious and Catholic, the Spanish republicans had been branded as "reds," and this simple and convenient classification had called forth such heavy commitments in terms of emotion that it had become almost dangerous to question it.

The truth was that each side in Spain was a motley group. The republicans included very active Communists with Russian support, very violent anarchists, Catholics and conservatives of the Basque provinces and Catalonia who were jealous of the autonomy of those regions which Franco opposed, and, I suppose, some who, fantastic though it may seem, believed democracy was possible in Spain. The Franco movement included monarchists, grandees, soldiers, churchmen, bankers and assorted reactionaries, and the Fascist Falange. The Falange came out on top when Franco achieved "unity" by pooling all groups and opinions under its banner — even including the Requetés, who were as different from the Falange as Loyola was from Hitler — and it was the Falange, with its original Fascist character dominant, which ruled Spain after the Spanish war.

There was ample opportunity for error in interpreting this confusion of forces and ideas, which reflected above all the fact that half-feudal Spain had virtually refused to enter the modern world but was now doing so with a vengeance. So regionalist as hardly to be a nation, so individualistic as to be almost anarchistic, Spain was adapted neither to Fascism nor to Communism nor yet to democracy. But it apparently could not go on living under the antique and antiquated institutions which no Reformation and no French Revolution had shaken and no nineteenth-century bourgeois capitalism had greatly modified. It is therefore impossible to describe the Spanish revolution and counter-revolution by any simple formula inspired by contemporary ideologies.

The confused internal causes of the turmoil were the more bewildering because they became complicated by an international conflict that was superimposed upon a social conflict. Consequently most of the passionate foreign onlookers were thinking not so much of Spain as of Moscow or Berlin or ecclesiastical Rome, or were responding emotionally under the influence of conceptions that were valid for England or the United States but had little or only remote relevancy to Spain.

The same confusion may well arise again when we deal with a disturbed foreign country which few understand yet where forces that we think recognizable may call forth immense investments of emotion on the part of Americans having opposing political philosophies.

Principle versus *Practice*

Some may object that adoption of immediate, tangible, and definable American interests as the sole criterion is too cold-blooded and selfish, that our policy should take cognizance of broader human issues, that we cannot be indifferent to tyranny in other countries even if it does no direct injury to our material interests. Just as the Hitler Reich eventually drew us into a world war, so any dictatorial or militaristic régime may not only threaten the existence in foreign lands of the kind of free society which alone is tolerable to us, but may in the end menace our own country. It seems obvious that a democratic world would better suit both our tastes and our interests, and therefore that our influence in foreign regions should be on the side of those who favor that sort of world and against those who do not. Close association with dictatorship, great or small, European or Latin American, seems inconsistent with our principles. In some countries those who are likely to prove our most trustworthy friends in the long run are not the rulers about whom our ambassadors are often rather too eager to make flattering speeches, but those who are in prisons or in hiding or in political seclusion because they believe in democracy.

Yet our diplomats — though they ought to be a trifle less effusive towards autocrats and oligarchies — cannot turn their backs on the major portion of the world which is not yet democratic. They cannot be so high-principled (or, as some would say, so doctrinaire) in their daily contacts with foreigners; contacts which in the nature of the case are not with peoples but with governments, whomever they represent or misrepresent, however they got into power, whatever their political philosophies or morals.

Although sincere democrats whom I met in various parts of Latin America spoke as if they would like us to intervene all over the place to upset dictators and feudal cliques, that is hardly a practicable program. For one thing, those democrats themselves would not really like it; for another, peoples who have experienced neither democracy nor elementary education are doomed to be ruled rather than to rule, and the only question is which minority shall wield the power and how rapid will be their progress (if any) towards fitness for self-rule. Meanwhile, unless we break off diplomatic relations with all non-self-governing peoples (which would include most of Latin America), we must carry on those relations with governments that do not derive their powers from the ballot box and perhaps do not believe in ballot boxes.

Consequently there is a perhaps inevitable and permanent divergence between our national ideals and our everyday diplomacy. It probably is no greater than the divergence between our ideals and our practical policies in the domestic field, or between the principles and practices of most individuals. Just as a man engaged in business must be ready for honest men and rogues alike, so in foreign affairs we are obliged to deal with such official material as fate happens to cast up in a somewhat capricious world.

X

WASTED VICTORY

Hopes of the Axis

IT was inevitable that the Germans and Japanese should hope that, if they lost, their defeat might be mitigated by the humanitarianism and war-weariness of the Allies and that the Allied coalition might fall apart, to the advantage of its enemies.

Let us frankly admit that neither of these hopes was without historical basis. This admission will be made readily by those who recall what happened in the year 1918 and afterward, and by those who are aware of the existing suspicions — likewise not without historical basis — between the Russian régime and its accidental allies, the British and Americans.

The pages that follow may seem unduly critical, especially of the British, who have amazed the world by their supreme courage in meeting an attack that should not have been permitted to materialize. They may seem too critical of the Americans, who have shown courage and ingenuity in winning a world war which — if they had had a foreign policy — could easily have been prevented. It does not detract from our appreciation of the qualities displayed in combat to recall that if these two peoples had shown a moderate amount of political intelligence there would have been no combat to face.

Let us therefore take due note of the historical basis for the Axis hopes of defeating us in the end. Let us recall the strange behavior of the Allies in throwing away their victory a quarter-century ago, after gaining it by immense sacrifices — behavior that has been forgotten or has grown dim in the memories of many.

Collapse of a Coalition

WHEN the massive Allied power, created slowly through four years of effort, had overwhelmed Germany in 1918, it began almost at once to disintegrate. The collective economic controls for mobilizing and allocating raw materials and foodstuffs and shipping were quickly abandoned. The United States and Britain dropped their financial aid to France. The Bank of England and the Bank of France let their co-operative agreement lapse. The United States withdrew from the Supreme Economic Council, which might have guided the reconstruction of Europe but which died in 1920. Within six months of the armistice, Polish forces, equipped and sent to Poland by the Allies, were resisting decisions of the Allied Supreme Council in Galicia; and shortly afterward Polish and Czech forces, both armed by the Allies, were fighting each other.[1] When the Senate rejected the Treaty of Versailles, the United States withdrew from the Reparations Commission, the Rhineland High Commission, and the Inter-Allied Military and Naval Commission of Control, leaving Britain and France to solve Europe's problems. But Britain and France parted company over reparations and became rivals with opposing policies in Europe and Asia.[2] The collapse of the Allied unity that had won the war was now complete. The reversion to extreme nationalism had begun, and Germany lost no time in profiting from it.

The stage was now set, in the early nineteen-twenties, for the recovery by Germany of her military power, the definitive break between Britain and France having come in 1923 over the Ruhr occupation. Meanwhile the victors in the war, who already regarded themselves as rivals, arranged to assist Japan along her path to future conquest. At the Paris Peace Conference in 1919 they had delivered to Japan under mandates the former German islands north of the Equator

[1] E. H. Carr: *Conditions of Peace* (New York, Macmillan, 1942).
[2] An excellent summary of the disintegration of Allied unity after the last war is that of Howard P. Whidden, Jr. (Foreign Policy Reports, Feb. 15, 1943).

which were to serve her so well in 1941 when she attacked the Dutch Empire, the British, and the United States. At the Washington Naval Conference of 1921 they went further by giving Japan naval mastery of the Western Pacific.[3] This was generally regarded at the time as a great feat of statesmanship. Thus, immediately after the first German world war, the United States and Britain in their innocence combined to create the conditions and to strengthen the aggressive forces that were to produce within two decades another and larger world war, this time a simultaneous German-Japanese onslaught aimed at the conquest of both Europe and the Pacific.

At the same time there began in the English-speaking world, under scholarly auspices, a kind of campaign to prove that Germany had been less guilty than France and Russia in causing the first world war of the century; that she was, in fact, comparatively innocent. This thesis was adopted by highly influential portions of the populations of Britain and the United States. Its effect was to undermine the moral basis of the peace treaty, which had provided for the disarmament of Germany on the ground that she had been responsible for the war. The conclusion to which this argument led could only be that it was unfair to disarm Germany — which soon became Hitler's plea; and that she should be permitted to rearm — which soon became British policy.[4] It almost seemed

---

[3] The resulting naval treaty limited capital ships (Britain and the United States having fifteen each, Japan nine) in such a way as to insure the impregnability of Japan and "an irresistible dominance of her power in Eastern Asia," as Professor Bemis expresses it. (Samuel Flagg Bemis: *A Diplomatic History of the United States*, New York, Henry Holt, 1938.) At the same time the United States agreed not to increase the fortifications of its Pacific possessions excepting those adjacent to the coast of the United States, the Panama Canal and Alaska.

[4] This conclusion was upheld officially as late as 1934 in Britain when Sir John Simon, the Foreign Secretary, said in the House of Commons that "Germany's claim to equality of rights in the matter of armaments cannot be resisted and ought not to be resisted." (Quoted by John F. Kennedy in *Why England Slept*; New York, Wilfred Funk, 1940.) At that time Hitler had been in power in Germany for exactly a year.

that the four-year struggle against German militarism had been a huge mistake, that the millions of lives which that struggle had cost had been spent under a misapprehension, that the whole affair should be written off like a bad investment and forgotten.

Never before, certainly not on such a scale, did great powers celebrate a victory in a life-and-death struggle by deliberately throwing away the power and the advantages it had gained for them, while reviving and arming and financing their enemies for still greater conquests. It was understandable that the Germans, just before surrendering their fleet at Scapa Flow, should scuttle it. It seems incredible that the democratic powers should have scuttled their hard-earned victory.

The British, having destroyed the rival German fleet, were not worried much by the prospect of a revived German army. The Americans were intent solely upon limiting the naval power of their former ally, Britain, and their potential enemy, Japan, and thought this could be done by treaties. The French, eyeing the Germans with a suspicion not shared by the British or Americans, striving to make Germany pay reparations, had come to be viewed in Britain and America as trouble-makers who perversely refused to forgive and forget what had happened between the years 1914 and 1918.

Filled with misgivings about the intentions of the French on the continent that their army now dominated, Britons and Americans thought that German militarism had been crushed only to be replaced by French militarism; and the British remedy was to support Germany against France. This was doubtless what Lord Tyrrell, British Ambassador in Paris, had in mind when he said that the British had concluded that the French had become Germans while the Germans had become Britons. It was as if Britain had for four years fought the wrong country.

This was the feeling of many British and American soldiers who returned from the Rhineland to report that Germany was cleaner and better organized than France and altogether a more congenial country. Meanwhile Britons and Americans grew weary of the complaints of the French, who seemed absurdly disturbed about future security against Germany and who objected to paying their war debts. Britons and Americans became anti-French and pro-German. At least, their feelings towards Germany were warmer than towards France. For Germany, who had lost the war, they felt sorry.

Helping Germany to Repeat

THIS CONQUEST of Anglo-American sympathy was Germany's first great post-war victory. It led to further victories — economic, political, and eventually military. It opened for Germany the road to escape from the restrictions of the peace treaty, to the re-establishment of her military power. Along with the sympathy came credits, eagerly proffered by American and British banks for rebuilding German industry and for municipal improvements. Approximately $2,500,000,000 of American private funds thus flowed into Germany to help restore her power. These funds exceeded the reparations which Germany paid to the Allies for the damage her invasions had caused. Germany later defaulted on these loans, which then dropped in value and were partly extinguished through repurchase by Germany of her own devalued bonds.

The sympathy of the English-speaking world was Germany's most useful weapon at a time when she had no other weapons. It was her most valuable asset down to the day Hitler began another world war by attacking Poland. The thesis, popular in Britain and America, that Germany had been no more responsible for the war of 1914 than France or Russia, supported Hitler's argument that Germany had been wronged by the peace treaty and should refuse to be bound by it.

This argument impressed many Britons as logical and natural, if not indeed laudable. Hitler, they thought, had a case. They thought so for various reasons — some because they disliked the Polish Corridor, some because they perceived the economic error of the reparations settlement, some because they did not like Frenchmen and thought they liked Germans, some because they were weary of war and opposed to any British commitments on the continent, some because they were wealthy and feared the revolutionary potentialities of either war or Communism. For whatever reasons, Britons suffered from an uneasy conscience about the peace treaty, which they believed had been harsh and unfair. Therefore, the thing to do was to liquidate the treaty, whereupon Germany would be grateful and as peaceful as Britain. What had been a kind of sportsman-like magnanimity towards a beaten foe became something very like a moral sanction for German rearmament and, especially on the part of those influential groups who said "Better the Nazis than the Communists," for German expansion to the east.[5]

It was for these reasons that upon Hitler's first real breach of the peace treaty — his adoption of conscription in 1935 without awaiting the permission which the British were preparing to grant on conditions — the British were not shocked or angered but promptly signed with him a new armament limitation agreement, this time for submarines, which Hitler would not need for the conquest of the plains and steppes of Eastern Europe. This incensed the French, who consequently showed little sympathy when, the same year, Britain belatedly grew concerned over Mussolini's seizure of Ethiopia, close to the British imperial water-route to Asia, and for once tried half-heartedly to mobilize the neglected League of Nations against aggression. The display of weakness and hesitation which resulted must have encouraged Hitler. At any rate he lost no time in taking, in March 1936, a step that affected the balance of Europe. He tore up another part of the peace treaty, a major military limitation, by occupying the demilitarized Rhineland, even though the army he then had

---

[5] The conservatives who summed up their tolerance towards Hitler by saying that anyhow Fascism was not so bad as Communism could not then conceive that Hitlerism was likewise a revolution which might prove similar to Communism in its consequences for Europe and the world. But they admitted that war, whatever caused it, was itself a revolutionary force, and the conclusion to which this thought drove them was that peace should be bought by concessions to Hitler. If you told them it could not be bought in that way, they put you down as a hopeless pessimist and warmonger.

was not formidable and could easily have been driven back by the French. This secured Germany's western frontier preparatory to her move eastward.

These easy treaty violations suggested aggression in a large way at no great cost or risk, particularly if undertaken jointly by Hitler, Mussolini, and Japan. They had already proved mutually helpful, fear of Germany having engendered French opposition to coercion of Mussolini. It was in these circumstances that the Axis was born. It was created by democratic lethargy, division, and ineptitude. The first result was an Axis-assisted civil war in Spain, where the German air force received valuable training in bombing nonmilitary objectives and in machine-gunning civilians in towns and villages and fields, thus placing in power a pro-German Spanish régime.

It was characteristic that this display of violence in Europe shocked the British as neither Mussolini's poison gas in Abyssinia nor Hitler's treaty violations could do. In the ruins of Guernica, the Basque town which became the first example of precision-bombing, they rightly saw a kind of omen for Europe and for Britain. But even that was not sufficient to persuade them that the Second World War had already started. Conservative minds in Britain and in America viewed the Spanish war chiefly as a crusade against Communism. That is, they adopted Hitler's contention; and British policy, oddly called "non-intervention," was in effect pro-Axis in the important sense that it enabled the Axis to win the war in Spain, its first military conquest on European soil.

That other conquests would follow and that at some point they would expand into a European war could not be doubted by anyone who knew Germany and the British attitude towards Germany. The only question was when the democracies would feel compelled to resist.

Hitler's long-heralded move eastward came while the Axis was approaching its victory in Spain — in March 1938, when he took Austria. His army was then larger and more mechanized, and he could take greater risks. Austria proved as easy as the Rhineland, both having met considerable British approval. Six months later it was the fortified western rim of Czechoslovakia — the first bite — that fell to Hitler with the somewhat shamed consent of the French and British, still trying to buy peace with other peoples' territories.[6]

[6] A disproportionate share of the blame for Britain's humiliation at Munich has fallen upon Mr. Neville Chamberlain, the Prime Minister at the time. It was an episode that brought shame to Englishmen. Mr. Chamberlain spoke very naïvely when he came back proclaiming he had achieved "peace in our time." Mr. Chamberlain's own explanation was that Britain was in no condition to go to war in 1938 and must play for time to arm. This he managed to do in extremely difficult circumstances. The real error, however, was not confined to the single year 1938 but was spread over a series of emotionally confused years when some in Britain were pressing the government to support the League against the government's will. Mr. Chamberlain, being a member of that government and of the Conservative Party, shared the blame; but the responsibility for Britain's diplomatic defeats in the succeeding years and for the risk she ran of military defeat in 1940 rests likewise upon Mr. Chamberlain's predecessor, Mr. Baldwin.

The disgust of many Britons with the results of their own folly and their leaders' negligence was well expressed just after Munich by "Evoe" (E. V. Knox) in the following verse in *Punch*, a classic example of British self-criticism (reproduced here by the kind permission of the proprietors of *Punch*):

A MATTER OF DEFINITION

I do not know what peace is. But I think
Some people write it in a different ink
From others. I myself could never state
What aspirations were legitimate.
I know that, seizing a heraldic chance,
Our good King Harry claimed the throne of France.
I know a broken-down republic stands
A vassal state just now in German hands.
And possibly the thing called peace will come
When we have given up to Nazidom
    Poland, Lithuania,
    Africa, Rumania,
    Hungary, Denmark,
    Turkey, the Ukraine.

I often ask what peace is. Some declare
When Hitler sighs it to the Autumn air,
When Goebbels, kneeling by his little bed,
Breathes it Heavenward ere he lays his head
On the white pillow, when von Ribbentrop

The first eastern bastion had now fallen without a shot, and, after the Munich agreement partitioning Czechoslovakia, Hitler seemed to have a kind of Anglo-French license to go as far as he liked towards the east so long as peace reigned on the Rhine, which Mr. Stanley Baldwin had called Britain's frontier. It seems certain that if Hitler had been wiser, he could have made German power effective and complete to the mouth of the Danube by utilizing his now tremendous diplomatic and military prestige and the economic weapon which Germany had already successfully wielded through her barter treaties with the Balkan countries. In this way he could easily have gained dominion of the continent for the German Reich and created a modern counterpart of the Holy Roman Empire. He had dreamed of doing that. But he did not know how. It was too great a task for the frenzied little corporal who saw life in terms of Wagnerian operas, who could incite Germany to violence but could not achieve statesmanship. He missed the great opportunity to consolidate in the form of lasting power the sympathy and assistance show-

---

>Ingeminates the word and will not stop —
>To them it does not mean a girl with wings
>And not much on except her underthings,
>But some large, bulkier lady, full of facts,
>Commercial penetrations, axes, pacts
>>And little bits of Asia,
>>Egypt and Dalmatia,
>>Persia, Madagascar
>>And Alsace-Lorraine.
>
>I want to know what peace is. Does it mean
>That half the countries that have ever been
>Ought to be seized and poisoned by a chap
>Who has his own ideas about the map,
>Whilst we look on and smile and call him friend
>And shake his hand and tell him at the end
>That everything he did was for the best,
>Whether in Timbuctoo or Bucharest,
>So long as Rule Britannia rules the waves,
>Britons never, never shall be slaves,
>>But only Patagonia
>>And Belgium and Estonia
>>Tartary and Iceland,
>>Portugal and Spain?

ered upon Germany by the democracies for nearly two decades.

Hitler misread his license and overestimated the tolerance of the British people as distinct from their government. When he broke his own Munich agreement, that license expired. For Britain there could not be a second Munich, even though Germany excelled in air power and London's defences were still far from adequate. Hitler did not understand this. There had been, it must be admitted, ground for misunderstanding. Unlike Sir Edward Grey in 1914, Mr. Chamberlain in 1939 did warn Germany that if she attacked Poland, Britain would fight. But such was the effect of previous British sympathy and tolerance that Hitler did not believe him. The consequence was not merely the attack on Poland but all the later attacks, including that on Pearl Harbor.

Having it Both Ways

BRITISH POLICY in the crucial years when Germany was rapidly rearming while Britain failed to do so was determined by a mood of easy-going, idealistic confusion. Like the Americans in the same period who wanted to eat their cake and have it too — who thought to prevent war by threatening to be neutral if aggression took place, who in 1940 and 1941 wanted Britain to win but did not want to help her by joining in her struggle — the British democracy clung to hopes that were mutually incompatible. The British people wanted a strong League of Nations to keep the peace but did not want the rearmament of Britain which alone could make the League strong. They wanted a guaranteed peace but not the means by which it could be guaranteed. The "Peace Ballot," a poll taken by supporters of the League in 1935, showed that a majority of the 11,300,000 persons consulted favored reduction of armaments by international agreement and at the same time favored forcible collective resistance to aggression. In the national election that followed none of the parties advocated rearmament.

The result was that just after the election a British Government felt authorized or commanded by public opinion to promise its full support of the League, although it had neither adequate armed force to carry through such a policy nor, apparently, any serious intention of carrying it through. This was indicated when, after solemnly promising to resist aggression, the Foreign Minister proposed to compromise with aggression by giving Italy about half of Ethiopia. An outburst of indignation in England then caused the Minister to resign and the government to adopt a policy which might be described — to use a later American phrase — as resistance to aggression "short of war." The result was the success of the aggression in spite of limited economic "sanctions" against Italy. For Britain had informed Italy that, whatever she did, Britain would not go to war — just as we had informed the world that, whoever was attacked and whatever the circumstances, we should remain neutral. Such attitudes virtually deprived the two greatest democracies of effective influence in keeping the peace which they both valued so highly.

Speaking in the House of Commons on November 12, 1936, Mr. Stanley Baldwin (now Lord Baldwin) made this amazing statement:

From 1933 I and my friends were very worried about what was happening in Europe. You'll remember that at that time the Disarmament Conference was sitting in Geneva, and there probably was a stronger pacifist feeling running through this country than at any other time since the war. . . . My position as head of a great party was not altogether a comfortable one. . . . Suppose I had gone to the country and said that Germany was rearming and that we must rearm. Does anybody think that this pacific country would have rallied to that at that moment? I cannot think of anything that would have made the loss of the election from my point of view more certain.

This was democracy right enough, since Mr. Baldwin had his ear to the ground, in the American phrase, and was watching the election returns. But it was democracy in one of its most careless moods, a mood to shake one's faith in democracy. For the Prime Minister naïvely confessed that he was thinking and acting "as the head of a great party" and not as the head of a great nation and Empire. As the leader of a great nation his duty, in the interest of that nation's safety, was to enlighten his people and awaken them from their lazy idealism. But as the head of a great party his job was to get votes — even, it would seem, at the risk of the safety of the country — and this he did, doubtless consoling himself with the belief that the return to power of the Conservative Party was likewise important to the safety of the nation.

Our own leaders faced a similar dilemma when public opinion seemed to compel them to accept a Neutrality Act which they knew would contribute to aggression and tie their hands in preventing war, an act that the President later said he regretted having signed.

From this one may conclude not only that the British people largely ignored or misunderstood the perils developing across the Channel, but that democracies in general are inclined to preoccupy themselves with their domestic affairs and to neglect dangers abroad. This seems inevitable since only a comparatively small minority can possibly be adequately informed of foreign affairs, though it must be said that during those crucial years the better newspapers of the United States presented an admirably clear picture of the trends that were at work. The problem of maintaining peace is to a very great extent the problem of informing the public in democratic countries where no defensive policies can be carried out without at least the tacit approval of the bulk of the people.

Pro-German Britain

THIS SINGULAR British mood would not have been possible save for the essentially friendly attitude of the British people towards Germany. It seems incredible today that the first great strategic move towards world war, Hitler's re-militarization of the Rhineland in 1936, should actually have been applauded by the majority of the British people. The explanation is to be found in the sympathy towards Germany and the remorse over the peace treaty which had colored British views of Europe for fifteen years. It is to be found also in the somewhat naïve assumption of the British that the Germans were sufficiently like themselves to respond to an act of fairness, even belated, and to look with horror upon a European war. These assumptions led to a mental confusion in which the aggressions, though they formed a logical sequence, were viewed as isolated incidents arising from specific local causes. The larger design of which they were mere parts was not perceived. Here both the British lack of imagination and a kind of "will not to believe" played their parts. Few Britons had any idea of the character of Hitler or the character of the German nation, and war was so far from their desires that it was kept as far as possible from their thoughts.

During those years I had seen the Nazi movement grow up, had visited German universities where it had taken deep root, had attended its meetings, read its press, and talked with Hitler and lesser leaders. But when I returned to London and was questioned about Germany in clubs and country houses, I found that many Britons declined to believe the simplest facts about the Nazi movement and about the Germans. "Do you really mean that they arrest people without warrants?" asked an educated Briton as late as 1938, when for five years concentration camps had been filled with men seized in their beds by Nazis without thought of trial or warrants, which had become virtually obsolete. The incredulous Briton must have read this in his newspapers, but he would not believe it.[7]

Even some Britons who had traveled in Germany came home emphasizing what they considered the redeeming features of Nazidom. The British always try to see the good in people instead of the bad, which they dislike to admit exists. They were impressed above all by the sun-tanned youths who

[7] He had his American counterparts, notably the American students at the University of Munich who in November 1938, just after the pogroms that swept over Germany on Nazi orders, wrote home that they did not believe any Jews had been injured since they had not seen anything of the sort happen. The injuries, many of them fatal, were of course inflicted in cellars, in the Brown House, in closed trucks or railway cars on the way to concentration camps, or within those camps; and to none of these vantage points had the young Americans been invited.

climbed mountains and worked in labor camps and marched about singing gayly, as British youth did not. They declined to associate these idyllic scenes with militarism and perhaps did not know that one of the charming songs they heard was "When Jewish blood spurts from the knife." This was a part of the incurable tendency among Britons of which Lord Tyrrell had spoken — their tendency to confuse the Germans with themselves. Others met Hitler, who told them how he admired Britain and how he longed for peace, and they came home feeling that Hitler might be a bit odd but was really not a bad fellow, and that, since he raved against Communism, he must be animated by conservative instincts. This view was widely held in "The City," London's financial district, where Dr. Schacht was cordially received in high places and where the belief persisted that a financial deal or two would fix everything up with Germany.

It happened that on the day after the occupation of the Rhineland I took tea with a company of educated and traveled young Englishmen and Englishwomen in a Hampstead garden. The great oaks, the old brick wall grown a deep russet in a century's weathering, the wistaria that half enclosed it, seemed to symbolize an old and ripe and secure civilization that none but a madman would think of trying to destroy. That there was any such danger had hardly occurred to those serene young Britons, though at that moment Hitler's army was moving into a strategic area which it had once been thought wise to demilitarize.

That action brought expressions of delight from some of the Britons present. The Rhineland was German territory, and why should not German troops march in? "How should we feel if we were told we might not march into Kent?" asked one of the company, as if the strategic significance of Kent were identical with that of the Rhineland. This question represented the unanimous view of the British party, who thought the removal of a genuine grievance would soothe the feverish German mind and facilitate better relations.

In the summer of the same year, desiring to sample the attitude of average Britons, I journeyed in the Midlands where

I questioned people of all classes, notably in the small town of Uttoxeter, Staffordshire, where I spent a week and met a large portion of the population. On the whole they knew almost nothing of Germany, save that some veterans of the last war and of the army of occupation thought the Germans rather pleasant people and felt sure Britain had made a mistake in fighting them. A few rare individuals thought the Germans were getting warlike again, but the overwhelming opinion was that Germany was a civilized nation with whom Britain could discuss and treat as she did with the United States.[8]

Yet many Britons knew, and all had an opportunity to know, what was happening in Germany and what it meant for Britain. The reporting of the British correspondents in Berlin was faithful and scholarly.[9] British consular officers scattered over Germany were well informed and without illusions, as I knew from talking with them and as their subsequently published reports proved. The Foreign Office, which Mr. Chamberlain brushed aside when he personally directed what is now known as his appeasement policy, looked at the German scene with a clear and realistic eye. The best British weeklies — the *Economist*, the *Spectator*, the *New Statesman and Nation*, and *Time and Tide* — supplied accurate and enlightened news and comment for the comparatively few who read them. The brilliant editor of *Punch*, Mr. E. V. Knox, in articles and verses managed the difficult feat of ridiculing Hitler while emphasizing the Nazi danger. But as late as the spring of 1939

---

[8] Thinking there might be a relationship between this state of mind and the newspapers the people of Uttoxeter read, I consulted the principal news agent, who told me that the popular London papers that did not take life seriously (except as it included crimes and horse races) circulated some 200 copies each in the town, while the London *Times* and the *Manchester Guardian*, which are designed to inform their readers about the world they live in, sold fewer than half a dozen copies each.

[9] Outstanding among those correspondents, and deserving places in the birthday honors list for the service they rendered their country, were Mr. Norman Ebbutt of the *Times* and Mr. F. A. Voigt of the *Manchester Guardian*.

each shaft of wit or irony directed at Hitler brought to *Punch* many protesting letters from conservative readers in England. Some were inspired by the belief that the British ought not to irritate Hitler, though one speaker in Parliament remarked that you could not irritate him because he was in a state of permanent irritation. Britain's full awakening did not come until the armed might of Hitler stood thirty miles from Britain's shores, when the courage of her people made up for their short-sightedness.

Meanwhile France, frustrated in her desire to maintain the Allied coalition of the last war as a guarantee against renewed German aggression, weakened by the inflation of the nineteen-twenties and the world-wide economic depression of the nineteen-thirties, dreading another war when her population had not recovered from the last, yet fearing social revolution almost equally with war, was weak, divided, inadequately armed at least in the air, and to a great extent at the mercy of Britain, her former and expected Ally.

The Maginot Line, which represented the hope of fighting the next war with steel and concrete rather than with the human flesh that France could ill afford to sacrifice, symbolized the delusions that in France developed from the hopeless position of an old and highly civilized nation living next a neighbor vastly superior in numbers, in industrial capacity, in warlike spirit.

The system of French alliances with satellite states — Poland, Czechoslovakia, Yugoslavia — was, like the Maginot Line, a makeshift designed somehow to fill the gap left by the absence of either a defensive coalition or a system of collective security such as the League of Nations might conceivably have become had the great powers willed it.

M. Aristide Briand, who may be called the first appeaser in the sense that he strove long and arduously for a rapprochement with Germany in her pseudo-republican period, was quoted as saying that "France is no longer the France of Louis XIV." That is, she could not manage Europe alone. Yet she received little aid from those who had helped her defeat Imperial Germany. France being unable to manage Europe, and Britain being unwilling, Europe could merely wait until Hitler undertook the task in his own way.

France's ability to play an effective rôle in Europe was fatally impaired by what some considered the threat of social revolution within. When Hitler was beginning his conquests in 1938 there was much talk of possible civil war in France, and the fear of working-class revolt created in certain important circles a longing for a strong state such as Hitler seemed to represent and a sympathy with Hitler's professed opposition to Communism. France, a house divided, fell at the first shock; and with that ancient bulwark gone, Europe was Hitler's until extra-European forces could come into play.

What Led to Pearl Harbor

THE ABOVE references to British faults do not imply any justification for American complacency. American faults ran parallel with British when they did not precede them. The United States was the first to withdraw from the Allied coalition that had won the war, the first to repudiate the peace settlement which, imperfect though it was, could have been revised and broadened and consolidated had the will existed to do so. Americans joined in the sympathy towards Germany which had such unexpected results. Americans contributed far more than British to finance Germany's recovery while assuming no political or military responsibility for what might follow. If the British were too preoccupied with sea power and paid less than due attention to the security of France, their own first line of defence, Americans on their side paid too little attention to the security of Britain which, though they did not usually admit it, was *their* first line of defence.

There is a striking parallel between Britain's policy and America's, or rather the lack of policy of both, in the years between the world wars. Britain refused until 1939 to assume any military commitments beyond the Rhine, while the United States refused to assume commitments outside the Americas and her own possessions. But to win the war both assumed the commitments which, if assumed earlier, probably would have prevented war. Both were guilty of letting their defensive power fall too low for fulfillment of the commitments they did take, Britain being unable to hold Singapore or Hong Kong, the United States being unable to hold the Philippines or Guam or Wake and very nearly losing Hawaii. Britons and Americans have much in common, including the blunders they have made.

Some of those blunders are described here because they show, more clearly than any argument can, the need for an American foreign policy that will take account of the realities which the blunderers of the past overlooked or denied or refused to face. Inexcusable as some of them are, those blunders should be kept in mind and memory for the good of the countries that were the victims of them.

"Remember Pearl Harbor" became an American slogan. Its purpose apparently was to prevent our forgetting the perfidy of the Japanese. But that perfidy was made possible by an American blunder, or rather a whole series of blunders. If somebody was caught napping at Pearl Harbor on December 7, 1941, what about all those who were napping when Japan was building up her aggressive power year by year and when Germany was plotting with her for a war which would give the one control of the Pacific, the other dominion of Europe and Africa? Mr. John Kennedy wrote in 1940 a book called *Why England Slept*. It dealt with the period of incredible lethargy described in this chapter. To it there should be a companion volume entitled *Why America Slept*. For both countries failed to perceive in time the perils that were developing before their eyes — and both have fought courageously to win a war that they should not have permitted to break out.

As a new victory approaches, it is well to recall the victory that was thrown away two decades ago. As a defeated Germany looks hopefully for a second withdrawal by the United States into isolation, for the break-up of another victorious coalition, for the resumption of the distrust and rivalry which divided Britain and America after the last war, let us remember all the blunders and fumbles and stupidities, all the mutual bitterness, all the nationalistic follies, all the futile talk of disarmament, all the blind provincialism, all the diplomatic nonsense, all the safety-first caution, by which the great democracies contrived in the last twenty years to bring on another world war.

"Remember Pearl Harbor," certainly. But let memory be capacious enough to embrace other notable events as well. Let Britons remember the days when their government seemed more intent upon rearming Germany than upon rearming Britain. Let them remember an editorial in the *Times* which first proposed to dismember Czechoslovakia in the interest of peace and, I believe, of Czechoslovakia. Let them remember Munich, and "non-intervention" in Spain, and all the things that made Britons a bit ashamed of their government in Hitler's heyday.

In American memories Pearl Harbor should stand not as an isolated event but as the final link in a connected chain of events, a logical sequence running through the years. When Americans think of that Japanese attack on their flag and their territory and their security, which resulted from the successes of Japan's partner, Hitler, they should think also of their refusal to help sustain the Allied victory in Europe which they had helped to win; of their government's refusal for several years to admit officially that the League of Nations existed; of the aid they gave in restoring German power; of the gift of naval supremacy in Asia which their Washington Naval Conference made to Japan; of the Neutrality Act which placed restrictions alike upon the democracies who were our inevitable allies and the dictatorships who were our inevitable enemies.

All these things should be filed in the same drawer of memory with Pearl Harbor, to which they led. Had the United States and Britain maintained the peace in Europe after defeating Imperial Germany, there would have been no aggression in either Europe or the Pacific and hence no Pearl Harbor.[10]

[10] Maintaining peace involves two things: safeguards against aggression, and the creation of economic conditions permitting nations to

The whole tragic pattern of those two decades was a mosaic of interconnected events in Asia and in Europe. Japan's attack on Manchuria in 1931 was followed by Mussolini's attack on Abyssinia in 1935, Hitler's march into the Rhineland in 1936, Japan's attack on China in 1937, Hitler's seizure of Austria and Czechoslovakia in 1938, and Mussolini's rape of Albania and Hitler's onslaught on Poland in 1939. Even after the war the pendulum of aggression swung between Asia and Europe, Hitler attacking Russia in 1941 and Japan following with her attack on British, American, and Dutch possessions the same year.

Let us remember Pearl Harbor. But let us remember also that it was the price paid for attempted isolation in a time when isolation had become an absurdity. It was, in other words, the price of not having a foreign policy.

---

live at peace. Wars are not always the product of internal social stress — Germany's war of 1914 was not — but the Nazi power that made this war throve on the unemployment and the economic uncertainty that followed the world depression.

XI

INVITATION TO AGGRESSION

Origin of a Partnership

THE intervention in Spain by Germany and Italy marked the début of the Axis. There for the first time those two powers experimented with deliberate and unprovoked military violence within Europe. The experiment was a success and consequently an augury of what was to come on an expanding scale. Thus the Spanish War was a prelude and a dress rehearsal for the European war. It opened what may be called the culminating phase of the Hitler period — the period from the spring of 1933 onward during which Hitler, absolute master of a newly armed and arrogant Germany, dominated the history of the world. That period was to end when Germany's power was broken.

The Hitler period embraced both Europe and Asia, for a kind of partnership in aggression was rapidly developing which increasingly linked the two continents and was to draw them both, with the other continents as well, into war. Yet it was Germany who was the leader and animator of this process. Germany was the protagonist in what Germans like to call a historic movement. Since Britain was accustomed to expect the New World to redress the balance of the Old, Hitler called in the Germany of the Orient to tilt that balance in favor of his conquest of Europe.[1]

[1] The German-Japanese alliance dates from 1936 when Berlin and Tokyo signed what they chose to call an "Anti-Comintern Pact" — doubtless because that name might cause it to appear harmless or even admirable inasmuch as practically everybody of any social or political importance in Europe, and perhaps in America, was as much against the Comintern as the Germans and Japanese said they were. It was like being against sin.

The real purpose of the pact was anti-British and anti-American,

INVITATION TO AGGRESSION

Thus the coincidence of aggressive impulses in Tokyo and Berlin was adroitly utilized to paralyze further the lethargic democracies by threatening them, including the United States, with a double war, a two-ocean war that would strain even their great naval power. It was amazing how slow the democracies were to perceive this maneuver and to act accordingly.

The democracies moved slowly even in their verbal resistance to aggression, and this behavior formed one of the major factors in the "historic movement" in which for a long while they played a passive rôle. On February 24, 1933, the League Assembly adopted the Lytton Report condemning Japan's invasion of Manchuria, which had taken place one year and five months earlier. The next day the United States, through the Secretary of State, Henry L. Stimson, expressed substantial agreement with the League's judiciously delayed conclusions.

Less than a month earlier — on January 30 — Hitler had become Chancellor of Germany through a combination of luck, intrigue, and violence. At the very moment of his grasp of power he had before his eyes the dramatic and impressive example of Japan's successful invasion, at which the democracies had looked on for a year and a half in slightly disquieted contemplation, finally responding with a dialectically shattering volume of printed paper. Such was the spectacle,

---

since it contemplated Hitler's engaging our attention in Europe to ease the way for Japan's aggression in the Pacific, while Japan for her part might prevent American intervention against Hitler by threatening simultaneous war in our other ocean.

This became clear — to all those who might have had any doubt about it — on September 27, 1940, when the Germans and the Japanese, this time disdaining ingenious labels, announced an alliance, taking Italy in as usual. Like the bulls of Pope Alexander VI, which divided the New World between the kings of Spain and of Portugal, the Axis agreement gave Europe to Germany and Italy and "Greater East Asia" to Japan. It provided that the three Axis partners would assist one another if any one of them were attacked by a power not then involved in the European or the Chinese-Japanese war — that is, the United States. Thus the Axis was striving hard, along with some Americans, to insure our continued isolation.

the lesson, the "tip-off," that the democracies offered to Hitler as an inauguration present when he began gathering into his hands all the reins of power to which a docile, state-broken people responded like a horse with a tender mouth. Hitler made haste to draw the obvious conclusion.

This acceptance of Japan's aggression was not an isolated event. It was the lineal descendant of the sympathetic, tolerant, and trustful attitude towards our past and potential enemies and of the suspicious, competitive attitude of the former Allies towards each other which are described in the preceding chapter. It was the result of the American policy of signing pacts with nothing to back them up, like the Briand-Kellogg Pact in which everybody joyfully renounced war, including those who were feverishly preparing for it. It was a result of our noncommital but verbally sympathetic attitude of making no promises whatever, yet of endeavoring, by acting independently, to "reinforce what the League does," as Mr. Stimson put it. It was the result of our policy of stiffening other powers against aggression while officially professing our neutrality between aggressors and their victims. It was the result of ten years of the Washington Naval Treaty which gave Japan mastery of Far Eastern waters in the hope that, being thus free to do as she would, she would not misuse that freedom. It was the result of what Professor Bemis calls "a face-saving retreat of United States diplomacy in the Far East under the cover of a multilateral international agreement for the observance of the traditional American policies for the open door and the administrative, political and territorial integrity of China."[2]

While the United States was thus backing out of the Far East, Britain was backing out of Europe by whittling down her commitments to the minimum (which was the defence of France, Belgium, and the Channel coast).

In these circumstances it may have been diabolical but it was also logical for Japan to assume that Asia had now become her hunting ground and for Hitler to assume that Europe east of the Rhine had become his. This, at any rate, is

[2] *Op. cit.*, p. 696.

INVITATION TO AGGRESSION

what they did assume. It was this assumption — which in the ensuing five years did not seem at all fantastic — that formed and shaped what we have called the Hitler period.

In fairness not to the aggressors but to ourselves — in the interest of that clear perception of realities that is vital to our security — let us remember not only the aggressions but the invitation to aggression which preceded and faithfully accompanied them.

That invitation was implicit, indeed more than implicit, in the whole policy of the democracies down to 1939 and, in the case of the United States, until 1941. It was implicit in that there was no assurance that the democracies would join forces to resist aggression at any given point in space or time. It was more than implicit in that the United States, through Congress and President, had proclaimed her intention to remain neutral — that is, not to resist aggression until it should strike against her own territory or her own hemisphere. We had virtually said to Hitler and Japan: Attack anyone you like so long as you don't attack us; we shall protest and denounce but shall not fight until our own domain or our own defensive sphere is invaded. Britain said almost the same thing by accepting a series of aggressions in Africa and in Europe between 1935 and 1939, though what she said to Hitler was: Attack anywhere you like so long as it is east of the Rhine.

How the Democracies Assisted the Axis

THUS DEMOCRATIC policies to a remarkable extent may be said in effect to have coincided with Axis policies through most of the Hitler period. The democracies sought to avoid a general war — that is, a war between great powers. This was also the purpose of the Axis. The democratic leaders thought that this could be achieved if aggression were confined within limits, which was the aim of the democracies in Spain. The Axis leaders fully shared this view. It fitted precisely the Axis design for a series of local conquests, no one of which would seem to the democracies to be important enough to resist at the risk of a major war. Consequently when Britain and

France, who had forbidden Germany to annex Austria, finally accepted that annexation without violent objection and followed it up by accepting the German invasion of Czechoslovakia and by implication the German threat towards Russia (Russia not having been called in even for consultation about defending Czechoslovakia), it appeared that the democracies and the Axis were in virtual agreement upon a scheme of authorized but circumscribed conquests. The merely verbal resistance to Japan's invasion of China in 1937, even when her forces sank the American gunboat *Panay*, certainly did not belie the impression of reluctant American acceptance of such a scheme in Asia.

This is not to say that the democracies welcomed those conquests. The truth is that they were confused and taken aback by a menace for which they were unprepared. They were unprepared in the double sense that they did not perceive clearly what Hitler's program was (in spite of his elaborate and explicit advertisement of it in his book, *Mein Kampf*, which few had read) and that they did not possess and were not creating the defensive power to resist it if and when they determined to do so.

As for those then governing or largely influencing the governments of Britain and France, the confusion was partly what may be called ideological; for in their decisions one factor was the impression that the fundamental conflict was that between Communism and Fascism, and as between the two they preferred Fascism. Some thought Fascism had admirable aspects, notably in the discipline it imposed upon the laboring classes by preventing strikes and controlling trades unions, and in Italy in accomplishing the miracle of running trains on time. But what influenced them was less the attractions of Fascism than the horror of Communism which they felt. That horror disorganized their thinking by inducing intense emotion at the mere mention of Russia and the "Reds" who seemed to be at the bottom of all the local trouble, such as the Spanish civil war.[3] The consequence was that, for cer-

[3] In his impressions of Fascist Spain (*Appeasement's Child*, New York, Knopf, 1943) Mr. Thomas J. Hamilton relates a conversation

INVITATION TO AGGRESSION 155

tain conservative minds, conquests towards the East that might erect new barriers to Russia (as Hitler promised to do) or that might include Russian territory (which was Hitler's avowed aim) appeared to be at least not unmixed evils.

Therefore in the minds of the democracies these impulses were at work: to avoid war at almost any cost, especially if the cost were paid by unimportant peoples far away, "people of whom we know nothing," as Mr. Neville Chamberlain said of Czechoslovakia; to wait and see how far Hitler intended to go, in the hope that relatively small conquests — a moderate use of overpowering force against defenceless nations — might suffice to content and appease him; to gain time for armament in case matters grew worse — though that time was not used to the maximum advantage by any of the democracies; to let Hitler move eastward where, from the point of view of the democratic powers, the damage would be less.

Since some Americans in those troubled years of the nineteen-thirties were prolific in advice to the European democracies, whom they urged to "stand up to the dictators," it is pertinent to note that a comparable situation existed in the Far East.

It is true that Japan was much farther from America than Germany was from Britain or France and seemed to be no direct menace to the United States. Yet there were these points of similarity between the growth of aggression in Asia and in Europe: We had lightly given Japan naval mastery of Far Eastern waters just as the British had assisted Germany to regain her dominant military position in Europe. We had tolerated — we had not forcibly resisted — Japan's invasion of

---

with Sir Walter Maxwell Scott which exemplifies this attitude in an extreme form. Sir Walter, as Mr. Hamilton describes him, was a supporter of General Franco in Spain and an appeaser regarding Germany, a combination common at the time. Sir Walter told Mr. Hamilton that he would prefer to "see the British Empire go down in honorable defeat" rather than see it win with the help of the Bolsheviks. Such a view, if it can be called a view, seems oddly anachronistic today when the British and the "Bolsheviks" are allied, but it was common in the nineteen-thirties and, I am convinced, had much to do with the course of British and French policy in those years.

Manchuria, which was less justifiable than Germany's occupation of the German Rhineland and half-German Austria. Japan virtually asked us to buy peace by sacrificing China, just as Germany convinced some in Britain that they were buying peace by sacrificing Czechoslovakia. We did not sacrifice China, but neither did we rush to her aid. China fought Japan alone for four years, and American assistance came only when Japan attacked the United States. On the other hand, Britain declared war long before she was herself attacked; she went to war when Germany attacked Poland.

It is true that when the American Secretary of State, Mr. Henry L. Stimson, proposed in February 1932 a joint Anglo-American statement invoking the Nine-Power Pact and the Briand-Kellogg Pact and proclaiming refusal to recognize Japan's conquest in Manchuria, the British Government — then at one of its low points, with Sir John Simon as Foreign Secretary — did not accept; though that government did introduce a month later a resolution adopted by the League Assembly declining recognition of that conquest. Mr. Stimson was disappointed, as were many Britons. But officials of the Foreign Office in London argued that neither Britain nor the United States was ready to go to war to enforce the pacts mentioned, that the Japanese knew this, and that Sir John's failure to support Mr. Stimson was therefore less culpable than it seemed. In higher British official circles there was a disposition to accept that Japanese action with a shrug of the shoulders, just as a few years later the conquests of Germany were to be accepted, though less lightly because of differences of geography. Britain was in one of her lazy moods when even the security of the Empire failed to excite her greatly. So it was that relations with the United States, soon to be regarded as of supreme importance, were treated with that short-sighted carelessness which so often has bitterly incensed those Americans who have been most friendly and most co-operative towards Great Britain.

Yet the facts remain that the permanent Foreign Office officials — always more realistic because better informed than their temporary chief, the Foreign Secretary — were right;

INVITATION TO AGGRESSION

that neither Britain nor the United States would then go to war against Japan, whatever her conquests of non-British and non-American territory; that Japan was aware of this, and that protests, however sharp, would have availed little.

Neither in Europe nor the Far East was anyone "standing up to" the aggressors. I recall well the complaints of Americans that Britain did not more vigorously oppose Hitler. I also recall that when in December 1937 the American gunboat *Panay* was sunk by Japanese aircraft in the Yangtze River, friends among English editors and correspondents in London rang me up to say: "Surely now you are going to stand up to the Japanese." They were on the point of writing articles to that effect. I advised them not to write such articles.

When we criticize the British for their lethargy and short-sightedness, as I have done in these pages, we should be sufficiently fair to remember that the short-sightedness of Americans — making all due allowance for differences of geography — was not wholly dissimilar. We both failed to take adequate note of the menace that was growing up under our eyes. We both protested and preached without doing or intending to do very much beyond that. The victims of that short-sightedness were ourselves.

Our Self-defeating Policy

ON NOVEMBER 11, 1935, when Mussolini was ready for his attack on Ethiopia and when Hitler, having re-introduced conscription, was rapidly preparing for many attacks, President Roosevelt in an Armistice Day address defined American foreign policy by saying that the primary purpose of the United States was to avoid being drawn into war. At the same time, he said, we sought in every practicable way to promote peace and discourage war.

But there *were* no practicable ways to discourage war so long as our primary purpose was to keep out of war. This, events were to prove. Yet if we could not successfully discourage war, we were destined to be drawn in. Thus our policy was contradictory and self-defeating. The only way for the United States to avoid being drawn into war was to make sure that no general war developed. This we did not do, and so the "primary purpose" of our foreign policy failed to be achieved. "Safety first" did not insure safety first — or last. In fact, it encouraged the aggressions that were eventually to reach American territory, since our announcement of our neutrality left the way open for the advance of aggressive power over most of the world.

President Roosevelt perceived that this might be the result of our neutrality as enacted into law by Congress. That law said that if war came we should withhold American arms from aggressors and their victims alike; that is, from friends as well as enemies. This was a departure from custom and American tradition in favor of our enemies, since the accepted practice had been that a neutral state might sell arms to any belligerent state that could buy them, and American policy had been to insist upon all our neutral rights upon the high seas in time of war.

We now did two very odd things: we abandoned those rights which we had hitherto stubbornly upheld by force when necessary, and we expressed our complete official indifference towards the nations that might be attacked by the powers which we ourselves regarded as the only possible danger to the United States. Those actions by Congress were far from being the most brilliant or glorious in our history. Nor were they in the interest of the United States. They were inspired by a logical absurdity and by a complete misconception of the national interest.

The President seemed aware of this when he said that the inflexible provision for an embargo of arms "might drag us into war instead of keeping us out." This was likewise the view of Secretary Hull. Yet the President signed the Neutrality Act. Four years later he frankly confessed that he regretted having done so.[*]

When the civil war began in Spain, Congress hastily amended the Neutrality Act so as to proclaim that our official

[*] He signed the Act on August 31, 1935; he expressed his regret on September 21, 1939.

indifference towards aggression applied also to that nominally internal conflict; and the President, though he did not share that indifference, again acquiesced. But in January 1939 the President criticized this legislation on the ground that it might give aid to an aggressor and deny it to his victim; and in May 1939 Mr. Roosevelt and Mr. Hull said that failure to repeal the embargo on arms "would weaken the leadership of the United States" in preserving peace. That leadership had already been weakened in the crucial years of the Hitler period by the Neutrality Act which the President had signed in spite of his misgivings in 1935. Yet even in the summer of 1939 Congress declined to alter the act, though it did so two months after the European war had begun. In other words, as soon as a major war broke out Congress dropped the arms embargo provision that was to keep us out of such a war, thereby admitting the folly of a policy that had been followed for four years. It is difficult to say what might have happened had the United States not thus advertised to the world its officially professed indifference to aggression. But so far as that policy may have influenced Hitler's actions, it could only have served to stimulate his aggressions by permitting the supposition that this time the United States would not enter a European war. That this was the sincere belief of many Germans seems beyond doubt to those of us who were in Germany in the years before the war.[5]

Shackled Diplomacy

THE COMPLETE absurdity of our policy can hardly have been made more luminous than it was by certain members of Congress who apparently feared that the armed strength of the

[5] In August 1939 Alexander Kirk, our Minister in Berlin, reported to the State Department that "the recent agitation on neutrality legislation . . . is viewed as an indication of isolationist sentiment that may delay America's entrance into the European war for a considerable period, and even then if the United States associates itself with Britain and France eventually it will not be able to make its influence felt decisively in time." (Quoted by Arthur Krock in the *New York Times Magazine* of July 18, 1943).

United States might be used to obtain the utmost protection for the United States. Discussing proposals for increased military and naval forces in the spring of 1938, several Senators and Representatives expressed the suspicion that the naval increases were based upon some agreement for naval co-operation with Great Britain.[6] In other words, they feared that in defending the shores of the United States our Navy might receive aid from the greatest naval power overseas, the power with whom we were to co-operate the moment we were attacked, and indeed earlier. When they read that eight American battleships had been put out of action at Pearl Harbor, were those members of Congress still disposed to insist that our Navy fight alone without assistance from the British Navy?[7]

This attitude was similar to that which led Congress, in the Neutrality Act, to adopt the thesis that the safety of any one foreign nation was no more important to us than that of any other, that war was an affair of aliens overseas which could be kept from these shores by treating alike the peaceful and the war-like, the free and the enslaved, those whose geographic position made them our defensive outposts and those who were threatening those outposts.

What this meant was that Congress by joint resolution had forbidden the government to have a foreign policy. It had tied the hands of the Commander-in-Chief and his diplo-

[6] *Peace and War; United States Foreign Policy*, published by the Department of State (Washington, Government Printing Office, 1942), p. 53.

[7] Congressional insight into the nature of American interests in the world was illustrated by two decisions of the Foreign Relations Committee of the Senate in the summer of 1939. One was to ask the State Department to "declare economic war against Japan by abrogating the commercial treaty," as Mr. Walter Lippmann puts it. "The committee's second decision was to refuse to lift the arms embargo which prevented Britain and France from buying arms here to resist Germany — the Germany which had been allied with Japan since 1936!" (*United States Foreign Policy*, Boston, Little Brown, 1943). Thus we affronted Japan and at the same time favored Japan's European ally against whom we were to have to fight — or did the committee not know that a virtual alliance existed?

matic staff who were charged with the defence of the United States against all enemies. It had almost said that the United States should not be defended, at least not adequately or promptly; that her defence should not begin until the danger had grown to proportions that made it unmanageable by diplomatic devices, should not begin until the natural allies and the outlying defensive frontiers of this country were broken or in imminent peril.

The consequence was that the President and Mr. Hull spent the better part of a decade warning Americans of the approaching dangers that Congress denied and going through the motions of trying moral suasion upon Germans and Japanese, who were completely pleased that this rich and powerful Republic should confine its activities to that harmless sphere.

Eleven months after Hitler came to power, on December 23, 1933, President Roosevelt told Americans that there was a threat to world peace and that its cause was the aggressive leadership of 10 per cent of the population of the world. (The President likes to talk in percentages even regarding quantities, like the world's population, that cannot be mathematically measured; here he was thinking of Germany, Japan, and Italy.) He believed that permanent peace would be possible if the 10 per cent would "do their own thinking and not be led." It was singularly Utopian to suggest that such a high proportion of the world's population should think for themselves — but that only showed how Utopian permanent peace was.

Twice in 1934 — on May 5 and on June 11 — Mr. Hull gave the same warning. He said that dictatorships and narrow nationalism led to "feverish" armament and that civilized peoples must not "fail much longer to take notice of present dangerous tendencies." He foresaw the threat of another dark age and urged Americans to awaken. But Americans generally were too preoccupied with the domestic havoc wrought by the economic depression to give adequate attention to the dangers abroad.

When the following year the President asked the Senate

to permit the United States to "throw its weight into the scale in favor of peace" by joining the World Court, the Senate refused. A few days later (February 16, 1935) Mr. Hull said it was futile for the United States to try to withdraw into isolation, for we could not fail, even if we would, to influence profoundly the relations of nations. We did not fail. We influenced them to believe we would strive above all to "avoid being drawn into war." It was not only Congress, it was the President, who so defined our intentions.

It was symptomatic of the mental confusion of those years, and doubtless of the hypocrisy imposed by the exigencies of domestic politics, that the President seemed to contradict his chief adviser on foreign affairs, and even himself. For both Mr. Roosevelt and Mr. Hull — like Mr. Winston Churchill in England — knew quite well what the Nazis were and meant and what Japan intended. Yet the President thought it necessary to adopt and apparently to sanction the very slogan of the isolationism that he and Mr. Hull knew to be impossible. This he did in proclaiming that our primary aim was to keep out of war.

Yet all this time the President was groping about, in spite of the manacles imposed by Congress, for something more positive in the way of a policy. He was feeling his way, testing public opinion, warning of danger abroad, and hinting that a great nation like this should do more than turn its back until that danger struck it. In his Chicago speech of October 5, 1937, he adopted the idea of a "quarantine" of aggression. He did not then define his views of the often discussed conception of economic action as a weapon to be used against aggressive nations.

Yet it was an idea that remained in the President's mind. He envisages the "quarantine" as an economic weapon. He imagines that an aggressive state might be simply cut off from the world by closing the frontiers around it, by cutting off all trade, all rail and sea and air traffic, all communications, so as to produce economic paralysis.[8] But economic paralysis is

[8] Article by Mr. Forrest Davis in the *Saturday Evening Post* of August 10, 1943.

itself a contagious disease that cannot be quarantined in this closely-knit world. Had Germany been thus blockaded in 1938 or 1939, her immediate neighbors whose economic life largely depended upon Germany's — Holland, Belgium, Luxembourg, Denmark, Sweden — would have been stricken along with Germany, and perhaps more severely.

Armed with Moral Suasion

MEANWHILE the only quarantine our shackled government could practice was in the moral sphere, if there was a moral sphere in international relations. Our policy of refusing to recognize the territorial gains of aggression was nothing more than an effort of moral suasion directed at governments which had not been notoriously sensitive to moral influences. Our notes and pleas and sermons to the same unresponsive ears were likewise vain gestures which could only be verbal since our government was authorized to seek to preserve peace only with its vocal cords and its typewriter.

It was hardly the most dignified position for a great power, and our official advances in the realm of moral suasion brought snub after snub from menacing powers like Germany and Japan and even from a second-rate power like Fascist Italy. But the authors of our negative policy apparently did not mind this humiliation of the United States so long as we carefully avoided having any acknowledged friends with powerful fleets, and so long as we made it quite clear we should not lift a finger against aggression until it should have crossed the Atlantic or the Pacific.

Our non-recognition weapon was used against Japan when she invaded Manchuria, and the whole moral force — such as it was — of the League of Nations was brought to bear in the same way. The League too was highly productive of moral suasion uncontaminated by vulgar intimations of violence, so we were working on parallel lines by similar means in endeavoring to reinforce what the League did, as Mr. Stimson put it. If one futile bit of moral suasion can reinforce another, we reinforced the League, and Japan reinforced her position in Manchuria.

A significant example of moral suasion was President Roosevelt's statement to Dr. Hjalmar Schacht, President of the Reichsbank, on May 6, 1933, that he thought Germany was the "only possible obstacle" to a disarmament treaty and that the United States would insist that Germany should not rearm while we made every effort to bring the armament of other countries down to the German level. He asked Dr. Schacht to make this clear to Hitler.[9]

Note the implications of the President's words, in the light of what we know, and what Hitler knew, our policy then to be. We were going to insist — by moral suasion — that Germany should not rearm. Meanwhile we would make every effort — by moral suasion — to get France to cut down her army to the 100,000 troops that Germany was then permitted by the Peace Treaty to have. Hitler was to be told of this momentous decision. What he thought of it, we know from what he did.

Ten days later moral suasion was at work towards the Far East. With the Japanese Ambassador Mr. Hull had "one of many conversations" designed to convince the Japanese that "their best interests lay in following policies of peace." Mr. Hull spoke of the advance of aviation, of the commercial and military possibilities that resulted for all civilized nations, of the need for the United States and Japan to "exhibit the utmost breadth of view and the most profound statesmanship."[10] The following year Mr. Hull spoke to Herr Luther, the German Ambassador, of Austria, Czechoslovakia, Memel, and the Polish Corridor, which the Ambassador solemnly denied that Germany wanted to seize. Mr. Hull then suggested that the Hitler government might take the lead in insuring peace in Europe.[11]

When Japan, doubtless by a heroic effort, resisted our moral suasion and attacked China in 1937, we offered to

[9] *Peace and War, op. cit.*, p. 10.
[10] *Peace and War*, p. 19.
[11] *Peace and War*, p. 22.

INVITATION TO AGGRESSION 165

both countries our good offices "towards composing the matters of controversy" — those "matters" being an assault upon China by Japan.[12] We even sent Mr. Norman H. Davis to Brussels, where he was instructed to tell the eighteen nations gathered there for similar good offices that "public opinion in the United States has expressed its emphatic determination" to keep out of war. With that major premise, Mr. Davis was supposed to do something or other to get the Japs to take a similar view and let China alone. The conference "reaffirmed" the Nine-Power Treaty that Japan had broken. It "urged that hostilities be suspended." Mr. Davis solemnly informed the State Department — which must have raised its eyebrows in amazement — that Japan was "unwilling to resort to methods of conciliation." Was there nobody in high quarters to ask: Why should she?[13]

This magnificent display of moral suasion by eighteen nations acting as a single morally impressive bloc was followed within eighteen days by the sinking of the American gunboat *Panay* by Japanese aircraft. Japan was very sorry about it and expressed the "fervent hope" that the "unfortunate affair" would not impair the notoriously friendly relations between Japan and the United States. Why *should* Japan want those relations impaired when they permitted her to invade Manchuria and China and even to sink American warships at the cost of an apology?

Meanwhile moral suasion was at work in Europe. It had no time to do anything for Austria, for Hitler seized that country too quickly. But during the succeeding months, when what the diplomats call "increasing tension" was threatening what President Roosevelt called "the fabric of peace," moral suasion was up and doing. Hitler felt the full force of it in September when the President in two messages insisted upon a "fair and constructive solution" of Hitler's desire to swallow up Czechoslovakia in order to dominate Eastern Europe. The "solution" solemnly signed at Munich was that Hitler got all

---
[12] *Peace and War*, p. 45.
[13] *Peace and War*, p. 50.

the fortifications which protected Czechoslovakia so that he could take the rest at will, which he did five months later.

Undaunted, the President tried moral suasion again when in April 1939 he asked Hitler and Mussolini not to attack anybody and gave a list of nations they ought not to attack. He reinforced his plea by the promise that, if the dictators behaved, the United States would "take part" in discussions of armaments and trade "in peaceful surroundings." On August 23, 1939, on the eve of war, the President sent a personal message to the King of Italy in a final effort to persuade the dictators to refrain from precipitating the catastrophe. He likewise appealed to Hitler and, for the sake of form, to the President of Poland. The reader will recall what followed.

But moral suasion insisted upon one more defeat, the most humiliating of all. It came when the President tried to persuade Mussolini not to attack France in 1940. Mussolini had told Mr. Sumner Welles, the Under Secretary of State, when he visited Rome in March 1940, that Italy was determined to limit the extension of the war and by so doing had kept the peace for 200,000,000 people in the Mediterranean region. On April 29 Mr. Roosevelt reminded Mussolini of that statement. Three days later Mussolini replied saying that Germany also wanted to limit the conflict but hinting that he wanted to make a few changes in the map nevertheless. But eight days later Hitler invaded Holland, Belgium, and France, and Mussolini saw changes in the map take place before his eyes with amazing swiftness. In another eight days (May 18, 1940) Mussolini had changed his mind about limiting the conflict and told Mr. Roosevelt he meant to follow along with his so successful ally, Germany, adding that "Italy cannot remain absent at the moment when the fate of Europe is at stake." In other words, Italy could not stand idly by when easy loot lay ready to her hand.

The President did not give up but became more stern. He spoke to Mussolini of the "historic and traditional interests of the United States in the Mediterranean" — interests which he was not authorized to protect — and he warned that if Italy went to war the result would be to increase the American

INVITATION TO AGGRESSION 167

rearmament program and American efforts to supply the Allies with war materials. Mussolini replied through his Foreign Minister that our aid to the Allies was of no concern to him and that "any attempt to prevent Italy from fulfilling her engagements is not well regarded." Thus snubbing the President of the United States, Mussolini gayly and heroically pounced upon prostrate France, only to find that the "fate of Europe," including Italy's territorial claims against France, was reserved for later decision by Hitler.[14]

The French Prime Minister, M. Paul Reynaud, was meanwhile sending frantic messages to the President urging him to save France. Mr. Roosevelt said the United States Government was doing all in its power to supply the Allies "because of our faith in and our support of the ideals for which the Allies are fighting."

This well-intended statement seemed bitterly ironical at the time because of its tragic inadequacy. M. Reynaud said the only chance to save France and Britain was for the United States to throw into the balance "this very day the weight of American power." But that weight was not the President's to throw.

If the United States would not do this, said M. Reynaud, "then you will see France go under like a drowning man and disappear after having cast a last look toward the land of liberty from which she awaited salvation."[15]

The President could not reach out a hand, or even throw out a life belt, to save France. Towards drowning France we were neutral by Act of Congress. All the President could do, as France went under, was to assure her that we shared her ideals. If that assurance carried any conviction in the circumstances, it was the highest possible tribute to the power of moral suasion.

[14] *Peace and War*, pp. 70–73.
[15] *Peace and War*, p. 75.

XII

OUR EXTREME NATIONALISTS

The Awakening of 1940

THE German tanks crashing into France in June 1940 destroyed once again the American dream of isolation. Americans who had hardly thought of it before became anxious about the French Fleet, as if they suddenly realized it was part of America's defences. The Atlantic seemed to grow miraculously narrower. It was as if Americans, though unwilling to admit it, had known instinctively all along that France formed a mainstay of the civilization which was theirs; that their frontier, like Britain's, was on the Rhine. Never did neutrality seem more fantastic.

The collapse of so much of the trans-Atlantic world to which Americans felt they belonged swept away a good deal of the laboriously self-induced American cynicism towards Europe which had served as a kind of intellectual vindication of isolationist impulses.

In the previous decade the first German world war had been popularly "de-bunked." It had been proved to the satisfaction of bright young nationalists that America's participation in that war had been a huge swindle; that we had been drawn in by propagandists and munitions-makers to serve British interests. We were now wiser. We should not again be taken in by European wiles or crusades to make the world safe for democracy.[1] It had been likewise demonstrated that we could lock our doors, ignore the neighbors, and live in seclusion — though, it was admitted, at an economic level that would hardly satisfy Americans. Mr. de Valera once told

---

[1] An example of this attitude was Mr. Quincy Howe's book, *England Expects Every American to Do His Duty* (New York, Simon & Schuster, 1937).

me quite seriously that Ireland could, if necessary, live without any relations with England, though she would have to get on without most manufactured goods and content herself with a simple, peasant existence. America would not fare so badly as that in isolation, but she too would suffer a reduction of her standard of life. Yet there were Americans who urged a nationalism of the de Valera kind as the way to avoid war.

Meanwhile the failure of democracy to solve its economic problems — the United States in the early nineteen-thirties being the most striking example — and the decline of democracy with the rise of dictatorship in Europe added to the disillusionment regarding both democracy and Europe. The result was a new type of nationalism — not that of the American Dream, as Mr. James Truslow Adams calls it in his *Epic of America*, not that of the daring, adventurous mood that had made the United States, but a nationalism whose principal aim was to keep out of trouble, a nationalism that was selfish, exclusive, cautious, cold, inhuman — and unreal.

Its unreality became clear the moment France fell, provoking profound emotion among Americans — emotion which might almost be called illegal, since Congress had in effect proclaimed that we did not care whether France fell or not. In the Neutrality Act we had virtually said that the civilized world and the uncivilized, democracies and tyrannies, aggressors and victims, were all one to us; for towards them all our official attitude was a cold and impartial neutrality, as if they were not parts of our world.

Even Congress did not really believe that, for long before the fall of France — in fact, sixty-five days after Hitler invaded Poland — Congress had weakened sufficiently to repeal the arms embargo which for four years it had professed to think would keep us out of war. Yet the Neutrality Act remained, even when the fictitious character of our neutrality had been further demonstrated by legislation authorizing the President to arm Britain on the ground that she was fighting our battle.

Was Britain Worth Saving?

THERE LINGERED also the aloof, chilly, calculating nationalism even towards people who (so Congress said in the Lend-Lease Act) were fighting and dying in our interests. Late in 1940 Britain, struggling to survive against our enemy, found cold skepticism in this country when she suggested she might need credits. Let her liquidate all her investments first, said the nationalists. Britain was not a good financial risk, wrote Mr. John T. Flynn.[2] The implication seemed to be that if she were not a good financial risk, we should let her perish rather than risk getting into war by lending to her.

Those who raised doubts about Britain's financial soundness were followed by others who disliked her social legislation and argued that if we helped her fight our battle, social changes might follow which some people would not like. Mr. Mark Sullivan cited Mr. Joseph P. Kennedy, who had just resigned as Ambassador to London, as the source of an impression widely held in certain American circles that Britain was going socialistic and, as Mr. Sullivan put it, ceasing to be a democracy. Mr. Sullivan concluded that in deciding whether we should "actually enter the war on the side of England" — which he seemed to think was something we could take or leave after coolly calculating the consequences — "we will be likely to take into account any surmised possibility that England is to be a Socialist country."[3] Our decision to rescue her or let her go down might depend upon what we thought of her social laws.

Mr. James S. Kemper, then President of the United States Chamber of Commerce, seemed to believe that the supreme question in that hour of Britain's fight for life was "the fiscal problem of this country and its possible effect on our form of government." Mr. Kemper had discovered that dictatorship in Europe was really a fiscal problem, since it resulted mainly from state bankruptcy which necessitated centralized con-

[2] Article dated December 9, 1940, in the *Washington Post*.
[3] Article dated December 2, 1940, in the *Washington Post*.

trol. This the dictator provided, so "dictatorships, more than anything else, are receiverships." Mr. Kemper — thoroughly Marxian in his materialistic theory of history — mentioned the cost of war and the danger of Federal bankruptcy and said that our participation in the war might change our social and economic system.[4] He apparently did not think that a successful conquest of Europe by the Nazi system was so great a danger for the United States as our participation in the war to prevent that conquest.

Russia's solution of the "fiscal problem" had long displeased many Americans far more than Britain's culpable departure from our standards; and the disposition mentioned by Mr. Sullivan to judge Britain's right to live by the orthodoxy or lack of orthodoxy of her social legislation placed Russia beyond the limits of tolerance, even after she too was fighting what we officially recognized was our battle.

This tendency to condemn our friends as well as our enemies, or perhaps particularly our friends, either because it was costing them a lot of money to fight for survival or because we might disapprove their conceptions of social justice within their own domains, was one of the strangest of all the manifestations of isolationism. In these instances it was what may be called ideological isolationism; for the thesis was that we should keep out of war because war might bring social changes (which presumably otherwise would not take place), and that we should avoid any far-reaching commitments not only towards countries that were geographically distant but towards countries that were ideologically distant — that is, countries whose internal affairs were not conducted in accordance with the Republican Party's platform.

The haggling in Washington over Britain's assets and the whispering campaign about Britain's "Socialism" (though a Conservative was Prime Minister and his party dominated Parliament), which took place when Britain was standing alone, hard pressed on the seas and in the air, holding off our enemy until we were ready to fight, did not add luster to the name of the United States. Like the cynical nationalism of

[4] *New York Times*, January 9, 1941.

the Left in the nineteen-thirties, this ruthless nationalism of the Right represented in an extreme form an aberration from which we were slowly recovering — but into which we might fall again in future.

Such financial haggling, displaying a disposition to measure the comparative war exertions of the Allies in terms of currency alone, continued after we and the British were fighting and sharing together. In a statement to the United Press on October 10, 1943, Senator Allen J. Ellender of Louisiana said that the per capita debt of the United States had risen more than that of the British, and that we were spending on Lend-Lease supplies alone nearly as much as Britain spent on her entire war effort. He said he did not want the British to assume "that Uncle Sam is going to do all the work and furnish all the materials needed." The Senator suggested that in return for Lend-Lease supplies the British and Dutch should supply to the United States "rubber, tin, nickel and other essential raw materials" and that our government should "make Lend-Lease aid conditional on these products being supplied without cost."

The Senator seemed to forget that the purpose of Lend-Lease, as defined by Congress, was to defend the United States by aiding those countries whose defence the President deemed vital to the defence of the United States — not to serve as a commercial transaction. He seemed to forget that those countries, above all Britain, had contributed not only materials but lives to this common struggle long before we got around to the Lend-Lease policy. His and similar statements seemed to be signs of a reviving economic nationalism which confused the security of the United States with sharp financial bargaining, and saw the future relations of Allies merely as a tussle for commercial advantages.

Thus the isolationist habit of thought, or rather of feeling, persisted in various forms after we had assumed our share of the burden of protecting the United States. It provoked constant criticism of Britain and Russia, often quoted in Berlin to indicate division among the Allies. It led to vehement protests against our fighting first in Europe instead of in the Pacific, protests which involved sometimes the expressed suspicion that Britain would desert us when the time came to attack Japan.[5] In many ways it seemed to foreshadow a revival after the war of the nationalism which had prevented any effective American action to avoid the war.

Conflicting Impulses

How LONG this kind of nationalism would have kept us out of the war if Japan had been wise enough to avoid attacking American territory or Australia or New Zealand but had attacked only British and Dutch Oriental possessions, it is difficult to say. But Americans from the summer of 1940 onward overwhelmingly desired a British victory and increasingly understood the relationship between such a victory and their own security, and doubtless these attitudes would have brought us in at some point even if Japan had not attacked Pearl Harbor or the Philippines.

How long this nationalism will prevent our committing ourselves to definite measures to insure the peace we shall have won at the end of this war is a still more pertinent question. It cannot be answered at this writing, although failure to answer it handicapped our policy even in the war — notably towards Russia, who likewise avoided commitments, for instance to help us against Japan — and will gravely handicap the policies we adopt for the peace.

Our relations with the foreign world have been paralyzed all along by contradictory motives. We wanted to prevent war, but we also wanted to make sure of not being drawn in. We wanted Britain to win, but we did not want to help her win, even though it was in our interest to do so. We shall want to insure peace but shall not be eager to assume the mili-

[5] Mr. Churchill's address to Congress on May 19, 1943, explaining the Atlantic-Pacific strategy and promising Britain's aid in the Pacific, was a direct reply to those suspicious, made in the very place where they had been expressed. It was also an amazing example of democratic methods on an international scale, the Prime Minister of one democracy addressing the Parliament of another much as he addressed his own Parliament.

tary and economic obligations necessary to do so. We shall want the world in general to be prosperous — so long as we are not obliged to open our markets to foreigners. In the past we have willed the end but not the means to the end, so the end was not achieved. The result will be the same in future unless these contradictions are resolved.

"Fear of war is no basis for a national policy," said President Conant of Harvard in 1940. He might have added that fear of war expressed in a determination to take no positive action against war was a way of making war probable. It had that effect in the Hitler period when both Britain and America sought to avoid war by negative or ineffective measures — that is, by measures that were not supported and were not intended to be supported by force.

The errors and contradictions attributable to extreme nationalism were even more notable in the economic sphere than in the political; for even when we most emphatically denied responsibility for the peace of Europe, as by our refusal to participate in the League of Nations or in the World Court, we did participate actively though unofficially in efforts towards economic reconstruction. We poured out loans to the foreign world.[6] The Dawes and the Young reparations plans were largely of American making. The Young Plan was particularly American in its optimistic assumption (even in 1929) that expanding world trade would absorb the huge international payments due from Germany to the British and French and from them to the United States. Within six months came the Wall Street crash and within two years a financial crisis struck Central Europe, putting an end forever to both reparations and war debts, and shortly thereafter much of the world followed the pound sterling in abandoning the gold standard.

This breakdown of the mechanism of exchange, like the American economic collapse which contributed to it, was at once the result of extreme and absurd nationalism and the

[6] The total in dollar bonds issued abroad amounted to $7,266,826,577, according to the 1940 report of the Foreign Bondholders' Protective Council, 90 Broad Street, New York.

occasion for still more of such nationalism, of which Hitler's militaristic economics was the German manifestation.⁷

Though the debts owed to the United States Government and to private American investors amounted to well over $20,000,000,000, we adopted in 1930 the highest tariff act in our history (the Hawley-Smoot Act). Here was the most amazing contradiction of all. We insisted upon payment of the debts while we raised our tariff wall to new heights to prevent that payment. We wanted to sell to the world in great quantities but not to buy from it in proportion. It was apparently little understood that this amounted to giving away our wealth; for what happened was that, by selling and lending abroad without buying equally, we got for our exported goods merely paper credits which to a great extent were not, and in the circumstances could not be, paid.⁸ Much of that wealth, government and private, is now written off as the cost of the follies of the past.

We were thus nationalistic in our days of ill-founded prosperity, and we remained nationalistic in the period of painful adversity which came as inevitably as the swing of a pendulum after that prosperity collapsed from its own inner contradictions, as the Marxists would say.

President Roosevelt will probably be distinguished in history for his enlightened attitude towards international affairs

---

⁷ It is not easy to apportion the factors which enabled Hitler to conquer Germany — German grievances against the world for the peace treaty; the almost instinctive German yearning to be bossed by someone, especially after the very un-authoritarian years of the un-representative Republic; Hitler's oratory, which had for Germans an odd magnetism that an outsider cannot possibly understand; the economic crisis which made some 6,000,000 Germans unemployed. But the economic depression certainly played its part in the growth of the Nazi ranks, in the opinion of many observers including myself, who was much in Germany in 1931 and 1932 and made a particular effort to understand the Nazi movement by reading its literature and talking with its followers in many parts of Germany.

⁸ The Foreign Bondholders' Protective Council at the end of 1940 estimated that the proportions of foreign investments in dollar bonds that were in default were: in Europe 75 per cent, in Latin America 77.4 per cent, in general 42 per cent.

in the years when the war was developing, but his original economic program in 1933 represented an extreme form of nationalism. In the summer of that year some sixty nations sent delegates to a world economic conference in London, summoned with the President's consent to seek stabilization of currencies. Soon after it met, Mr. Roosevelt sent a message to say he could not participate in stabilization, since he sought a further rise in American prices. Thus the United States, one of the major factors in the economy of a disrupted and disturbed world, took its stand on the side of instability and purely nationalistic action and so prevented an international accord regarding currencies. With currencies uncertain, nearly all else in the economic life of nations must remain equally uncertain. So the depression was fought by each nation alone, or groups of nations like the sterling bloc and the gold bloc, and broader common action was impossible.

To suggest what might have happened if the great democracies had been united in their efforts to rebuild the shattered exchanges of the world instead of being in three different camps — Britain leading the sterling bloc, France leading the gold bloc, the United States going its own way in experimental instability — would take one into the realm of hypothesis. But there is no doubt on one point: the division among the nations that was displayed and accentuated at the London conference intensified extreme nationalism everywhere, including the German nationalism which was to prove the major cause of the world war that was to come. Economic nationalism, in which the United States took the lead in the prosperous nineteen-twenties and again in the depressed nineteen-thirties, accelerated the militaristic nationalism in which Germany took the lead in Europe and Japan in Asia.

President Roosevelt was one of the first to perceive clearly the nature of this aggressive nationalism and to warn his countrymen against it. It is one of the ironies of history that, by measures which seemed to him at the time to be compelled by domestic exigencies, he himself contributed to that nationalism.

Ideology and Foreign Relations

THUS THE economic attitude of the Left, as represented by Mr. Roosevelt and his associates in planned economy, and the economic attitude of the Right, as represented by Mr. Sullivan and Mr. Kemper and conservative businessmen generally, were both nationalistic factors working aganist our cooperation with the rest of the civilized world in the interest of our safety and prosperity. The first group took the position that the depression must be cured and Utopia created in the United States alone and by a strictly national program, even if that retarded the recovery and the unity and hence the peace of the democratic world. The second group took the position that the United States might be well advised to hold aloof from the war because participation might bring undesirable social changes of the kind that had been sought by the Left in this country and carried out — largely by the Right, that is, by the Conservative Party — in "socialistic" Great Britain.

Although German and Japanese violence awakened us to the urgency of our common interests with Great Britain and the civilized world in whose defence Britain fought in heroic and honorable solitude for an entire year, these nationalistic impulses and attitudes have persisted and will remain as obstacles to common action in the future.

As we have seen, nationalism is neither Left nor Right but reaches across ideological lines. Yet the danger in the immediate future seems likely to be rather from the extremely conservative nationalists who look askance at Russia because of her unorthodox economic practices, and even at Britain because she may, they fear, carry her democracy from the purely political field into social and economic life.[9]

The fallacy in this attitude is its assumption that we may

[9] By many Americans Britain has been criticized because, while democratic politically, she was not democratic socially but aristocratic and caste-ridden. But now that under the impact of the war she has grown more democratic socially and more conscious of the obligations of the state to its people economically, she is again criticized by Americans, this time for being too socialistic.

choose our partners in world affairs according as we like or dislike their domestic arrangements or their national philosophies. This was the attitude, to some extent, of Nazis and Fascists, who professed to represent together a kind of social revolution in the international sphere. The consequence of such an attitude would be to divide the world again, as our enemies divided it, on ideological lines. In that case the Americans who find Britain and Russia alike too radical to associate with would be at a loss to find any power in an unpleasantly evolving world which was sufficiently conservative to meet their standards, and they could only advocate the same kind of isolation for the United States which President Roosevelt sanctioned, for different ends, in 1933.

But we obviously cannot choose our foreign relationships on the basis of common economic prejudices any more than we can choose them on the basis of similarity of language or culture or race or religion. Nations sometimes imagine they choose their allies on such principles, but actually they do not. They choose them on the basis of common interests. Those common interests have been chiefly defensive in the past and are likely to remain chiefly defensive for a considerable future. We aided Russia to fight not because we were fond of Russia or of her social system but because Germany was our enemy as well as hers.

It may be regrettable that relations between nations cannot be more complicated than this, cannot be shaped by congeniality of ideas, as conversations are shaped in clubs, Pullman cars, and drawing rooms. But the fact is that foreign affairs are absurdly simple, at least in principle, since they are determined purely by the self-interest of the nations. The problem is to discern our national interests and what they are likely to be in the future, and to choose our companions accordingly.

That is in fact what we do, but hitherto we have done it with a great and dangerous time-lag imposed by such ideological conceptions as those mentioned and by the illusion of geographical security. To have a foreign policy meeting our requirements it is therefore necessary to simplify our views of our national interests by getting rid, at least in this connection, of emotions about Russia and Britain and other peoples, just as we are getting rid of the illusion that we can defend ourselves without adequate weapons and overseas bases.

The fall of France helped this process of clarification, and the attack on Pearl Harbor carried it farther. Possibly we were fortunate that the nationalism of Germany and Japan was so violent and unbalanced; for if it had been tempered with a moderate amount of wisdom Hitler would have conquered Europe peacefully with the lazy consent of Britain and France, and Japan might have conquered more than Manchuria with no more than official protests from us.

Another time, if there is another time, our enemies may be less violent and unbalanced and may not repeat the shocks which in 1940 and 1941 awakened us in the nick of time.

PART FOUR: *After Victory*

XIII

GERMANY AFTER DEFEAT

The Reich and Europe

THE great overwhelming problem of Europe is that of Germany. So it has been for seventy-five years and so it will long continue to be. Two world wars within a generation leave no doubt on this point. But there is doubt how that problem will be met. It was not solved after the first great German defeat because few understood the character of the problem or the character of Germany.

Germany is the largest country in Europe outside Russia (which is not really European though playing a rôle in Europe). Her people are the most advanced mechanically and industrially of the great European nations. They are the most inventive, enterprising, laborious, energetic, the best organized and disciplined. They have the greatest continental industrial apparatus. They live in the center of Europe, at the crossroads of Europe. Their territory extends to the North Sea and the Atlantic lowlands neighboring England, to the borders of Italy, to the Scandinavian region, yet touches on the east and southeast the vast and prolific world of the Slavic countries.

Germany in a sense is the central point about which Europe revolves and through which a large part of the European trade and exchange passes. She is at the same time the greatest continental producer of manufactured goods consumed in Europe and the greatest single European market for the farm products of Europe. She has lately aspired to be for Europe what industrial Britain used to be for her Empire when that Empire was agricultural, dependent, an economic and military appendage of Britain. This, in substance, was the "new order" which the Nazis sought to create by outdoing Bismarck in "blood and iron."

So favorable were the geographic and economic circumstances that this project might have succeeded, and Germany might have made Eastern Europe in effect a German colonial domain, if only Germany had had rulers possessing the political genius of the British in dealing with other peoples. The road to such a goal was wide open in 1937 and 1938, when Germany was succeeding in her economic conquest of southeastern Europe with little opposition from the British or the French, who wanted above all to avoid another European war and would have sighed with relief had Germany continued to throw her weight progressively towards the East and Southeast by the economic diplomacy she then used while avoiding that threat of armed attack which all Europe feared.

The prolonged negotiations of the summer of 1938, which culminated in the Munich agreement, and the succeeding negotiations of 1939, which proved unable to prevent the German attack on Poland, were in reality persistent efforts by the two great democratic powers to persuade Germany to take the dominant position in Europe which she sought, but to do so without throwing Europe into war.

Until March 1939, when it seemed almost if not quite hopeless to expect Hitler to forswear military conquest in favor of the less rapid and less dramatic conquest of barter and trade and political pressure, Britain had no commitments to defend any part of Europe east of the Rhine, and France's previous commitments had in effect been abandoned before Munich. Until September 1, 1939, when Hitler took his great and fatal gamble, the British continued to hope that the commitments they had assumed in March of that year to defend Poland and Rumania would not have to be made good by force — that Hitler would avoid violence but would avail himself of the otherwise almost unlimited free hand that was left to him in Europe.

But it was not in Hitler's nature, and perhaps not in Germany's nature, to take this moderate and restrained advantage, as it seemed, of the opportunities which were offered by the accommodating apprehensiveness of the Western powers. Germany, after her triumph at Munich, was "on top of the world," as a British official put it at the time, and the German conception of the use to be made of that happy position was not one of modesty or moderation. Germany has not known, on this or other occasions since Bismarck, how to use her great power or her naturally dominating position in Europe with the restraint which alone could have assured the retention of that power. In this sense Hitler was not un-German.

This is the very essence of the German problem — this apparent incapacity of a great nation to be a great power without being a great menace; this apparent unfitness of Germany as a collective entity to live at peace with the world around her; this primitive thirst for violent acquisition of that which so far has been unattainable by violence, yet has been readily attainable — as the history of Germany from 1871 to 1914 proved — by the peaceful exercise of the superior inventive and productive skill of the German people. Germany refused to come to terms with Europe because Germany would accept nothing less than domination of Europe. In view of the events of 1938–1939, it seems accurate to add that she would not even accept that domination unless she could seize it quickly and violently instead of acquiring it in less primitive ways.

Their great defeat in 1918 did not persuade the Germans that this domination was unreasonable or impossible. Nor did the behavior of the victorious Allies after 1918 serve to further such persuasion. It seems unlikely that a second defeat in itself will persuade the Germans any more than the former one did, though it could contribute to such persuasion if this time it were properly utilized to that end. The process, however, will be neither automatic nor rapid nor certain. For there is in Germany an impulse towards violence and mastery which will not readily yield save to superior force long maintained.

Therefore the immediate issue is not what Germany will do — which is indicated by her character and history — but what the Allies will do; not whether Germany can suddenly become a good neighbor, but whether the power and the will outside Germany will be such as to further Germany's adaptation to the civilized community with which she must, in one way or another, come to terms. This in turn will depend mainly upon the ability of the people who hold the power to understand Germany.

Two Views of Germany

AN EXAMPLE of what may be called the pessimistic view of Germany, held by many who know Germany best, is that of Professor Bernadotte E. Schmitt of the University of Chicago.[1] Recalling the abundant literary evidence of the German will to mastery, the German exaltation of the military state, the German view of war as ennobling and profitable, the German belief in ruthlessness, he finds that these trends in German thinking were not broken but were intensified by the defeat of 1918. The old bureaucracy and the old military caste continued dominant in the days of the Republic, for Germany had little experience of self-government and a long tradition of what Thorstein Veblen called "subservient alacrity" under the regimented Prussian system.[2]

Professor Schmitt does not think that greater sympathy by the Allies towards the German Republic would have enabled it to survive, and argues that every concession made by the Allies was followed by more demands. When the Allies evacuated the Rhineland in 1930, five years earlier than the time prescribed in the Treaty of Versailles, the Germans took it as a sign of weakness, and in the November election of that year

[1] *What Shall We Do with Germany?* (Public Policy Pamphlet No. 38, University of Chicago Press, 1943).
[2] *Imperial Germany.*

the Nazi members of the Reichstag increased from twelve to 107. Thus the more the Allies yielded, the weaker the Republic became, contends Professor Schmitt, who believes that the great mistake was in failing to enforce the treaty. He speaks of the "sadistic traits in the German character" and warns that we shall have to deal "not with a people like ourselves or the British but with a nation of fanatics." He concludes that German history does not justify the assumption that a mild and generous settlement would induce the Germans to live at peace with their neighbors.

The first essentials for the future, in the opinion of Professor Schmitt, are complete and unmistakable defeat of the Reich, its effective disarmament, the restoration of goods stolen from the occupied countries, and such restraint of humanitarianism as will insure that the Germans' distress will not be relieved until that of the victims of Germany has been relieved. These policies, with punishment of Germans guilty of crimes in occupied territory, would at any rate tend to persuade the Germans that war does not pay. To the question whether the Germans then will "reform and re-educate themselves," Professor Schmitt thinks that only time can give the answer; though he believes it is not unreasonable to hope that the Germans, like the French after the Napoleonic period, can learn from experience.

This American historian takes in 1943 a view of Germany which resembles in its skeptical "from Missouri" attitude the view held by many in France in 1920 — a view not then dominant in Britain or America. Marshal Foch thought the peace should insure permanent French or Allied occupation of the Rhine bridge-heads. M. Gabriel Hanotaux, the historian, argued that Prussia should be pushed back not beyond the Rhine but beyond the Oder. M. Jacques Bainville thought the only cure for German aggression was the dismemberment of Germany so long maintained by the French kings but abandoned by the Republic and by nineteenth-century idealists who believed that national unity was a principle to be favored for all countries.[3] Professor Schmitt does not believe in divid-

[3] *Histoire des Deux Peuples.*

ing Germany, which would stimulate nationalism, but his doubt of Germany's rapid adaptation either to democracy or to a peaceful existence sustains the skeptical French view of a quarter-century ago.

On the other hand, Mr. E. H. Carr, a brilliant historical writer who was professor of international politics in the University College of Wales and is now one of the editors of the *Times* of London, takes a much more hopeful view. He rejects the thesis of "the inherent and irremediable wickedness of the German people," attributes their warlike qualities not to "supposedly ineradicable national characteristics" but to the lateness of German unity which turned Germans against individualism and internationalism; and he questions whether "we shall, for any length of time, feel morally justified to adopt towards Germany a political attitude fundamentally different from that adopted towards other states."

Mr. Carr believes that the occupation of Germany should serve as the starting point for German co-operation in creating a framework of European order and for convincing the Germans they have a part to play in such an order, which would bring them greater "spiritual, social and physical wellbeing" than the old. He places his faith in economic co-operation on a European scale and suggests that while the postwar German mind may again become a potential prey to aberrations, it will also "be accessible, as it was after 1918, to nobler inspirations." [4]

Thus Mr. Carr reflects today in England the hopeful attitude towards Germany which characterized England and America after 1918, an attitude which Professor Schmitt rejects in contending that concessions do not conciliate the Germans, who understand only force. Mr. Carr would doubtless reply that after the last German defeat the hopeful view was not expressed in the right economic or political measures.

[4] *Conditions of Peace.*

Germans on Probation

It seems probable that these two views, the intensely skeptical and the determinedly hopeful, will come again into sharp conflict in future months as the suitability of differing policies towards Germany is debated.

That suitability must be judged not merely by the character and mood and reformist potentialities of Germany but by the will and power of the victors to apply any given policy over a long period — upon which the record of the last two decades casts considerable doubt. Therefore it seems logical to recognize the historical proportions of the German problem as emphasized by the less sanguine like Professor Schmitt, and to restrain and qualify our hopes for the future by continued awareness of the persisting German traits which have destroyed such hopes in the past.

We are free to believe that eventually the Germans may become amenable to the more civilizing influences, on condition that we remember the obstacles which history reveals and which forbid us to be very optimistic in a short-range view. It would be fatal to assume that when the Nazis' power was broken, the character of Germany would quickly change. It would be equally unjustifiable to assume that the character of Germany would never change. The question is how much and how soon it may change. On this point we shall do best to take the more cautious and skeptical view, and to suspend judgment pending tangible proof in the form of behavior over a considerable period.

The possibility of such proof must be assumed. For, in spite of Germany's violent past, there is not adequate evidence for giving her up as incurable. Moreover, this assumption is the only possible working hypothesis, inasmuch as it is difficult to devise a practicable treatment for a nation assumed to be irredeemable, though in time nature or the forces of history may devise one, as Professor Toynbee suggests in speaking of nations in general.[5]

It would be misleading to believe, as some do, that Hitler

[5] *A Study of History, op. cit.*

was an exotic and alien and un-German figure that somehow got imposed upon Germany against her will. Hitler was a slightly distorted personification — not so distorted as many imagine — of those German qualities which inspire the pessimism of Professor Schmitt and have long been visible. Hitler was not non-German, or un-German; he was an expression of Germany in one of her least civilized moods, a kind of laboratory specimen of the virus from which Germany has long suffered and has made her neighbors suffer.

I first visited Germany in 1927 when I was studying its language, exploring its cities and musuems, reading its books and magazines, enjoying the company of university teachers who were then as keenly aware of the German problem as Professor Schmitt is today and whom, it is only fair to say, I counted among the most charming and cultured of the Europeans I met in a dozen countries. In that year and succeeding years (my last visit being in 1940) I returned again and again to Germany, to its universities, its forests and mountains, its music, its neat and well-ordered cities, its friendly and exceptionally honest people.

As a student and correspondent I became fond of Germany because of the erudition I found there, the organized knowledge, the love of knowledge, the eagerness to study and discuss contemporary politics in an objective spirit, the cordiality towards foreigners and their points of view. Visiting German universities as a stranger, I was invited to students' clubs and to professors' homes and urged to exchange ideas with complete frankness. Young men and women I met on mountain tops almost invariably asked me to join up with their groups or to share their lunch of black bread, wurst, and cheese, to attend dances in the village towards which we descended. It was such a comfortable, friendly, pleasant country to move about in, at least for an American, in that republican interlude of German history when militarism was in the background of life and the next war seemed distant — a period when, according to Hitler, Germany was "a pile of ruins." It was long before I understood that phrase; for to me Germany was anything but that, and in fact she had made a rapid and remarkable recovery from the material effects of the First World War.

Nazi Youth

IT WAS LONG before I understood Hitler and his movement, which gained ardent adherents among precisely those young men whom I had met at universities and on mountaineering expeditions. Under his influence they became even more solemn than German youths normally are as compared with British or Americans of like age, and acquired a kind of collective ferocity that had not existed, or that I had not remarked, before. Yet even when they became Nazis and yearned for war, many of these young men remained companionable and urbane as if, like Faust, they were torn between two spirits — that of the excellent education they had received before the blight of Hitlerism fell upon the German universities, and that of the de-civilizing gregariousness of the Nazi creed. It was a kind of national recidivism. It was somewhat as if a member of Phi Beta Kappa should join the Ku Klux Klan.[6]

The transformation that thus came over many of my German friends amazed and puzzled me. They could not explain it to my satisfaction because it was the work of emotions difficult to translate into intellectual terms. But they were very sincere; and if they seemed suddenly to cease being lucid and enlightened young Europeans and to become obscure, sentimental, and passionate Germans instead, they retained enough of their former selves to permit them to discuss the matter with an air of objectivity and to consider without a trace of anger all the uncomplimentary things I said about their *Fuehrer*.

Indeed Germans of all classes, as well as these universit

[6] When I met him in Munich in 1931, Rudolf Hess (then secretary to Hitler, later his Deputy as *Fuehrer*, who flew to Scotland in 1941 on a diplomatic errand and has since been a prisoner of the British) explained to me that the Nazi movement was a good deal like the Ku Klux Klan. He had not the faintest notion of the ingenuousness of his remark.

graduates, retained in their fierce Nazi mood that politeness which I had found almost universal in the pre-Nazi era. I have talked with Nazis, educated and uneducated, from Koenigsberg to Hamburg, from Vienna to Duesseldorf, from Bremen to Innsbrueck, with the utmost frankness without ever offending them, so far as I could see. One Sunday in June 1939 I sat with a dozen Germans upon the veranda of a country club near Hamburg. They sought to defend Hitler and quoted some of his utterances. Finally I said: "Don't you understand that outside Germany nobody believes any promise your *Fuehrer* may make?" They replied, in effect, that they had gathered that such was the case, and none gave the slightest sign of resenting my candor. But this did not mean that their views or feelings were at all affected by the fact I had stated or were even accessible to any argument I might make.

Hitler, whom I first met in 1931, appeared willing to argue with an air of appealing to reason, though on the occasion when I spent an hour talking with him he behaved much as if I were the Sport-Palast and made impassioned speeches for my private benefit as he marched around his small office in the Brown House in Munich, shouting and gesticulating. When I asked him about armaments, he said Germany wanted only an army equal to France's — which, taken at its face value, seemed a somewhat reasonable argument. At that time he was even willing — though he ceased to be later — to discuss his anti-Semitism; and in response to my questions he retorted that the United States, in its immigration law, had practiced racial discrimination (which was true).

Yet Hitler was very difficult to interview, for he wanted to make a speech instead of answering the questions he had asked me to submit in writing in advance. But I interrupted his speech and urged him to stick to the questions, which he then did fairly satisfactorily. I interjected new questions where his answers, in rapid, nervous German, required further clarification. He spoke so fast that he said a good deal in that hour, and his emotional outpouring did not exclude occasional interludes of canny lucidity when he was pressed for direct and specific answers to questions or arguments put to him.[7] But he impressed me, and I believe most foreign correspondents at that time, as a fanatic without education or great ability, in spite of the visible appeal he had even for many educated Germans.

He seemed a dumpy little fellow in his brown Storm Troop uniform as he sat in that party building which had become a kind of shrine to the Nazi enthusiasts who visited it with adequate awe. He spoke no foreign languages and knew little of the outside world, but his advisers had convinced him of the importance of what they called the "world press," and the courtesy he showed me was at least partly the result of this concern for foreign opinion.

This same politeness, in a kind of studied and disciplined form, was shown by the German armed forces, at least towards Americans. When I was awakened by gunfire at Narvik at 5 a.m. on April 9, 1940, and ran down to the harbor to bump into German soldiers coming ashore in that Norwegian port, my American passport insured courtesy from any army or navy officer. At the railway station a naval captain showed my passport to the sergeant in charge, saying: "Do you see this passport? You don't understand English? Well, take a look at this and remember it is not an English passport and this gentleman may depart whenever he likes." When I left for Sweden, the captain said: "Perhaps you'll come back with the American Army." "It will be coming all right," I replied, and we parted with courteous farewells.

Unlimited Aims

TO ONE of the brightest of these educated young Nazis, who had by then become an important official in Vienna, I said in the summer of 1939 as we sat over drinks in the Grand Hotel: "Your *Fuehrer* has made his greatest mistake. If he had taken advantage of the Munich agreement, he could have had control of Europe without effort. Instead, he had to break the Munich agreement by marching into Prague. Now the deal is

[7] Much of what Hitler said in that conversation was reproduced in an article in the *New York Times* of December 20, 1931.

off and we shall probably get a war which Germany will lose. How do you explain that mistake?"

He did not agree that it was a mistake, but this was his answer:

"Every nation desires to be powerful and dominate its living space. Imperialism is a natural expression of a healthy people. Germany's living space includes at least all of the former Austro-Hungarian Empire and the Balkans. The Munich agreement could be only temporary because it did not acknowledge that the Czechs belong logically within Germany's living space. Treaties are valid only so long as they serve their purpose, their duration depending upon the power of the nations concerned. There is no right or wrong about it. Vital needs are the dominating factor. Whatever serves the nation is right, and what does not serve it is wrong."

This was not at all a novel doctrine, but coming from one close to the fount of Nazi inspiration it made perfectly clear why no well-schooled Nazi could admit that the aggression of March 1939 was a mistake. It was a part of what Americans once called "manifest destiny," which was another name for what the Nazis called "living space."[3] There was, however, this important difference: American expansion had taken place mostly in an empty continent, while German expansion involved the conquest and subjection of a long-settled region whose inhabitants were not ready to serve as Germany's living space.

It was this urge to seize "living space" by dominating Europe, the same aspiration which Kaiser Wilhelm II described as a desire for a "place in the sun," that inspired young Nazis to follow Hitler. They sometimes attributed it to the oppressive Treaty of Versailles, forgetting that it had existed prior to that treaty and had been one source of the war which re-

---

[3] ". . . the phrase Manifest Destiny, first coined in 1845, but invoked in spirit, in words and deeds by American statesmen from Jefferson and John Quincy Adams to Seward and Charles Sumner, not to mention the expansionists of 1898, the Mahans, the Lodges and the Roosevelts." Samuel Flagg Bemis: *A Diplomatic History of the United States* (New York, Henry Holt & Co., 1938), p. 215.

sulted in that treaty; so that the German expansionist fever was not a result, but a cause, of the treaty that many Americans and Britons agreed with the Germans in considering unduly harsh.

While Britain and France attained national unity and reached out for "living space," Germany, divided by the Reformation and the Thirty Years' War and feudalism, remained weak and frustrated until Bismarck created the German Empire in 1871. Rapid economic expansion of Germany followed and won the admiration and envy of the world. But the ancient grudge remained and could not be removed by that peaceful conquest — any more than it could be removed by the peaceful conquest offered to Hitler's Germany in 1938, when Europe lay, so to speak, at his feet, on the sole condition that he seize it gently. The growls of the German encyclopedists of militarism echoed from the eighteen-eighties onward, and Germany's defeat in 1918 only deepened her sense of frustration and her anger at destiny.

If neither the economic conquests of Wilhelm II's reign nor the peaceful dominion proffered to Hitler were enough, the question may be asked: What, if anything, is enough for Germany? Perhaps one reason why Germans think they have never succeeded as a nation is that there is nothing they will accept as success. The German mind dislikes limits and boundaries, and this may account for the admiration of the power that breaks through barriers, even though it may end in breaking Germany.

German Freedom

STRETCHED ACROSS great halls where Hitler spoke was often a banner reading *"Freiheit und Brot"* ("Freedom and Bread"), which seemed an odd phrase for Nazis, who did not believe in freedom in our sense of the word, but in dictatorship. For Hitler, freedom meant release from the Treaty of Versailles and from armament limitations. It meant freedom for conquest. To Germans that banner suggested no such paradox as it suggested to me, as I sat not far from Hitler and watched him slowly cast a kind of spell over his audience. In it they saw no contradiction. In their minds the word "freedom" is not associated with any Bill of Rights or with individual liberty, as it is for Americans and Britons. To Germans it has a collective rather than an individual meaning.

"Freedom in the mouths of German philosophers has a very special meaning," said Santayana. "It does not refer to any possibility of choice nor to any private initiative. It means rather the sense of freedom we acquire when we do gladly and well what we should have to do anyhow. You are enlarged by sympathy with your work, your country and the universe until you are no longer conscious of the least distinction between the Creator, the State and yourself. Your compulsory service then becomes perfect freedom."[9] Santayana would have understood the Nazis instantly, for this was their idea of freedom.

The German historian, Oswald Spengler, explained the German conception of freedom by contrasting it with the English conception. "There [in England] we see personal responsibility, self-determination, resolution, initiative," he wrote. "Here [in Germany] discipline, selfless renunciation, self-training. . . . Service is the old Prussian ideal; no 'I' but a 'we,' a common feeling in which the whole being of the individual is merged. The individual does not count; he must sacrifice himself to the whole. Not each for himself but all for all with that inner freedom . . . freedom in obedience."[10] Veblen thought that the Prussian system was "beneath the human dignity of a free man," but he conceded that it was a source of strength to the German State and to the German economy.

An American would be disposed to infer that this "German freedom" carries somewhat ominous implications for the German as an individual, since it involves his complete subjection, and equally ominous implications for Germany's neighbors, since it creates a powerful, regimented, militaristic state which can only lead sooner or later to conquest of other states.

[9] *Soliloquies in England.*
[10] *Preussentum und Sozialismus.*

A good deal of historical evidence would support this inference.

But if one goes on to argue that the remedy is to make the Germans free in our sense of the word, thus removing the internal foundation of the military state, the question arises whether such a remedy would be acceptable to Germany, where the individualistic tradition has not shaped the national life as it has done in democratic countries. Though there have been many liberals in Germany who admired the English system which Spengler contrasts with the Prussian, they have been a minority. In general the Germans have shown no consuming passion for liberty, no marked discontent with the Prussian tradition. Meanwhile in democratic countries some believe that individualism needs to be tempered with a far greater sense of duty to the community and nation — that is, with a dash of "German freedom." Discipline and the sharing by youth of all classes of the hardships and risks of life were among the military virtues that William James believed should be inculcated by other than military means so as to offer a "moral equivalent of war." [11]

If Germany is disarmed, she will desperately need some "moral equivalent of war." For her youth will be suddenly deprived of this "German freedom," this "freedom in obedience," in its most characteristic, most conspicuous, and most universal form, while Germany will be deprived of her army, which throughout modern times has been regarded not as a mere adjunct of the state but as the foundation of the state if not the state itself.[12]

---

[11] See Chapter III above.

[12] "The writer will never forget his last conversation with the greatest German sociologist and one of the greatest liberals of modern Germany, Max Weber, in his seminar at the University of Munich a few months before the latter's death in 1920. When asked about his political plans, Weber (who had been a member of the German delegation at Versailles) smiled wanly and sadly, then answered: 'I have no political plans except to concentrate all my intellectual strength on the one problem, how to get once more for Germany a great General Staff.'" Gustav Stolper: *This Age of Fable* (New York, Reynal & Hitchcock, 1942).

Can Germany Change?

THE German problem is that of the possibility of a transition from the military state of Frederick the Great, and the philosophic and social tradition and "way of life" associated with it, to some form of national expression which we should regard as more civilized or more befitting "the dignity of a free man." The military state to us seems anachronistic and evil. But along with the "subservient alacrity," as Veblen called it, it developed an ideal of public service and a staff of extremely efficient if unimaginative public servants.

The British developed a similar ideal and an equally competent, if not a uniquely competent, civil service, but on other principles. But it took them a long time, and we cannot expect the Germans, accustomed to their more rigid discipline, to acquire the British type except possibly after a long evolution.

I have often heard educated and traveled Germans contend that the British were far in advance of Germany since they had acquired a kind of instinctive discipline, while the only discipline possible in Germany was that imposed by a strong state built upon "soldierly" principles. This British superiority they attributed to the fact that Britain was an island and hence had long been secure and able to afford individual freedom and an unmilitary state, while Germany had to the east no natural frontiers and must be armed and on guard against the Slavic world.

Germans have long felt this admiration, amounting sometimes to a kind of awe, of the British, who seemed to control much of the world with a kind of lazy ease, without half trying, in a way that the Germans had never been able to do with all their highly organized, carefully calculated, and strenuously executed efforts. Hitler long ago dreamed of an alliance with Britain; and when he faced Britain across thirty miles of water after the fall of France, a Britain that had practically no army, I suspect that he was restrained not merely by the obvious physical obstacles but also by the profound respect he had always felt for the capacities of the British, so mysteriously successful, as it seemed to Germans.

One reason is that Britain is an older nation. She has received comparatively little immigration since the year 1066, and time has enabled the various racial strains in her population to merge and settle and form a singularly homogeneous people. Another reason is that the apparently lazy Briton instinctively saves up his energies for an emergency and declines (if he can avoid it) to waste them in strife and worry as the less self-controlled German does. In this sense the Germans were right in saying that the British had an instinctive discipline which Germans lacked. (The fact is that Americans lack it also and consequently expend a disproportionate amount of nervous energy in all they do. We have neither the Prussian discipline of the Germans nor the discipline of tradition and custom and manner which distinguishes the British; nor have we found an adequate substitute for either.)

Germany's Disarmament

MR. STALIN believes that the disarmament of Germany is both impossible and undesirable.[13] Probably he assumes that the democracies will not have the determination to make it effective for any prolonged period or to subject Germany's heavy industry to the rigid control that would be necessary to insure against rearmament. This may be one reason why he thinks it would be undesirable to make the attempt. Another reason may be his belief that Germany must remain an important and strong power in any event and his calculation that in certain contingencies the existence of such a Germany might serve Russian interests.

On the other hand, the disarmament of Germany in a more thorough and lasting manner than that of a quarter-century ago has been one of the primary aims of Britain and the United States. Though the precise means of doing this have not been made public, consideration has been given to the assumed need to control German industry, the source of armaments, even at the expense of Germany's productive

[13] Speech of November 6, 1942.

power for peacetime reconstruction of Germany and Europe. Some officials have taken the view that security against another German aggression transcends in importance the need of German industry for rebuilding Europe. Their theory is that, even if reconstruction should be slower as a consequence, Germany's heavy industry must be subjected to close surveillance. Here the two attitudes indicated at the beginning of this chapter come into conflict; the pessimists believing that Germany's military and economic power are inseparable and that both must be curbed in the interest of peace, the optimists contending that the solution lies in making Germany a partner in the new Europe even though this necessarily involves a revival of her power.

Alluding to the plans being made by "the ruthless gentlemen," Mr. Roosevelt and Mr. Churchill, then meeting at Quebec, Mr. Brendan Bracken, British Minister of Information, said on August 19, 1943, that the intention was "to bomb and burn and ruthlessly destroy in every way available to us the people responsible for this war."

Those violent words represented the feelings of the British people as a result of the German air attacks on the civilian population of Britain in 1940. They represented the American intention also, though America has not suffered as Britain has; and it seems unlikely that after the second German war British or Americans will relent so far as they did after the first.

When Mr. Bracken spoke, the Allied bombardment of Germany from the air was intense and plans called for making it ever more intense. Hence his words and the circumstances in which they were uttered seemed to have a possible bearing upon the question of Germany's military and economic disarmament. For if the result of the bombings should be to reduce materially the capacity of German heavy industry, they would be in themselves a part of the process of Germany's disarmament. They might answer Mr. Stalin by proving that effective disarmament of Germany is possible, and by so diminishing German heavy industry that Germany's value as a future ally of any other power would be small.

This would be a quite logical outcome of what the Germans themselves called, and made, a "total" war. It would be the application to Germany of the methods Germany had herself applied to other countries.

Destruction as a Cure

SUCH A DEFEAT — complete, visible, devastating, leaving its mark of horror upon Germany's own soil for years — might serve as one of the most potent factors in changing the German mental attitude towards war and militarism. The profound German respect for physical force, which so long has sustained the military state, would then be turned against it. The Germans as a nation might conclude at last that, unlike their easy nineteenth-century Bismarckian wars against Denmark, Austria, and France, war in the future will not pay. Towards this psychological end the crippling of German industry might serve particularly, since the industrial superiority of Germany tends in any case to diminish relative to Russia, an industrially advancing nation whose fighting power amazed friend and foe alike, and more especially relative to the United States, which probably may henceforth be counted upon to oppose Germany whenever she seeks to conquer Europe.

The problem then would be to induce the democratic countries, always prone to forgive and forget after wars, to retain the physcial power and the moral readiness to prevent by force any effort by Germany to rearm. This would involve acceptance of the doctrine of preventive war which was so repugnant to the conscience of the democratic world in the years between the world wars.

The retention of the power necessary to this end and the readiness to use it are far more important than the actual disarmament of Germany. They are so much more important that they might conceivably be preferable to Germany's total disarmament. For if Germany is officially regarded as disarmed, the democratic powers may tend again to relax their surveillance and neglect their own armaments, while if there is visible danger of further German aggression the democracies will be more likely to remain armed, both physically and morally. The ideal situation might be the disarmament of Germany sufficiently to deprive her of the power of aggression, but the continuance on the democratic side of the suspicion and alertness necessary to maintain permanent democratic superiority of armament, particularly of a quick-striking air force.

If this should involve the permanent diminution of Germany's predominant industrial power in Europe, as compared with that of France, Belgium, Holland, Sweden, Poland, and other countries, and the consequent diminution of Germany's population in the long run (which vital statistics have long indicated), that would not necessarily be tragic for Europe or for Germany herself. It might tend towards a better balance in Europe, though the immediate effect would be to reduce the aggregate productive capacity of Europe.

The German birth rate, like that of Western countries generally, had already begun to decline before the Nazis managed to give it a temporary upward stimulus, and German students of population growth have predicted a falling-off of population as well.[14] This "demographic" decline in face of the more prolific Poles, Russians, and Balkan peoples was depicted as a peril for Germany before the Hitler period. It was a bit difficult for Germans to express alarm at their falling birth rate while at the same time claiming greater "living space" for their population, but this was done by arguing that Germans were superior to Slavs and must keep their dominant position both by fighting and by breeding. Consequently the trend towards reduced population pressure, which logically should have been a factor making for peace, became a factor making for war. Propaganda to this end was active in 1930, when I visited Danzig and the German-populated regions of Poland.

[14] Dr. Friedrich Burgdoerfer calculated that Germany's population would begin to decrease about the year 1950 and would drop sharply in the following years. (*Bevoelkerungsentwicklung im Dritten Reich*, Heidelberg and Berlin, 1935).

To dismember Germany or to seek to impose upon her any system of internal administration would only stimulate her nationalism and her thirst for vengeance. To restrain her productivity in peacetime would be in a sense illogical and probably impracticable, and the attempt would create a new grievance. It seems likewise doubtful whether the democracies will sit on Germany, so to speak, in order to keep her completely disarmed for a generation or so. Pending the choice by the Germans of more peaceful paths, the best insurance lies in continued preponderance of armaments on the part of the victors, with the willingness to use them preventively to control any future aggressive moves such as Hitler's march into the Rhineland in 1936 and into Austria in 1938. Meanwhile the Germans should receive every opportunity to live down their militaristic reputation by diverting their skill and discipline and intelligence into constructive channels.

XIV

THE ENIGMA OF RUSSIA

Russia and the West

ON August 23, 1939, two Junkers aeroplanes landed in Moscow from Berlin. From one of them stepped Joachim von Ribbentrop, Foreign Minister for Adolf Hitler who, in his political program entitled *Mein Kampf*, written some sixteen years before, had said that Germany's destiny was to expand eastward at the expense of Russia. But the time for that had not yet come. Ribbentrop's mission was a peaceful one — for Russia, and for the moment. A story told in Moscow at the time was that the Russians skirmished about for a Nazi flag to do proper honor to Ribbentrop, but that the only one available was a swastika banner that had been used in an anti-Nazi Russian film. Late the same night a non-aggression pact between Russia and Germany was signed. Hitler had eliminated the only great power that might form an eastern front against him. Eight days later he attacked Poland, and a European war, destined to become a world war, began.

Seventeen days later Poland was partitioned between Germany and Russia, Soviet troops moving in when Warsaw fell to the Germans. At the end of November 1939 Russia invaded Finland and by the following March forced the Finns to make peace by ceding the naval base at Hangoe and some 11,000 square miles of territory. When France fell in June 1940, Russian forces invaded the three Baltic states: Estonia, Latvia, and Lithuania. The following month Russia took Bessarabia from Rumania. Meeting a German diplomat in The Hague on the day Russia attacked Finland, I remarked that the Russians evidently were preparing for war with Germany, and he agreed. Russia took advantage of the fall of Warsaw and the fall of Paris to push her strategic frontier as far westward and southward as possible against the day when the nonaggression pact, so solemnly signed in Moscow, would be broken.

That day came in June 1941, when Hitler attacked Russia. Many observers in the West thought Russia would last only a few weeks or months. When she retreated but held out, especially when she finally threw back the Germans from Stalingrad, we found that Hitler had raised up for us a valuable ally — the only one then capable of resisting him on the continent which he had very nearly conquered in three years of continuous victories.

Russia, who had signed a pact with Hitler, now signed one with the British and later with us — with, we hoped, somewhat less cynicism than she had signed with Hitler. In July 1941 she and Britain made a mutual assistance pact, extended a year later for twenty years. On January 1, 1942, Russia, through her Ambassador in Washington, Maxim Litvinoff, signed a joint declaration by the United Nations in which she subscribed to the Atlantic Charter and agreed — as she had done in the treaty with Britain — not to make a separate peace.

But neither those apparently clear and definitive documents nor two years of fighting against a common enemy sufficed to remove the ambiguities and suspicions that through the years had accumulated between Russia and the Western powers. Nor will they soon be removed by any document or declaration.

If in the West it is argued that the Second World War began when Mr. Stalin and Ribbentrop signed a pact in Moscow which assured Russia's neutrality when Hitler attacked his next victim, it is argued in Moscow that the decisive moment was approximately a year earlier when Britain and France failed to call in Russia in settling the fate of Czechoslovakia. The absence of Russia was significant in view of the fact that the sacrifice of Czechoslovakia to Hitler meant that he was free to move eastward, in accordance with his plan for German expansion at the expense of Russia. The British and the French governments knew of this plan. They knew

THE ENIGMA OF RUSSIA

that the surrender of the Czech fortifications opened the way for its execution. Some believe they favored its execution. They certainly did not resist it very strenuously. They certainly were more keenly concerned for the security of the West than for that of Russia.

Russia concluded she must look after her own security in her own way. Britain's policy underwent a sharp change in March 1939, when Hitler invaded Prague. Britain then gave to Rumania and Poland the guarantees she had previously been unwilling to give, and those guarantees automatically covered much of Russia's Western frontier. But Stalin — like Hitler — was unconvinced that the guarantees represented a determined policy, particularly when in the summer of 1939 British-Russian discussions of a mutual defence pact failed, the British being then unwilling to concede that Russia should occupy the Baltic states and doubting Russia's military strength. Moreover, Russia's eagerness to challenge Hitler in battle, which seemed very great when the battle was in Spain, diminished as the drama moved eastward to Czechoslovakia in 1938 and to Poland in 1939; and by her pact with Hitler she gained a respite. So in August 1939 she evened the score with the West by showing as little concern for the democratic powers as they had shown for her the previous year. By so doing she gained time and territory for her defence.

The most significant conclusion to draw from these events is not that the democracies let Russia down and that Russia then took her revenge, but that in acting as they did neither the democracies nor Russia achieved the security they were seeking. The democracies gained no more than a short respite in sacrificing Czechoslovakia, and Russia gained less than two years of immunity from attack by facilitating Hitler's aggressions against Poland and Western Europe — though by acting together the Western powers and Russia might have prevented the war.

Distant Allies

PARTLY no doubt because of vivid memories of these recent efforts by each to thrust Hitler upon the other, partly because of still older memories of antagonism, Russia and the Western coalition continued to be, not reluctant allies since each welcomed the help of the other, but distant allies destined both by geographical remoteness and by incomplete mutual confidence to fight what in many ways remained two separate though related struggles. For more than a year after the Hitler attack on Russia, Moscow accorded to Allied military observers only limited opportunities, as if unwilling to share her military secrets. For more than two years the complaint continued that the Western powers were not helping Russia enough. The Western coalition had changed with the fall of France and the later entrance of the United States into the war, but Russian distrust apparently remained.

When Mr. Molotov, Soviet Foreign Commissar, visited Washington in June 1942, a White House statement said that he and President Roosevelt had reached a "full understanding" regarding "the urgent tasks of creating a second front in Europe in 1942." This was widely interpreted as indicating there would be such a front that year, and when the Allies landed in North Africa in November many said that this was the second front. It was in the European war zone, if not in Europe, and it proved to be a stepping-stone towards an invasion of Europe. But the Russians did not agree that it was adequate, since it did not draw German forces from the eastern front.

Mr. Stalin had indicated his impatience for this aid from the West. On October 4, 1942, in a statement to Mr. Henry W. Cassidy of the Associated Press, he said that compared with the aid Russia was giving the Allies by drawing upon herself the main German forces, Allied aid to Russia had "so far been little effective" and that the Allies should "fulfill their obligations fully and on time." On November 6, 1942, he again complained of the absence of a second front which had enabled the Germans to throw their reserves against Russia "without risk to themselves." This last was an odd phrase, since the risk the Germans took was shown at Stalingrad to have been very great. Long after the Allied invasion of North Africa, on February 22, 1943, Mr. Stalin once more complained in rather bitter terms by saying that because there was no second front in Western Europe, "the Red Army alone is bearing the full weight of the war" — a singular statement in view of the fact that the war at sea, including heavy losses in convoying war materials to Russia at Murmansk, was entirely borne by the Allies, and in view of the increasing Allied air attacks on Germany which were materially impairing her war production and transport. In August 1943 the Russian complaint was revived, this time by an article in the official newspaper, *Pravda*, although by then the Allied armies had almost conquered Sicily, had bombed Rome and thus caused the fall of Mussolini and virtually put Italy out of the war. To the Russians a second front meant a massive attack on the western shores of Europe, and no substitute seemed acceptable. They counted the divisions of the enemy that were occupied in Sicily, but apparently failed to count the vastly more important wreckage of whole cities in Germany by Allied bombs.

These strategic arguments were reflections of other differences. Although Russia had subscribed to the Atlantic Charter, which declared against territorial changes that did not accord with the freely expressed wishes of the peoples concerned and in favor of restoration of self-government to conquered nations, she clung to a program that seemed incompatible with these principles. Moreover, the Charter declared for the disarmament of aggressive nations, but Mr. Stalin apparently opposed the disarmament of Germany.

An article in *Pravda* of February 8, 1943, officially circulated in this country by the *Information Bulletin* of the Russian Embassy, clearly claimed for Russia the retention of Bessarabia and the three Baltic states, all annexed in 1940. In his order of the day of February 22, 1943, Mr. Stalin spoke of those under the German yoke as including Ukrainians, Byelo-Russia (White Russia), Lithuania, Latvia, Esthonia,

Moldavia, Karelia. The bulk of the Moldavians live in Bessarabia, which Russia took from Rumania while Hitler was fighting in the West. Many White Russians live in the part of Poland taken by Russia in 1939 when she and Hitler partitioned the country. The Karelians are about half in Finland and half in Russia, as the border was fixed after the Russo-Finnish war in March 1940.

These official and semi-official utterances were interpreted in Washington as indicating that Russia was staking her minimum territorial claims for the future. That minimum included the regions held by Russia in 1941 when Hitler attacked her — that is, the territory she had seized in the period when she had a non-aggression pact with Hitler and was using his embroilment with the democracies as an opportunity to extend her own frontiers in anticipation of the German attack that was to come.

It is true that the three small Baltic states were Russian until the end of the First World War, as were Bessarabia and a large part of Poland, while the grand duchy of Finland was under the Russian Crown. Russia had recognized the independence of the three Baltic states and of Finland, though not the cession of Bessarabia. She was annoyed that the United States continued to recognize the Baltic states even after Russia had annexed them. With the Polish Government in London Russia signed a treaty in July 1941, declaring void the partition of Poland by the German-Russian agreement of 1939, but no provision was made for restoring the Polish territory then appropriated; and in its official note breaking off relations with the Polish Government on April 26, 1943, Moscow accused the Poles of carrying on a campaign to obtain this Russian territory.

Russia would doubtless have contended that in much if not all of this territory the inhabitants wanted Russian rule. To this the answer might have been made that the only way to determine the point would be to hold plebiscites. The Russians argued that this had been done in the Baltic states and the annexed Polish territories. But those were the kind of plebiscites which were denounced by the father of the Soviet

Revolution, Lenin, on November 8, 1917, when he declared that "plebiscites" held during military occupation by the annexing power were plain annexations.[1] They were not unlike the plebiscites that Hitler and Mussolini had held, resulting in almost unanimous endorsement of their régimes.

Cordon Sanitaire *in Reverse*

BUT IT seems unlikely that European frontiers can be fixed by restoring the pre-war territorial situation and thus wiping out all the changes since made by violence in favor either of Germany or Russia, and adopting the principles of the Atlantic Charter as the criterion for any readjustments for the future. We must recognize Russia's special interest in Eastern Europe, though it can hardly be denied that that interest has been qualified by Russia's voluntary acceptance of the Atlantic Charter.

The British treaty with Russia and British deference to Russian desires (as, for instance, an article in the *Times* of London on March 10, 1943, suggesting that Russia should be the judge of her own security and implying that Russia should therefore draw her own frontiers) did not facilitate satisfactory consideration of the questions of principle and strategy involved in the Russian claims. Nor was the American Government in a position to exert great influence, since it was unable to offer Russia any guarantees for her future security in return for an agreement on her part to apply the principle of self-determination to the countries on her borders. It could only argue that the possibility of such guarantees might be affected by the impression made upon American opinion by Russia's attitude towards her smaller neighbors, towards the democracies, and towards the Charter which she had herself accepted.

The question of Russia's frontiers and her relations with the states to the west was largely strategic. Allied policy after the first world war had been animated by the doctrine of the *cordon sanitaire,* the desire to create west of Russia a series of

[1] Lenin: *The State and Revolution.*

buffer states which would limit Russian influence, or Communist influence, in Europe. The Western powers at that time were essentially hostile towards Russia. In 1918 Allied troops, including American, were at Archangel and Vladivostok. Britain did not recognize the Soviet Government until 1924, broke off relations in 1927, resumed them in 1929. The United States did not recognize the new Russian régime until 1933. Russian distrust in 1942 and 1943 probably owed something to memories of those troubled past relations — down to 1938, when the Western powers at Munich had sought to divert Hitler in Russia's direction. At any rate, Russia seemed to seek a kind of *cordon sanitaire* of her own — first, frontiers fixed as far west and south as she fixed them in 1939 and 1940; second, beyond those frontiers a string of states sufficiently under Russian influence or control to be permanently friendly to Russia. It might have been argued that the additional territory she had taken did her little good as a defence when Hitler attacked her, but she wanted it nevertheless. She assumed that Germany or other powers might again threaten her, and none could deny that historical ground existed for such an assumption.

Russia and German Disarmament

YET RUSSIA, to judge by statements of Mr. Stalin in 1942 and other evidence, was not desirous of completely destroying German military power, even though British and American power was so remote as to cause little apprehension to Russia. She seemed reluctant to entrust all her eggs to the democratic basket, so to speak, even by accepting the unprecedented position of power which she would hold if Germany were effectively disarmed, leaving Russia the only Great Power in Europe. Mr. Stalin thought that German power could not be really destroyed in any case and might be useful to him again, and he may have thought Russia's growing industrial capacity gave her new assurance against Germany, or that a potentially friendly power in Europe might be more desirable than potentially friendly powers overseas. When he spoke of Russian frontiers, he appeared to be filled with apprehension of Germany, but when he spoke of German armaments he seemed to regard the Germany of the future as a benevolent institution.

In his address of November 6, 1942, Mr. Stalin said: "It is not our aim to destroy all military force in Germany. To attempt the compulsory disarmament of a defeated Germany would not only be impossible but inadvisable from the point of view of the victor." Yet he had instructed his Ambassador in Washington to subscribe the previous January to the Atlantic Charter which declared for the disarmament of "nations which threaten, or may threaten, aggression outside their frontiers." Did Mr. Stalin believe that at the end of the war Germany would not be in that category?

Mr. Stalin meanwhile, in the same address, said that "the Hitlerite army" could and must be destroyed; and in his order of the day of May 1, 1943, he spoke of the unconditional surrender of the "Hitlerite armies," in contrast to the Roosevelt-Churchill doctrine of unconditional surrender of the Axis powers. Mr. Stalin's words suggested that as soon as the German army ceased to be a "Hitlerite army," it would become eligible to preservation instead of destruction.

This view seemed indicated likewise in a broadcast from Moscow to Germany on December 13, 1942, which (as translated by the *Daily Worker* of New York) said: "The German nation has a way out. . . . The German army must return to Germany. Germany will retain none of Hitler's conquests. . . . To this end must the will of all Germans be bent, from workers to noblemen, from private to General. Thus can Germany win freedom. . . ."

This was the theme also of the manifesto of a group of Germans in Russia calling themselves "Free Germany," broadcast from Moscow in July 1943 (as translated by the *Daily Worker* of July 22, 1943). It called on the Germans to get a new government, to withdraw the German armies to German soil "and embark on peace negotiations, renouncing all conquests." It thus suggested a negotiated peace as opposed to the "unconditional surrender" doctrine of the British and American governments.

This manifesto was regarded as having Russian official approval, especially since it appeared to conform to officially expressed Russian aims and was broadcast from Moscow. Consequently it was interpreted in Washington (a) as Russian psychological warfare against Germany, (b) as part of the propaganda visible in other forms, as indicated above, to assert Russia's leadership in the continent of Europe as opposed to that of Britain or the United States, and (c) as a hint that Russia at any rate would be ready for peace with Germany under the conditions set forth in the manifesto and in Mr. Stalin's speech. (Russia had, of course, given her pledge on January 1, 1942, not to make a separate peace or armistice.)

But in October, 1943, it appeared either that this last interpretation was erroneous or that Russian policy had changed. For in the British-Russian-American program then adopted at Moscow, Russia agreed to insist upon unconditional surrender of Germany and to join with the two other powers to maintain the peace thus to be won.

Differing British and American Views

BRITISH and American conceptions of relations with Russia — or, rather, Britain's adopted policy and the official American views as to what our policy might conceivably be if we could have one — were far from identical. For Britain, security in Europe was an immediate and vital interest with which no chances could be taken. For the United States it might have been regarded as an ultimately but not immediately vital interest, a vital interest which on two occasions it had taken us more than two years to recognize (since we entered the first German world war two years and eight months after its start, the second one two years and three months after its start). Moreover, Russia — in getting attacked by

THE ENIGMA OF RUSSIA 211

Hitler, whatever the cause — had come directly to the relief of a hard-pressed Britain, who then fought alone against Germany. Russia had rendered us no comparable service, although we recognized the direct relation between our military task in Europe and the share Russia was taking in the defeat of Hitler. Hence our attitude towards Europe and Russia's rôle in Europe could be rather more objective and even academic than Britain's. It did not, at any rate, express the same degree of dependence upon Russian collaboration.

The result was that, while Britain took a cold-blooded, realistic, even slightly cynical view, we felt more bound — or felt we could afford — to inject broad issues of principle, even at the risk of preventing an unprincipled but useful Anglo-Russian entente. The British could say, and practically did say in signing their treaty with Russia, that Russia could do just about what she would in Eastern Europe if she helped Britain hold Germany in check. This, at any rate, was the interpretation of British policy given in the article in the *Times* of London cited above. It accorded no better than some of Mr. Stalin's statements with the Wilsonian doctrines of the Atlantic Charter which the *Times* seemed to cast aside when it opposed "any organization based on the conception of national independence which entails the partition of Europe among twenty separate and jarring military and economic sovereignties" (this being precisely what the Wilsonian doctrine of self-determination, repeated in the Atlantic Charter, had done a quarter-century earlier).[2]

The British aim was friendship with Russia at almost any

[2] "The new political frontiers of Europe are Wilsonian and so drawn that 3 per cent only of the total population of the Continent live under alien rule. Judged by the test of self-determination, no previous European frontiers had been so satisfactory." (H. A. L. Fisher: *A History of Europe*.) They must be judged, of course, by other tests as well — for instance, durability. Those frontiers, practically ideal from the point of view of the Wilsonian and Atlantic Charter doctrines of the right of peoples to choose under what state and under what kind of government they will live, lasted barely twenty years, after which there was, for several years, complete lack of self-determination.

cost, because of Russia's rôle in the war and possible rôle in the maintenance of peace. The American aim seemed to be to clarify Russia's enigmatic position towards the war in the Pacific, for which we wanted air bases in Siberia, and towards the reconstitution of Europe in accordance with the will of the peoples involved. And Russia was in no mood to vouchsafe clarification on either point. On her side Russia might have asked, and perhaps did ask, for a definition of American policy after the war — which, of course, our government was in no position to give. Mr. William Henry Chamberlin, long a correspondent in Russia, expressed the belief that we might have Mr. Stalin's aid against Japan at a price, and that the price might include Russian annexation of Manchuria,[3] which China would hardly like. Mr. Walter Duranty took a similar view, suggesting that Russia might covet the recovery of Port Arthur.

Affecting all these discussions of the relations of the three great powers in war and in peace was the fact that Mr. Churchill and Mr. Stalin could sign treaties and otherwise fix the terms of their countries' long-range relationship, while President Roosevelt had no such power. On the one hand our interests, though they might be as great, were not so obvious. On the other hand our Constitution does not permit a President or a government to undertake commitments such as other governments can undertake.

The three-power agreement signed at Moscow in October 1943 exceeded expectations, and it seemed to find Senatorial approval a few days later in a resolution favoring American participation in an international authority to prevent aggression. It thus raised hopes that the obstacles cited above might be removed. The agreement was a diplomatic triumph which confounded the pessimists and which seemed to offer hope that this time the victorious coalition would not dissolve when the war had been won.

[3] In the *Progressive*, Madison, Wis., of March 22, 1943. Quoted by Harold Kellock in *American and British Relations with Russia* (Editorial Research Reports, Washington, Vol. I, No. 13).

XV

BRITAIN'S POLICY AND OURS

Defending Our Neutrality

WHEN Sir Wilmot Lewis, the distinguished Washington correspondent of the *Times* of London, was asked at a meeting of Americans how long Britain would continue to expect this country to pull her chestnuts out of the fire, he replied with another question: How long would the United States continue to expect Britain to fight in defence of American neutrality? His hearers laughed. Sir Wilmot then remarked that he thought both questions a bit beside the point since the fact was that the defensive interests of the two countries were related and should be so treated.

This incident took place before Congress had passed the Lend-Lease Act, which in effect officially acknowledged that Britain was fighting in defence of our neutrality. We seemed at that time content to let her do so, and to arm her without otherwise assisting her. The Lend-Lease Act applied to countries whose defence the President deemed vital to the defence of the United States, and it applied first and foremost to Britain. She was fighting, of course, in her own defence, but it was the Congressionally acknowledged fact that she was fighting at the same time in our defence which resulted in the Lend-Lease Act.[1]

Twice in our lifetime Britain has been in the front line while the United States has been a long way behind it — two years or more, if we measure the distance by the time it took us to join in what we recognized on both occasions to be our

---

[1] Britain's share in the burden of war, as compared with that of other parts of the Empire, was indicated by official figures showing that the casualties of the United Kingdom between September 3, 1939, and September 3, 1942, formed 53.6 per cent of the total Empire casualties. while the number of United Kingdom men killed was 79.8

battle. The result was that Britain, exposed first and more perilously, had more cogent reasons to perceive the trans-Atlantic community of interest, of which Americans became aware more slowly and reluctantly. It has thus inevitably appeared to the more suspicious that Britain somehow got into trouble and then asked us to get her out. It has seemed that we were repeatedly called upon to do favors for Britain, whereas in fact she has been in the position of holding off our enemy until we were ready to admit that he was an enemy. Our defen-

---

per cent of the total for the Empire. The comparative figures are as follows:

	Killed (including deaths from wounds and injuries)	*Total Casualties*
United Kingdom	73,477	275,844
Australia	6,192	53,959
Canada	3,142	10,422
New Zealand	3,219	19,345
South Africa	1,439	22,615
India (including losses at Hongkong and Singapore)	3,286	101,979
Colonies	1,334	30,829
TOTALS	92,089	514,993

In addition to these casualties in the armed forces, British civilian casualties from September 3, 1939, to August 31, 1942, were: killed, 47,291; injured, 53,643. (Mr. Clement R. Attlee in the House of Commons, June 3, 1943.)

Seventy-six per cent of the troops in General Montgomery's British Eighth Army, which drove Rommel's forces out of Egypt and Libya, helped drive them out of Tunisia, and then invaded Sicily, were from England, Scotland, Wales, and Northern Ireland; 20 per cent were Dominion and Indian troops; 4 per cent were French. In the British First Army in North Africa 90 per cent of the men were from the United Kingdom, 10 per cent were French. (British Information Services R. 2561.)

As regards war materials sent to Russia, in the period from October 1941 to the end of 1942 the United Kingdom sent 3,000 aircraft (250 more than she had promised), while the United States sent 2,600; the United Kingdom sent 2,974 tanks, while the United States sent 3,200. Britain sent to Russia also 70 million rounds of small-arms ammunition and 50,000 tons of rubber from her limited stock. (British Information Services, weekly war notes, Feb. 26, 1943.)

Nor should Americans forget, when they measure Britain's contribution to victory, that before the European war began Britain invested

sive interests were less immediate and direct than hers and therefore were not recognized as comparable to hers. The sea power of Britain had so long effectively defended our neutrality that Americans were unaware that it was doing so.

It is an interesting fact that the late Senator Borah, ardent protagonist of American neutrality, was fully aware of the advantage the United States derived from British sea power. Though he had not traveled in Europe, he had studied its past and contemporary history. In a conversation in January 1937 he remarked to me that the British Empire was a tremendous force for stability in the world, and that if it should collapse there would be chaos in many regions from which the United States would suffer.

In other words, the neutrality which had become traditional for the United States depended upon the stability which Britain's power assured. Consequently when Britain's power was endangered, the foundations of our neutrality were threatened, and in fact we ceased to be neutral.[2]

Britain's power has now undergone a change and her policy takes account of that fact. Britain's changed position in the

---

$1,500,000,000 in the American aircraft industry for construction, expansion of plant, and orders placed. Some $200,000,000 took the form of direct capital assistance to American corporations making tanks, guns and other armaments. From September, 1939, to August, 1942, Britain made contracts with American industry aggregating $3,250,-000,000. Thus British funds materially helped to transform our industries to war production long before it appeared that this production would be required for the United States also. In other words, Britain helped us to arm by financing the expansion of plants making armaments in this country.

[2] Mr. Walter Lippmann (*op. cit.*) has most lucidly and impressively analyzed the relationship between American security and British sea power, though with perhaps less than due emphasis upon the fact that at certain times, notably during the American Civil War, British sea power came very near being used against the United States, then not a major naval power. But now that Britain's fleet can never again provide the general protection it provided in the nineteenth century, incidental to its primary task of protecting British territories and trade, and can never again be a potential danger to this country, Mr. Lippmann's argument in favor of a partnership between British and American sea and other power seems altogether sound.

world has been well described by Mr. E. H. Carr.[3] He points out that she can no longer blind herself to the relative decline of her power by assuming that the French army and navy form an adjunct to her defences, and that the British know they could not have won the second German war single-handed. Not only Britain but Western Europe is weaker than formerly in relation to the rest of the world. In future there will not again be a single economic and financial center managing world trade, as London did in the nineteenth century. Britain's creditor position will have been altered, and her former annual income of some $1,000,000,000 a year from overseas investments will drop to a fraction of that sum. She will be obliged to increase her exports at a time when the growth of manufacturing in other nations will have limited further her overseas markets, and her prosperity may depend upon a general rise of the standard of living in the world which would create new demands and the purchasing power to meet them.

Britain and Russia

IN THE ABSENCE of France as a great power and ally, Britain inevitably turns to Russia as an indispensable factor in the European stability she hopes to create in the interest of peace and of her own security — and, incidentally, of ours. She cannot again adopt the policy, beloved of the British as well as of Americans, of isolation. She alone cannot "contain" German power from her extra-European position off the western coast of the Continent. Nor can Russia practice isolation, as she has tried to do in the last two decades; for the result would only be the domination of Europe by Germany, which both powers have fought a long war to prevent. Consequently hostility or distrust between Britain and Russia could only lead to an early revival of German power since it would divide the only two great nations which can counter that revival or that power.

This primary requisite for the safety of Europe must condition British foreign policy and that of other powers, in-

[3] *Op. cit.*

cluding the United States, whose interest in the safety of Europe has ceased to be merely academic or humanitarian. Only great powers can insure that safety. It cannot be done by the small nations, desirable though it is for them to continue to exist and even increase in the interest of the cultural diversity which gives Europe its unique character and makes it worth preserving, apart from our vital selfish interest in its preservation. Hence there must somehow be a reconciliation between the interest and duty of the great powers in preserving peace and the rights and independence of the small nations which might be infringed by what the great powers regard as their strategic necessities. We see an example in the case of Russia, who apparently maintains that her safety requires her retention of the territories she acquired in 1939 and 1940 when she was in effect collaborating with Hitler, though those acquisitions impaired the integrity of Poland, Finland, and Rumania and destroyed the independence of Latvia, Lithuania, and Esthonia.[4] We may see an example closer home when we mark out on the map the bases for aircraft and ships that we think the United States will require in South America, Africa, Asia, and in the North Atlantic, which inevitably would give us power over the adjacent countries — power which may not everywhere be regarded as beneficent.

It was this reconciliation of the needs of great and small states which Mr. Churchill had in mind when he suggested, within a world organization of the United Nations, a Council

[4] The extreme lucidity and completeness with which this situation of Britain, Russia, and the smaller nations has been described in three articles in the *Times* of London is such that I have included those articles in full, with the kind permission of the editor of the *Times*, in Appendix C at the end of this volume, for the benefit of American readers who otherwise might never see them. The articles deserve to be read and weighed because they present the British point of view regarding these major post-war relationships with a candor which no official spokesman could permit himself but which a great newspaper can indulge in with almost equal authority, and because they analyze the basic facts with classic clarity. The difficulty which some Americans find in accepting the British point of view supplies an additional reason for their careful study of this brilliant presentation of it.

of Europe and a Council of Asia and groups and federations of smaller states side by side with the great powers.[5] These two continental councils suggest a Council of the Americas which would supplement them and, with them, emphasize the gradations of regional interest and responsibility which may arise from the fact that the defensive range of each power is necessarily limited and compels a division of labor which may tend constantly to threaten the universality of the defensive organization contemplated by Mr. Churchill.

Effect of American Tradition

THE TRADITIONAL foreign policy of the United States is essentially regional in being preoccupied almost exclusively with the integrity of this hemisphere but universal in its aversion to fixed alliance with any power or group of powers. President Wilson sought to overcome this limitation by presenting the League of Nations not as an alliance but as an association in which the United States could take part without abandoning its aversion to alliances. Those in President Franklin D. Roosevelt's government who have contemplated another attempt at forming collective safeguards against war have assumed that this "universality" of the traditional American policy, this opposition to special commitments to any nation (other than those in this hemisphere), must be accepted as the basis for American action.

This tradition is the opposite of that of Britain, who has been compelled by her semi-European position to make alliances, now with one power and now with another, as circumstances and the needs of her safety dictated. Americans sometimes call this a policy of expediency, though they admit its necessity, as contrasted with our adherence to broad principles without special commitments. One such principle is the refusal to recognize territorial gains acquired by force. It was so interpreted as to prevent our recognition, and perhaps to prevent Britain's recognition, of Russia's annexation of the three Baltic states. Here our universalism came into

[5] Speech of March 21, 1943.

conflict with what might have been regarded as a British interest, since recognition of that annexation might have improved Britain's relations with Russia, whom she needs as an ally. Yet we were in no position to offer to Russia, as an alternative to her territorial gains, any guarantees for the security to which she seemed to believe those gains contributed.

This difference of tradition forms what may be called the Anglo-American problem. Britain, uncertain regarding the future American contribution to security, feels compelled to protect her safety by an alliance with Russia. But that alliance apparently implies a rather free hand for Russia in Eastern Europe which may — and, as interpreted by Russia, already does — conflict with our doctrine of self-determination, written into the Atlantic Charter. Russia says in effect that she moved her frontiers westward to be safe and intends to keep them there. The British believe Russia's safety is necessary to the safety of Europe. We say, in effect, that safety must not be attained at the expense of the right of small nations to independence and the integrity of their territories. We now seem disposed to help in resolving this dilemma in the way in which some think it could be resolved; that is, by creation of a system of collective security which would remove the need or the pretext for encroachment upon small nations for strategic reasons.

Our Aversion to Power Politics

IT IS A PART of the American tradition to think of power politics as something immoral, necessary though it has been for nations that did not enjoy our happy aloofness. Russia's frank cynicism in asserting her frontier claims came as a shock to those Americans who like to formulate policies in ethically unexceptionable terms. For the same reasons many were shocked by the military expediency, as President Roosevelt called it, which dictated American negotiations in North Africa with Admiral Darlan, who had collaborated with the enemy and suddenly proved useful to us. Americans shrink from the admission that the power of guns and bombs, not the opinion of enlightened humanity, is the decisive factor in the relations of states. They like to imagine that the destinies of nations can be settled by reasonable conversations — though the destiny of the United States has not been settled by that means.

In the coming years it seems certain we shall be more power-conscious, so to speak, because of the perils that have faced us in the recent past and that we must avoid in future. Our naval experts insist upon bases extending far into the southwestern Pacific; and when we recover Guam and the Navy desires to fortify it, there is hardly likely to be a repetition of the Congressional refusal that met that proposal a few years before the Japanese took Guam with its garrison. In the Atlantic we have acquired from Britain a string of bases from Newfoundland to Trinidad. A year before we were at war our strategists and members of our State Department decided that North Africa was a vital defensive area for the United States, and they took the first of a series of steps which were to be followed by the occupation of North Africa as a base for achieving command of the Mediterranean and for the attack on Italy. West African points like Dakar are even closer to our hemisphere and cannot be permitted to fall into hostile hands. The strategic interests of the United States have expanded across the two oceans and will not shrink to their previous proportions.

The consequence is that we shall be compelled to think in terms of power politics, as Britain long has done, and for precisely the same reason — that we, like her, are now concerned by potential causes of war everywhere. A decade ago Mr. Stimson, then Secretary of State, said that neutrality was obsolete. He was thinking in the somewhat legalistic terms of the Briand-Kellogg Pact. Today much more realistic evidence supports his statement; the evidence of events which compels us to assume that an aggressive power anywhere is potentially a danger to the United States, as Germany and Japan have demonstrated.

It does not follow that we need agree that Russia may swallow as much of Finland and Poland as she likes, or that we shall leave small nations to their fate. For if we accept our logical rôle as one of the leading powers and protect ourselves by sharing in guarantees against aggressive power, we shall be in the best possible position for insisting that no great power need dominate small states in the interest of its own defence. It is the absence of guarantees against aggression which supplies grounds, or pretexts, for making *glacis* and buffers of boundary states. It has been suggested that Russia should practice towards her smaller neighbors a European version of our Good Neighbor policy. The logic of this is not perfect since we have no Germany on the other side of our good neighbors and able to march against us by land. But the most potent influence in favor of a more generous Russian policy towards the small nations of Eastern Europe would be the certainty that the United States as well as Great Britain intended to insure that Germany should not again threaten Europe. If Britain alone is allied with Russia to this end, Russia will have her way in Eastern Europe and will establish her frontiers where she will, with none to interfere. If Britain and the United States form parts of a collective system in which Russia believes, the incentive for advanced frontiers will have disappeared.

The British feel more cordial and more tolerant towards Russia than Americans do. For Russia, by an accident of history, by the will of Hitler, came to the defence of Britain because she was compelled to defend herself — for the same reason that Britain came to our defence. Moreover, under stress of war that has been immeasurably more intense for Britain than for us, the British of all classes have become resigned to extensive social changes in the direction of wider distribution of wealth and privilege and security within their country by means of greater state control over economic life. One consequence of this is that the unorthodox economy of Russia, which after all proved capable of sustaining a war that was in Britain's interest and ours (little though 90 per cent of the Western World expected it so to prove), appears less frightening to the British than to the more conservative-minded among Americans.

There are some who fear that Russia may dominate the Continent in the post-war years, and that a revived and highly nationalistic France, as well as other nations, will turn to her and to a "continental policy" as against the British and Americans, who are outside Europe and foreign to it. So far as such a trend exists, it would clearly be strengthened if the United States reverted to aloof neutrality. For that would leave Britain and Russia only to look after the security of the Western World; and in that case Britain would be compelled to accede to a Russian desire for a free hand on the Continent, while Russia would have every reason for taking such measures as seemed to her necessary for her safety against Germany, probably at the expense of the small countries lying between the two.

American Prejudices

HAVING TWICE recognized, rather more clearly in the second German war than in the first, that Britain was in effect our first line of defence against a European power which threatened the Atlantic and therefore this hemisphere, having felt gratitude and admiration for the way in which she held that line against tremendous odds in 1940 when we were doing extremely little to help her, we should be able to view British faults and weaknesses in generous perspective as we relate them to the essential greatness of the British people, to whom Americans as a whole have never done full justice because comparatively few have really known the British.

They are not easy to know. They display towards foreigners not the eager interest that Americans show but often a chilly indifference. Sometimes it is by calculated rudeness that certain well-bred Englishmen make their special contribution to the reputation of their country, and that rudeness is long remembered by Americans in spite of all the kindness they have experienced. Probably the Americans who have visited England, including the many soldiers who have gone there in the last few years, would agree that it is one of the most polite and socially civilized countries in the world, giving more time and attention to good manners than Americans mostly do. The sharp edges of life have been smoothed, the friction of social contacts of all kinds has been reduced. Strikes are almost always completely peaceful. Policemen are unarmed. Crimes of violence are at a minimum that would appear incredible to the chief of police of any large American city. In this sense Britain is the most civilized large country in the world, and this atmosphere of quiet, unhurried politeness, tolerance, fairness, and reasonableness goes far towards explaining the successful working of British democracy.

Many Americans are prejudiced against monarchy, aristocracy, and imperialism without at all understanding the peculiar forms which those institutions have taken in the British Realm, where nothing is quite what it seems, especially what the British call their Constitution, though they do not themselves quite know what it is. Americans are impatient of the foggy indefiniteness that surrounds so much which they think requires to be defined and written down but which the British prefer not to be too precise. Accustomed to their cloudy island, upon which through most of the year the sun shines only in what the weather report calls "bright intervals," the British instinctively recoil from excessive light and logic. They are content that many things inherited from the dim past should remain dim, like the British landscape at most seasons, like the British Constitution, like the nature of the Monarchy, which Bagehot hoped would never be subjected to the luminous examination which would deprive it of the mystery which was its life.

We may speak the language of Shakespeare, more or less, revere Magna Carta, live by the English Common Law. But we have not inherited the English climate or the mental attitudes which may owe their origin to it, or the national homogeneity which permits a cohesion and placidity which hardly seem likely ever to exist in the United States, or the oddly modernized and efficient yet ancient institutions of political life, or the leisurely habits and quiet manners that are almost universal in Britain. In many ways our national life would be improved if we not only understood but learned from the

British, whose democracy is superior to ours at least in the sense that it permits revolutionary change with less fuss and friction than are generated by even minor innovations in this country.

These differences of view and viewpoint prevent mutual understanding and handicap relations between the American and British peoples, who probably understand each other least when they think they are nearest to an understanding. But they should not prevent recognition of such basic facts as that our safety is closely linked with Britain's strategically, and that politically we have similar ideologies or *Weltanschauungen*, as the Germans would say, which cause our conceptions of the relations of men and nations to be much alike. The British have acquired a certain worldliness and catholicity (some would call it a sense of expediency) which comes of their long experience of world power and has no American counterpart. We see it in their alliance with Russia, whose whole history, manner of life, and ideology are different from theirs but whose national interests happen at present to be similar to — or at least, they hope, reconcilable with — their own. Here again is a British trait from which we shall have to learn in our relatively new rôle of a world power that can no longer sit back in comfortable neutrality while the destiny of humanity is decided by others.

Accompanying this British sense of expediency, this canniness or "perfidy," as the French called it when their interests were in conflict with Britain's, accompanying the British power which stood guard over British security and British property, there has been a moderation and restraint which the Germans have rarely displayed when they were "on top." It is this which has lent permanence to British power. For it was exercised on the whole for the good of the smaller nations of Europe whose integrity became a British interest. The German historian Dibelius testified to this fact.[6]

If its purpose were the maintenance of peace through restraint of any aggressive great nation, such would be, one hopes, the character of the force at the disposal of Britain,

[6] Dibelius, *England*.

the United States, and Russia as leaders of a system of security. Some will object that these nations cannot be trusted with power, and, if this means that the power would be used in their interests, it is true. We must assume that power will be so used. We cannot assume that great nations will at once become pure altruists or that they will always be perfectly just to smaller states. But if they safeguard the small states against future Hitlers and wield their power as fairly as Britain has done, the result, while falling short of Utopia, will be one that every state should welcome.

XVI

WHAT WILL AMERICA DO?

The World Looks to Us

IN the preceding pages it has been suggested that the victory of 1918 was not enough because the defeat of Imperial Germany did not insure a real peace or genuine reconstruction of the world's economic life, and that it remained to be seen whether the results would be substantially better this time. It seems probable that the decision, and therefore the fate of the world, will rest with the United States. What we do or fail to do may well determine whether the second victory over aggression within a generation will prove as barren of lasting fruits as the first.[1]

The greatest single enigma that has hovered over the whole course of the war has been that of the United States. Sharply divided by the depression preceding the war, by the domes-

---

[1] I do not mean to imply that the tragic aftermath of the earlier victory was entirely our fault, though we bore our share of the responsibility. We certainly did our part in inspiring hopes which proved excessive and led to depressing disillusionment. A singular combination of circumstances caused a treaty that might have maintained peace to be rejected by the American Senate and thus deprived of much of its force, though there was no overwhelming opposition to it either in the Senate or in the country. It is my belief that Britain and France, had their governments so willed, could still have sustained the forces for peace and counted upon the benovolent neutrality of the United States. But the American defection served as a pretext for a return to isolation on the part of Britain, which in turn stimulated the French policy of alliances with small states which was doomed to futility by the potential superiority of Germany in population and industrial resources. The result was that after the three democracies had set up a peace, two of them walked out, so to speak, and left the maintenance of it to France, who was not strong enough.

tic program of the New Deal which grew out of the depression, by economic philosophy, by the issues of the war, and to some extent by the racial groups within this country who have their political importance, could the United States achieve sufficient unity regarding foreign affairs to adopt a policy befitting her defensive needs in the new circumstances that would follow the war?

The question was asked in Whitehall, in the Kremlin, in Chungking, in Washington, and perhaps most earnestly of all in Berlin. For the answer would determine the degree of the ultimate success of the Allies, the degree of the defeat which the Germans came to see was unavoidable. Having had some acquaintance of the German mentality, I have no doubt that far-seeing Germans reasoned that defeat might not be irretrievable if America again walked out of the concert of powers, with only Russia left as a great continental power now that France was eliminated for the present from that rank, and with Britain probably reluctant to engage in another continental conflict. The favorable circumstances for recovery of her power that were offered to Germany after her defeat in 1918 might, to some extent, recur. In other words, this victory might prove as temporary in its results as the last. None could blame a German for reasoning, and hoping, in this way.

Thus the enigma of the United States cast its shadow over all the battlefields; over all the Roosevelt-Churchill conferences to plan strategy and, towards the end, to plan what must follow the success of the strategy; over all the scholarly designs for peace that were being drawn up in Whitehall and Washington; over all the hopes of the Chinese, who would face at the end of the war a strong Russia close by while America might be far away in more than a geographical sense; over all the calculations of Mr. Stalin, who surveyed his frontiers to the west and to the east on the assumption that, pending more specific evidence to the contrary, the game of power politics would continue as before.

In the early stages of the war I was in London, The Hague, Copenhagen, Stockholm, Norway, and, for a short time, Germany and Italy; and even then the question asked eagerly in all those countries was what, if anything, the United States would do. The Germans counted confidently upon our neutrality, and the British feared it. Yet President Roosevelt's speech of May 16, 1940, which I heard in Stockholm, gave encouragement to non-Axis Europe because he spoke of creating an American air force of 50,000 planes. This suggestion of increased American power lifted the peoples' spirits, in spite of our neutrality policy, which said in effect that we would not use our power to prevent aggression abroad.

When a few months later I made a tour of the Pacific, where Japanese aggression was expected, the same anxious question met me at every point where I got out of clipper or land plane — in New Zealand, Australia, the East Indies, Singapore, Hongkong, Manila, Honolulu. It was asked alike by the highest officials, by the leaders of the armed forces, and by the average citizen.

The same question pursued me, as it must have pursued other traveling Americans, to every capital of South America in the spring of 1941. At that time the greatest single handicap of our Good Neighbor policy was the widespread belief, especially among Latin American soldiers, that Germany would win the war and that we would not stop her — a belief which naturally increased the reluctance of Latin Americans to assume too definite ties with the United States, which could not buy their raw materials, as opposed to a German-controlled Europe, which would need them desperately.

After visiting the President of an important South American state, I met our Ambassador there. I related to him the questions — including, of course, the supreme one mentioned above — which the President had put to me.

"What did you tell him?" asked the Ambassador.

"I told him," I said, "that we would be in the war and that Germany would be beaten."

"That's the stuff," said the Ambassador. "But I wish I felt as sure of it as you feel."

In various capitals in South America newspaper editors and writers put the same inevitable, persistent, unvarying question: What would the United States do? I answered it al-

WHAT WILL AMERICA DO? 229

ways in the same way. Newspaper articles appeared quoting the prediction — which seemed bold indeed at that moment, when the British were losing Crete, Germany was tightening her grip on the whole Balkans, and speeches by Charles Lindbergh (widely republished in South America) seemed to contradict my view. I was not sure how far the attention paid to my opinion was attributable to the fact that I had recently come from Europe, Asia, and Washington, how far to the fact that what I said seemed odd and startling to readers of Mr. Lindbergh's and some other Americans' speeches. In any case, to Presidents, Foreign Ministers, Bishops, Generals, and journalists from one end of the continent to the other I gave the one answer, with perhaps a shade more confidence than I felt.

We Question Ourselves

THAT PERSISTENT, unvarying, unanswerable question, which I had encountered in five different continents, was not by any means left behind when I returned to the United States to spend a year in Washington beginning in the autumn of 1942. For at that slightly later stage of history it was as persistent, and as unanswerable, in our own capital as it had been in London, Berlin, Canberra, Batavia, Singapore, Bogotá, Rio de Janeiro, and Buenos Aires. It particularly dogged my steps in the Victorian corridors of the State Department, where theoretically the answer should be found. The members of our foreign service were as eager for the answer as the President of a South American republic or the Prime Minister of Australia or the average European. If they listened to all suggestions — such as that the President should summon the Senate in secret session and tell it what was going on in the world and what we must do — that probably was a measure of their desperate anxiety lest another great victory should prove less than enough.

The question now had become more urgent, since we were in the war and knew that Japan and Germany were doomed. The question was not what we should do about the war but what we should do about the peace. It was essentially the same question as before: Would the United States take part in deciding the destiny of the world? — a part that all agreed would be decisive. This was the query in every capital in 1943, just as it had been in 1939, 1940, and 1941 when we were apparently neutral.

It seemed quite clear that while we probably had the power to decide the fate of the world for generations, a wise decision could be reached by considering the long-run interests of the United States — which lay neither in imperialism nor in isolation but in sustaining the powerful forces abroad which represent interests identical or reconcilable with our own and which are capable, in combination, of preventing war.

Our Negative Policies

OUR OFFICIAL attitude towards the world has thus far been largely negative. Neutrality and isolation were negative — and, be it noted, they failed of their purpose, which was to keep us out of war; for we have been in two world wars within a quarter-century. Our proclamation that we would not recognize territories acquired by violence in breach of treaties was negative, and in Asia and Europe it had negative results since it failed to prevent such annexations. Our disapproval, on this principle, of Russia's absorption of the Baltic states (Latvia, Esthonia, Lithuania) in 1940 was likewise negative, as was our coolness towards the British-Russian mutual assistance pact and the suggestion of Mr. Churchill for a Council of Europe and a Council of Asia — both of which to some of our officials seemed to be potentially inconsistent with the more inclusive system of world-wide security which our leaders had in mind.

The Jeffersonian phrase "no entangling alliances," usually attributed to Washington, has received an almost exclusively negative interpretation in recent times; although that was not the intention of its author, who after uttering it contemplated an alliance with Great Britain as a necessary consequence of a possible occupation of New Orleans by the French, and who twenty-one years later urged upon President Monroe "a concert by agreement" with Britain by saying: "With her on our side we need not fear the whole world."[2] These are not the words of an isolationist.

In those days, even though America was a small power with limited interests, her policies were less negative than when she became a world power of the first rank with territorial possessions off the shores of Asia and strategic interests extending to Africa's coast. Washington's warning in his Farewell Address against implicating ourselves "by artificial ties in the ordinary vicissitudes of her [Europe's] politics" was inspired by the effort of the French to defeat John Jay's treaty with Britain through intervention in the American Presidential election, and it was this foreign entanglement that he had chiefly in mind in drawing a line between America's and Europe's interests. He counseled against "interweaving our destiny with that of any part of Europe" on the ground that Europe was "engaged in frequent controversies the causes of which are essentially foreign to our concerns." Yet even in the eighteenth century the American colonies were involved in European wars, and later our destiny became still more closely interwoven with that of Europe, whose controversies had become our concern by menacing our security and by affecting our relations with Asia and Latin America.

Our defensive needs tend to draw us outward towards wider fields of activity and broader responsibilities. So do our very real desire for an insured peace and the growing realization of our indispensability to such a peace.

But even as our strategists insist upon bases far away and

[2] Quoted by Walter Lippmann, *op. cit.*, pp. 63–65, who shows that among the statesmen who founded the United States, Jefferson, Madison, and Monroe at least were not isolationists but were willing to act with other powers when it was in the American interest to do so. He further argues that Washington, whose Farewell Address is so often cited as authorizing isolation, while opposed to permanent alliances which would involve the United States in disputes within Europe, took it for granted that where American interests were at stake, temporary alliances with European powers were desirable.

our minds recognize that peace is a world-wide problem, not a continental one, our emotions and our traditions, our sense of inadequate experience of world leadership, our partisan and domestic prejudices, and our fears of vast economic projects which appear revolutionary, all tend to pull us back into the familiar paths of the past.

It is as if our intellects perceived clearly enough that the safety of the United States is now inevitably affected by the causes of war everywhere and hence that isolation means insecurity, yet the habits of a century and a half impelled us almost automatically to shrink from the implications of that perception.

The Lesson of Wilson

WOODROW WILSON understood that peace depended upon a concert of powers ready to act against aggression, and his doctrines and speeches made him for a moment the leader of the world, to which America seemed to bring a new and inspiring message. But the hopes he inspired throughout Europe dwindled as the often sordid wrangles of the Peace Conference of 1919 dragged on, and they were shattered when finally our Senate rejected the peace treaty and repudiated his doctrines. America's prestige, which had been so high, suddenly dropped, and the mood of depression and cynicism which followed introduced a period of disorganization and growing fears that was to lead to another and greater world war.

Franklin D. Roosevelt strove to succeed where Wilson failed. He sought, during a second world war, to create safeguards for the future. Fundamentally they resembled those Wilson had advocated, since they involved some system of collective guarantees against war in which the United States must play her part.

In a sense one may say they were ominously similar to Wilson's. For the striking parallel between the idealistic generalities of the Atlantic Charter and the more specific principles of Wilson's Fourteen Points, while it emphasized the persistence of hopes for equity and liberty among nations, recalled also the comparative brevity and the troubled character of the peace that had followed the Wilsonian effort. "The new political frontiers of Europe are Wilsonian and so drawn that 3 per cent. only of the population of the continent live under alien rule," wrote H. A. L. Fisher. "Judged by the test of self-determination, no previous European frontiers had been so satisfactory."[3] Yet those frontiers lasted less than twenty years. The careful justice they dispensed to nationalities proved transitory, and Europe was so divided and weakened that it became an easy prey to Hitler. No economic unity was created to draw together the states and peoples who had been politically divided by a somewhat academic application of the principle of nationality, essentially disuniting in its effects. No guarantees against aggression existed that were sufficient to prevent Germany from taking advantage of this division. Having split Europe up politically, the great powers were unwilling to join in preserving their collective creation.

Answering a question in the House of Commons on July 14, 1943, Mr. Churchill said the Atlantic Charter was not a treaty but "a statement of broad views and principles which are our common guide in our forward march." Which meant that the Charter remained to be defined in specific terms, and one could not deduce from it more than a vague hint of the kind of peace that its authors would frame. Its "broad views" gave no answer to the question whether self-determination would this time frustrate itself through one-sided and unrealistic application. It left frontier questions open. It told little of economic relations, upon which political relations depend. It was only the roughest sketch of what the two leaders thought should follow the war. Vice-President Wallace questioned its fourth provision — equal access to trade and raw materials for vanquished and victors. Mr. Stalin apparently questioned its eighth point — disarmament of aggressors.[4] One could see indications of the disputes and problems which its application would bring, not unlike those Woodrow Wilson faced. It was a mere beginning, or a hint of the beginning, of a program for security.

[3] *History of Europe.*   [4] See Chapter XIV.

234   A PREFACE TO PEACE

Though he had spoken in alluring generalities, as perhaps statesmen must do in wartime, Mr. Roosevelt was less academic than Wilson was, more the politician and realist and man of the world. Moreover he had Wilson's defeat as a warning. His advisers, notably Secretary Hull, kept close contact with members of Congress during the war in order to smooth the way for an understanding about the peace by giving due recognition to the prerogatives of the Senate and by striving to get foreign policy lifted above the plane of partisan conflict.

The Constitution as a Barrier

THE NEGATIVE character of our foreign policy in recent years, and of the attitude of the world towards America, has been attributable to two causes: the constitutional restrictions upon foreign policy, and the dramatic and memorable failure of Wilson to get his policy adopted. I think these causes are, to some extent, separate, and that Wilson's defeat has tended to exaggerate in American and foreign minds the obstacles imposed by the Constitution as compared with those created by the mood of the country.

It was the defeat of Wilson's policy, resulting partly from narrow partisan politics, which caused so many to believe that the constitutional restriction — a relic of the days when the United States had not yet become a democracy, when the Senate itself was not elected by the people, when manhood suffrage was not universal — was a fatal obstacle to any foreign policy. That inglorious episode, contributing much to the instability that led to another world war, caused the Senate to be regarded as a body of men determined to prevent the United States from having any consistent, continuous policy in foreign affairs; determined to proclaim to the world that no nation dare make any arrangements of importance with an American President with hope of their endurance. The notorious conflicts between President and Congress which frequently arose — impressive examples of the constitutional balance of powers in its negative working — confirmed the impression that the American Government was hopelessly handicapped in comparison with foreign governments.

In the summer and autumn of 1943, when President Roosevelt and Mr. Churchill were seeking a conference with Mr. Stalin, foreigners and Americans were constrained to ask what the President could achieve if he succeeded in meeting the Russian leader, in view of the constitutional manacles which he alone wore. Mr. Stalin could propose and decide; Mr. Roosevelt could not. Mr. Churchill could sign, with Mr. Stalin, a twenty-year alliance; Mr. Roosevelt could not dream of such an act. The two foreign leaders could make policy for their countries in the form of agreements for years ahead; Mr. Roosevelt could not, and so he was at a tremendous disadvantage. Russia and Britain could have foreign policies; the United States could have none — not until the Senate had debated and decided, in its unhurried way, some formal treaty submitted to it by the Executive. This was not good enough in a time when much might depend upon a quick decision.

The Commander-in-Chief is authorized to make such decisions in the military sphere, but not in the equally important and perhaps equally urgent political sphere. The President of the United States can order the whole Navy or Army or Air Force to attack an enemy in a given way and at a given moment, but he cannot facilitate that attack by telling enemy or ally just what the United States will do when the attack is successfully completed. He may concert with our Allies how the enemy is to be beaten and the world saved from his clutches, but he may not promise that this country will help the world to stay saved.

It was to bridge this difficulty that, after long discussion, the Senate adopted in November, 1943, a resolution in favor of our participation in an international organization to keep the peace; though the Senate, of course, retained the power to accept or reject any particular form of organization or any future treaty to create one. The resolution, and the public opinion to which it was a response, indicated the direction in which we seemed to be moving as the advance of military events increased the urgency of the issues.

The People Must Decide

THE CONSTITUTIONAL rule that treaties must be ratified by the votes of two-thirds of the Senators present is undemocratic in the sense that it is an exception to the principle of majority rule and places in the hands of a minority the final decision on foreign policy. Nowhere else in our system are the dice so loaded on the negative side.

There is one other application of this two-thirds rule. A vote of two-thirds of both Houses of Congress is required to override the President's veto of a bill passed by Congress. That is, Congress may act by majority in adopting laws which the President approves, but only by a two-thirds vote in adopting them against the President's approval.

If this same principle were applied to treaties, Congress — not the Senate only — could ratify treaties proposed by the President by a majority vote but could reject those treaties only by a two-thirds vote. Such a rule would at least be in accordance with the balance of constitutional powers as it affects other legislation, and it would meet the objection that at present foreign policy may be frustrated by a minority.

When a nation sufficiently desires to do something, it does not permit a constitution to stand in the way. The American people can amend the Constitution and abolish the two-thirds rule, or they can make their support of a co-operative policy so plain that not even one-third of the Senate will resist it.

It is true that our Constitution is far more rigid and more difficult to change than the British, which is not written and in many ways not even clear. The power of the House of Commons is infinitely greater than that of our Congress. There is, for instance, no Supreme Court to overrule it, no sharp distinction between constitutional and statute law, and the House of Commons in effect makes the Constitution as it goes along. Thus the political institutions of Britain — some Americans may be surprised to learn — are far more democratic than ours, since the legislature chosen by the people is subject to no such restrictions as our Congress. Possibly one

WHAT WILL AMERICA DO? 237

day we shall come to trust our national legislature with powers as great as those of the British legislature. Meanwhile there seems little doubt that both Congress and the Supreme Court follow the election returns, as Mr. Dooley said, or that the people can make their will felt in foreign as in domestic affairs.

Our system has not the suppleness of the British. We lack the periodic by-elections which in Britain give more than hints of changing sentiment to a Parliament and government which always have their ears cocked for such echoes from the country. We have not the habit of trusting our government to deal with foreign powers as the British trust their government, which is constantly in touch with the House of Commons and subject to its questions and its approval. We have at times what seem like two governments, one at the Capitol and one at the White House, while in Britain the two divisions are merged since the government springs from, and in a sense is simply a committee of, the House of Commons. Our system is awkward and slow and often self-paralyzing, in domestic as in foreign affairs. Theirs can act quickly, even changing Parliament and government by a national election on short notice, while our elections are determined by astronomy (that is, by the calendar) rather than by the political needs of the country.

But even with this cumbersome, archaic political system — representing in some respects, notably in the two-thirds rule and in the judiciary control of legislation, distrust of democracy which has lingered in this country longer than in Britain, at least in a constitutional sense — cannot prevent the American people having a foreign policy if they make up their minds to have one, though it certainly will retard the process of expressing such a decision.

The Legend of Our Incompetence

AMERICANS have not always been victims of a sense of helplessness in the field of foreign policy. They have not always been afraid of alliances. They have not always, as Will Rogers expressed it in a witty remark, won the war but lost the peace. They have not even waited for the sanction of two-thirds of the Senate to adopt major foreign policies. It is only in recent times that there has grown up the legend of American incompetence in foreign relations.

We won our independence through an alliance with France which was an adroit stroke of power politics, since the motive of the French was to cause damage to their enemy, England, and the motive of the Americans was to accept aid from any quarter in their struggle for freedom. The smuggling of munitions to America from the royal arsenals of Louis XVI by Beaumarchais, the activities of the secret committee of the Continental Congress in getting in touch with allies within Britain and outside it, the dealings of Benjamin Franklin and Silas Deane with British secret agents in Paris by way of bringing pressure upon the French to make an alliance with the American colonies, show that even before they had attained the status of an independent nation the Americans knew their way round in diplomacy. They did not regard themselves, as Americans were to do in the twentieth century, as innocents abroad who would "lose their shirts" in any transactions with the sharper negotiators of the Old World. They skillfully played one power against another in the interest of the independence of the United States. And when Franklin, Jay, and Adams negotiated the peace, far from "losing" it, they won triumphantly, getting far more favorable terms than Congress had expected, terms that astonished Vergennes.[5]

Our greatest and most enduring act of foreign policy, the Monroe Doctrine, rested upon an understanding with Great Britain whose naval power sustained it, but it was not a treaty and so was never ratified by the Senate. It became a basic principle of the United States because it eminently suited our interests and contributed to our safety. It was therefore accepted by the American people.

The requirements of our interests and safety are equally

---

[5] The diplomacy of this period is described by Bemis, *op. cit.*

clear today in the illumination of two great wars. But there is not now the unity about policy in this country that there was in Monroe's time.

The Needs of Today

AN AMERICAN Doctrine of today might be somewhat on these lines: That the United States is concerned in potential causes of war everywhere, that she is determined to unite with other powers great and small by disarmament of the present aggressors and by the use of force not only to resist but to prevent aggression, that she means herself to retain sufficient armaments for this purpose, that she intends meanwhile to co-operate with other nations in the expansion of production, employment, and the exchange and consumption of goods, as agreed in Article VII of the master agreements made under the Lend-Lease Act.

The implications of such a doctrine, both political and economic, would be enormous. In the political sphere they would involve a close understanding, accompanied by military commitments, with Great Britain and Russia. For these will be the only two great foreign powers that remain, and for a time at least the fate of the world will be in their hands and ours.

But we cannot brush aside as subordinate or unimportant the nearly 400,000,000 people of Europe living west of Russia and east of Britain, as some writers seem to do in their absorption in the spectacle of three great powers wielding the influence that six or seven powers enjoyed in the past. Europe is far more populous than any one of the three giants, except for the British Empire the bulk of whose population is Asiatic and at a lower level of culture and energy than Europeans. Nor should we assume that because Germany may be prostrate and France severely wounded, Europe will remain negligible as an element in the power complex. Europe is the most highly civilized of all the continents — the mother, so to speak, of the Americas and the British Dominions — and in her western parts one of the most advanced of continents by any standard. For lack of unity, for lack of sufficient cynicism to judge the Hitler Reich correctly, Europe has been overrun and submerged and oppressed. Her vitality has been impaired. She longs for bread and revenge and freedom. It may require years for Europe to recover from her ordeal. But let us not forget that Europe, despoiled and trodden upon though she has been, is a power in the world. She may perhaps be regarded as a fourth great power, or soon to become one.

The face of Europe has been scarred, her frontiers blurred, her personality maltreated by Hitler and somewhat forgotten by the Allies as the great extra-European powers have come to grips with the German oppressors of Europe. We have come to think of Europe as a mere helpless victim of a somewhat un-European barbarian invasion having its origin within Europe, as a continent for which we are sorry and which we must rescue and revive and, in a sense, support through relief and reconstruction. European faults have played their part in creating this conception of a powerless Europe. But we shall soon see that Europe is not powerless, will revive quickly, and will require to be taken more fully into account than our somewhat too "global" thinking has done as our eyes have moved over the Pacific and Africa and Asia.

In its northeastern corner are the Finns, who oddly and paradoxically found themselves at war with Britain, their natural ally, because they were attacked by Russia in 1939 (and cheered by the British in their heroic resistance), and consequently fought Russia again in 1941, not to aid Germany but to defend their country and to regain what Russia had taken from them by violence in March 1940. I was in Stockholm at that time and wrote from there the story of the Finnish-Russian peace negotiations, which were kept secret in Moscow and Helsinki and became known only in Stockholm. Neither the Russian nor the Finnish Government — for different reasons — was eager to advertise to the world the results of the Russian aggression which the Finns could no longer resist. It was a peace which spread apprehension throughout Scandinavia, where Russian power has long been feared. If in Sweden and Finland it was feared more than German power, there were historical reasons.

The Finns, an advanced, democratic people, were profoundly disturbed by their plight; for they became by force of events, and by their government's grievous error in signing the anti-Comintern Pact, in effect allies of the Axis — not because of their sympathies but because of the simple facts that Russia attacked them to strengthen her position against Hitler, and that Hitler then attacked Russia. By being technically an enemy of Britain, Finland may be considered by some to have lost its claim to the self-determination promised by the Atlantic Charter. But such reasoning would be a distortion of the principles of the Charter and of the United States. Since Russia seized Finnish territory — let us say — to protect herself against Germany, she will have no ground for retaining it once other protection is afforded by the disarmament of Germany and possibly by great power guarantees. It will be difficult for us to make an arrangement with Russia that does not re-establish the pre-1939 integrity of Finland and the independence of Poland and of the Baltic states, and does not apply the principle of self-determination to states and territories in Eastern Europe.

In the exuberance of her revived nationalism Poland was too quick to annex non-Polish territories — on the same defensive principle adopted by Russia in despoiling Poland, Finland, and Rumania in 1939 and 1940. Her corridor to the sea and the special status of Danzig as her seaport were untenable the moment Germany grew strong again, and possibly it is not too fantastic to hope that a degree of economic collaboration in Europe may be attained which will diminish the importance of seaports under a given flag.

Mr. Stalin has said he favored a strong and independent Poland but has not indicated its frontiers. It has been suggested that we return to the frontiers of 1938, prior to Hitler's first aggression against Czechoslovakia (by which Poland did not hesitate to profit in seizing Teschen from Czechoslovakia, impairing her own claims against greater aggressors). Thus the fruits of all the aggressions — German,

Polish, and Russian — would be restored to their original possessors as a kind of moral foundation for the future. It seems doubtful that Russia will agree, especially regarding Bessarabia. In any case self-determination would again prove futile — as when it took the form of the Wilsonian frontiers — unless the European states liberated from Hitler should agree to profit by their ordeal and create a unified but free Europe in which frontiers would not represent points of deliberate restraint of trade and of the movement of men and capital. It would seem today sufficiently clear that the only kind of nationalism that can endure is that which permits the economic unity of the Continent.

Here too there doubtless will be opportunities to make American influence felt in removing causes of future war, not in imposing economic freedom but in assisting European states to adopt it by eliminating the strategic incentives to self-sufficiency — a self-sufficiency that even the greatest states cannot attain. Our policy towards freedom of trade will help turn the policy of other states in the same direction. The scope for our influence will be unusually great since we shall be feeding and supplying materials to much of Europe, and our industrial output, given suitable trade relations, can hasten the physical and economic recovery of that Continent and of Russia.

If we use this tremendous power, as we should, to create freer trade the world over, we need not resort to altruistic principles to justify it. We may say that we are doing so in the interest of our own high standard of living, which requires an expanding economy and access to foreign sources of raw materials that we do not produce and shall need in growing quantities. We may say, too, that we are doing so in the interest of a lasting peace for ourselves and the world, since we cannot have it unless the world has it. There would be no Santa Claus generosity in our assisting to create a Europe that can unite and live, or in our export of capital to enable less fortunate peoples in all continents to develop their resources and live at a higher level.

This is one of the advantages we could offer Russia to induce her to demonstrate her good will by according to her smaller neighbors the same security and independence which she asserts for herself. Only on some such terms of mutuality will Russia's co-operation be genuine. The Lend-Lease agreements, providing for co-ordinated efforts among the nations for expansion of trade and employment, supply the opening for such a policy; for in them the United Nations have already committed themselves to the economic co-operation which can solve many of the major political problems on the road from war to peaceful reconstruction.

Outlines of an American Policy

THE capitulation of Italy provided the occasion for a revelation — which was very cautious and almost casual in manner — of American policy for the immediate, and possibly a prolonged, future. That policy moved in the direction of collective responsibility for peace; and it seemed to respond to an unmistakable desire of the American people, who probably are ready for participation in the task but not yet united regarding the precise means. But the continuance into the armistice and post-armistice periods of the machinery of co-operation created during the war — military and civil — may serve to crystallize opinion. For it may provide a tangible example of the international organization endorsed by the Senate, rather than a lawyer-like document in the form of treaty or covenant which few can understand and which many will suspect conceals menaces to sovereignty and freedom of action.

Less than twenty-four hours after the armistice with Italy was signed, a high British official, sitting at luncheon and tapping the ashes from a cigar, remarked lightly that Mr. Roosevelt and Mr. Churchill had agreed upon a Mediterranean Commission in which Russia would be represented. Three days later President Roosevelt, at a press conference, confirmed the statement, equally casually, saying that the purpose of the commission was to get the Mediterranean out of the war. But perhaps the chief importance of the commission lay in the fact that, in getting the Mediterranean out of the war, it was to get Russia into our war as a full collaborator, which she had not previously been — as the President had himself emphasized in his efforts to bring Mr. Stalin into a conference with himself and Mr. Churchill. This or some similar commission might well develop into the supreme Allied civil authority that would bridge the gap between Russia and the Western Allies and between the armistice and the peace period. It might become, not a commission to negotiate peace (for peace probably will be not so much negotiated as slowly constructed by military, economic, and political means alike) as an instrument for uniting the three great powers in the task of reshaping Europe.

At almost the same instant that the commission was mentioned, Mr. Churchill — in his speech at Harvard on September 6, 1943 — suggested that the Combined Chiefs of Staff Committee, which has directed Anglo-American strategy, should be continued "probably for many years." It was thereupon confirmed in Washington that this was the intention of the President and Mr. Churchill. The war would not be over with the final armistice, it was pointed out; and meanwhile the Chiefs of Staff would have to meet and watch events, ready to maintain peace by force if necessary. It was hoped that the other United Nations would appreciate the value of this procedure and would join in it.

Later an Anglo-Russian-American commission was decided upon, to co-ordinate the political relations of the three powers, united by the Moscow agreements of October, 1943, which supplemented what was in effect a military understanding between Britain and the United States for an indefinite period. The day before Mr. Churchill's Harvard speech, Governor Dewey of New York, at the Republican Party's conference on post-war plans, had advocated a military alliance between Britain and the United States — which perhaps indicated that this desirable pillar of peace was not necessarily a partisan issue in this country since public opinion was tending to favor it. This, if true, was even more important than the informal creation by Mr. Roosevelt and Mr. Churchill of a scheme for common military guardianship by the two great English-speaking powers. For it seemed to indicate that an American policy was in the making with every hope of full approval of the people. Charters and covenants and treaties might follow, perhaps. But more valuable than any written document would be the general agreement by Americans and Britons to stick together in the difficult days that will follow the end of actual warfare in Europe and, later, in Asia. That agreement seems approaching. Let us hope that no quarrels about the terms of it, no disputes over trade or shipping or air routes, will delay or impair it. Let the Combined Chiefs of Staff go on together as a stabilizing force and as an inducement to Russia to cooperate also. And let the economic boards imitate the Chiefs of Staff. If this can be done, half the battle for peace will have been won.

The British likewise have ambitious plans in the realm of economics, to judge by a statement made by the late Sir Kingsley Wood, Chancellor of the Exchequer, that Britain after the war intended to provide full employment for her people.[6] This can hardly mean anything else than the provision by the state of whatever credit may be needed to maintain full employment. Meanwhile in the United States the National Resources Planning Board has urged that it be the policy of the government to maintain production and consumption by planning for a national income of $100 to $125 billion, and Mr. Sumner Welles points out that the post-war problem is not that of production, which has been solved, but that of the distribution of what can now be readily produced.[7] To that end we must promote increased trade among nations, as the Atlantic Charter and the Lend-Lease agreements promise.

Both in Britain and America the conviction is growing that the economic maladjustment and want which have been contributing causes of war are avoidable, though in Britain the conviction is more general among the conservative classes than in America, where isolation has taken not only a politi-

[6] Speech in House of Commons on May 12, 1943.
[7] Speech of May 30, 1942.

cal form but an economic form in the high-tariff tradition. Incidentally, we shall finish the war with a merchant marine greater than that of Britain when the war began, and there are already demands that it be maintained. A large merchant marine implies a large world trade, and that in turn implies that we shall buy as well as sell and shall adjust our tariff accordingly.

In this sphere likewise, international links are close and isolation is difficult with anything like full employment. If Britain should adopt a state-financed plan of expanding economy to provide full employment, not only would she set an example among great nations which would impress the others, but her capacity to export would increase and thus affect the world market and world finance.

We must expect the trend in Europe to be towards increasing state finance and guidance in economic life, a trend that existed before the war and doubtless will be accelerated by the war. The same trend existed, but was more stubbornly resisted, in the United States, where it seems likely to meet greater opposition in the post-war period than it will meet in Europe. But the United States will be potently affected by developments abroad, which reach into the world market; and if Britain attains full employment, it will be the more urgently demanded by Americans.

"A workable plan for maintaining full employment that would not blight the development of personality or check social progress would be one of the greatest achievements in history," writes Wesley C. Mitchell.[8] Peoples like the British, who in fighting and resisting have found themselves capable of one of the greatest achievements in history, apparently will be satisfied with nothing less in their economic life. So, at any rate, their leaders believe. We must therefore be prepared for the prospect of novel and unorthodox economic measures in Britain which may place her in the lead in social progress — radical departures undertaken by conservatives (as so often happens in Britain), or at any rate by conserva-

[8] *War-time "Prosperity" and the Future* (New York, National Bureau of Economic Research, 1943).

tive methods and in a conservative spirit (which nearly always happens in Britain). Consequently the United States may appear as the most conservative of the great nations, and we may find again in America an impulse to withdraw from a world that seems unpleasantly radical. For the war will not have shaken us so deeply as Britain, where conservatism has in any case not been so rigid in recent years as in America.

Both in political and in economic relations — the two are inseparable — we shall face a greatly changed world which will be, in a real sense, closer to us and will more directly affect our safety and our prosperity than ever before. As our industry expands we shall need more imports to build up stock piles depleted by the war and to provide new materials for the magic productivity which the future offers if only we organize its distribution. Our planes will soar over and our ships sail around an essentially smaller and tighter world in which no great power can be neutral or isolated and none would want to be who realized the possibilities offered by co-operation among nations in eliminating war and poverty. Let us hope that our country, which in so many ways has led in political and social advance, will not lag behind but will take her part in creating a new era of civilization.

XVII

OUR SOUTHERN NEIGHBORS

Where We Have a Foreign Policy

THE one region of the world in which it was possible for us, before we entered the war, to have a full-fledged foreign policy, including military commitments and bases, was Latin America. Ever since the Monroe Doctrine was promulgated, it has been generally accepted in this country that the region between the Rio Grande and Cape Horn was one of American defensive responsibility — though in the confused period of 1940–1941 some isolationists argued we need defend only the region extending as far south as the "hump" of Brazil. It was taken for granted that the safety of the two American continents was bound up with the safety of the United States; and it was the proximity of the easternmost point of Brazil to the coast of French Africa, which we feared might fall into German hands, that enabled many to visualize the relationship between the European war and our security. Our strategic frontier was fixed in North Africa because it was so near South America, where our strategic frontier had been for a century.

Since 1933 our policy towards Latin America has been what President Roosevelt called the "Good Neighbor." We have abandoned all pretension of intervening in its internal affairs. We have recognized its republics, great and small, advanced and backward, white and Indian or mixed, as fully equal sovereign states — juridically equal, that is, for they are equal in no other sense. In a long series of Pan-American conferences we have made persistent efforts to develop among those states a sense of common interest that had hardly existed before and a sense of common responsibility for defence. We have studiously adhered to the doctrine of sovereign equality even when the real inequality of these states was emphasized by their reliance upon American financial and military aid for their sustenance and their security during the war.

Although much that was done in the name of the Good Neighbor policy was fantastic or futile, such as some of the "good will" tours which served principally to advertise our hopelessly un-Latin mentality and our profound misunderstanding of Latin America, and although in many cases (as in the oil settlement with Mexico) American interests were lightly sacrificed with perhaps considerable damage to the credit of the countries which profited momentarily, it must be said that on the whole the policy has succeeded beyond the expectations of some skeptics, including myself. It has succeeded in that Latin American states generally, with the single conspicuous exception of Argentina — who has all along been the most aloof and recalcitrant — have collaborated with us during the war.

It was to their interest to do so. They were compelled by circumstances to line up with us, since the war and the British blockade had severed them from their European markets and the United Nations offered the only markets and the only sources of supplies. They received economic aid from the United States in the form of purchases of their raw materials, notably minerals, and loans and credits to sustain their economies. They received from the United States the military protection which none could have supplied for itself. From 1942 onward they realized which side would win the war, and this was an added reason to be co-operative with us. But to say that the American republics, in spite of long-standing distrust of the United States, acted in accordance with their interests is merely to say they acted intelligently.

Eloquent hypocrisy may perhaps be necessary in diplomacy, and Latins rather like it, but the fact is that our policy would have failed had it been obliged to depend upon good will or mutual confidence or such faint cultural links as exist. It succeeded because, in spite of the pretense of ideological bonds, it rested really upon mutual vital interests. Yet for a time, notably in 1940 and 1941 when the outcome of the war seemed doubtful, many Latin Americans were unconvinced that their interests lay with us rather than with Germany. For Germany, if she had won, would have been able to offer them the European market, which was far more important to their economies than the American market.

Britain's Contribution

IT HAS NEVER been recognized, though it should be recognized and remembered, that in those crucial years it was Britain who made the decisive contribution to our Good Neighbor policy. She made it by fighting Germany when most of the world thought she could not do so. She made it by thus casting doubt upon the general belief that Germany would win and that therefore Latin America had better get ready for a totalitarian world — which some Latin Americans were eager to welcome.[1] By giving a demonstration of the tenacity

[1] In a speech made on June 11, 1940, President Vargas of Brazil said that "the era of improvident liberalism, sterile demagoguery, useless individualism and the sowers of disorder has passed," and that "political order is no longer made in the shadow of vague humanitarianism which sought to abolish frontiers and create an international society without friction." He spoke of the "exasperation of nationalism," of "strong nations imposing their will by the sentiment of nationality." Those words might have been uttered by Hitler. They were the pure milk of totalitarianism. They were uttered a day after Mussolini had declared war on Britain and prostrate France — a day after President Roosevelt had described that declaration of war by saying that "the hand that held the dagger has struck it into the back of its neighbor." So sharp was the contrast between Vargas's speech and Roosevelt's — between Vargas's mental processes and those of the democratic world — that Vargas's press bureau issued a statement saying that the speech did not mean a change of foreign policy.

It may seem ungracious to recall this incident in view of Vargas's behavior later on, when he decided that the "era of improvident liberalism" still had a lot of fight in it. On the other hand, it would be still more ungracious not to emphasize, by citing such historical facts as this one, the hitherto unrecognized service rendered to the United States in her relations with this hemisphere by the British, who had been on the right side even when it seemed the losing side. Moreover, the change of viewpoint, if not of policy, on the part of President Vargas

and stamina of a great democratic country at a time when the non-democratic world, including much of Latin America, thought the democracies were decadent, the British amazed and dumbfounded the Latin Americans who had lightly taken it for granted that the future belonged to Hitler and Fascism and authoritarianism in all its forms.[2] The Royal Air Force — the few to whom so many owe so much, in Mr. Churchill's classic phrase — won in 1940 not only a victory for Britain but a victory for our Good Neighbor policy.

I trust that one day this simple historical fact will be so noted that it will never be forgotten. It would probably be regarded as inappropriate to erect a memorial to the Royal Air Force in the Pan-American Union building in Washington, since this would carry the invidious implication that Latin Americans had been sufficiently realistic to act in accordance with their interests as affected by the balance of power in the world. Yet such a memorial would be immediately understood by every intelligent Latin American, who knows that Latin America's good-neighborliness towards us was directly affected by the tide of battle in Europe which determined the degree of the future dependence of Latin America upon the United States.

If I emphasize this fact with great confidence, it is because from the beginning of March to the end of July 1941 I toured South America by air, visiting every capital in that continent, meeting all but two of the heads of states, nearly all the foreign ministers, many soldiers, businessmen, scholars, archbishops, and priests, as well as humbler and more nearly average members of the populations. At that time the outcome of the war was doubtful. In the spring the British lost Greece

throws more light than any other single fact upon the problem we faced in Latin America, where in 1940 and 1941 many spoke as Vargas did.

[2] Sitting in the pleasant Buenos Aires military club in May 1941, one of Argentina's most distinguished soldiers, himself of Spanish descent, who believed even then that Germany would win the war, expressed in superlatives his unbounded admiration of the British people for the way they behaved in the prolonged German bombardment of London by air. "We admire it the more because we Latins would be incapable of holding out as the British did," he said.

and Crete and the Germans overran the Balkans. Britain's naval power was spread very thin over the world, and we were still officially neutral towards those who stabbed their neighbors in the back or assaulted them by invasion and terror. None could blame Latin Americans for assuming that Germany might win, or for remembering that the Europe which Germany dominated was economically complementary to raw-material-producing Latin America and therefore necessary to its prosperity. Indeed a Latin American statesman would have failed in his duty to his country if he had not taken due note of these possibilities and facts and shaped his policy accordingly. In saying that Latin Americans did just that, I am simply saying that they exercised common sense and political realism. Every small nation, and every great one for that matter, must take account of where its economic interests lie and where the dominant power in the world.

Britain's resistance through 1940 and 1941 did not convince Latin Americans that she would win, but it convinced them she would fight hard and it forced them to qualify their previous belief that Germany would win. It compelled suspension of judgment and a more receptive attitude towards our good-neighborliness. Even in the spring of 1942, when the Japanese had crippled our Fleet at Pearl Harbor and German submarines were sinking merchant ships with ease throughout the Caribbean and along our coasts, Latin Americans wondered whether our naval power could really reach as far as Cape Horn and whether the Good Neighbor policy would be justified by our ability to protect that vast coastline in two oceans. "Where is the United States Fleet?" was a question asked anxiously throughout the American republics as American defeats were added to British defeats in the Pacific and our shipping in our own coastal waters seemed unprotected against submarines. Our prestige in those months was at a low ebb, as Britain's had been previously.

To offset the effect of this military adversity and of the economic link with Europe there was no enormous or overwhelming ideological or cultural bond between Latin America and the United States. Some in the southern continent contemplated with equanimity the possibility of a United States defeat, and still more declined to be frightened by the prospect of a German victory. Not only did the predominant economic interests of Latin America lie in trade with Europe, not only were its cultural ties almost entirely with Europe, not only were the social and political views of the dominant classes anti-democratic and in some places totalitarian, but Germans as individuals and traders had established throughout Latin America closer personal relations than Americans or Britons had done. In many countries Germans had married natives and settled down, though without ceasing to be Germans; whereas Britons and Americans, even when they lived in the Latin countries, often failed to bother about learning the language and largely confined their social relations to the English-speaking colonies. Germans on the whole entered far more into the local life, while Britons and Americans often left the impression that they regarded themselves as superior outsiders. Moreover, Germans sold machinery and aspirin and cutlery and a thousand articles more cheaply than we did, and the Latins — without inquiring into such questions as German export subsidies and labor costs — thought that North Americans habitually overcharged. Consequently when we told the Latin American world in 1940 and 1941 that the Germans were a menace, the Latins did not instantaneously adopt our view, especially since many had habitually thought the United States was the menace and had looked upon Germans as dispensers of excellent goods at low prices.

Motives and Policies

THOUGH the Argentine government steadfastly resisted our good-neighborliness, while the Mexican Government enthusiastically accepted it and all that went with it, it does not follow that the people of Argentina were more suspicious of us than were the people of Mexico. They may even have been less so. They had less reason to be, for while we have taken about half of what once was Mexican territory, we have taken nothing from Argentina. The principal difference was that the Mexican Government thought it best to ignore, and even to deny, the obvious and widespread and profound Mexican suspicion of the United States in order to take full advantage of the Good Neighbor policy, which was financial as well as political; while the Argentine Government of Señor Castillo thought the Germans would soon win the war and save Argentina from Pan-Americanism and good neighborliness. When the Germans betrayed this confidence by failing to win, and Brazil received armaments from the United States as a result of going to war with Germany, the Argentine army revolted and put General Ramirez in power chiefly in order that Argentina might get from us armament to match that of her good neighbor, Brazil, and so maintain what Ramirez's Foreign Minister, Admiral Storni, called the equilibrium of power in that part of the world.

This shocking realism on the part of the military government at Buenos Aires, when in August 1943 it asked President Roosevelt for a good-neighborly gesture in the form of American arms, revealed above all the diplomatic plight into which Argentina had got herself by betting on Germany at a time when, to military minds almost everywhere, Germany seemed a good bet. It revealed little, if anything, about public opinion in Argentina (which was sharply divided but may have been all along more for us than against us); for the actions of governments in Latin America bear comparatively little relation to public opinion, even when the governments are civilian, as sometimes happens. Throughout Latin America the ballot box has failed as yet to acquire the status or the serious attention or the decisive influence in government which it has acquired in this country.

Argentina's official antipathy to almost everything the United States does or proposes, including Pan-American unity against the Axis, should not be taken as necessarily representing the predominant feeling among the people of Argentina, though it represents the feeling of many thousands. Nor should it be taken as representing something exceptional in Latin America, isolated though Argentina has become through her official policy. It would be more nearly true to say that Argentine governments have expressed officially the fear and suspicion towards the United States which other Latin American governments feel but wisely conceal and which a large proportion of the people of that region feel and do not conceal.

Some of those suspicions may seem quite fantastic, such as the Catholic suspicion that our democracy must be anti-clerical because French democracy was, such as the soldier's suspicion that we wanted bases in Latin America in order to exert military dominance over it, such as the suspicion of youth in Argentina that we seek a kind of economic imperialism there. Others have some historical basis, such as the Mexican fear of us that results from memories of our invasion of Mexico; such as the fear among feudal landed classes (in Chile, for instance) that our conception of democracy may undermine their position; such as the fear among dictators that too great familiarity in their countries with the American liberal tradition may ruin their popularity. The great Yankee menace to Latin America today is the doctrine that all men were created equal.

Portrait of a South American Democrat

A CHARMING, European-educated member of an old Peruvian family prefaced a conversation on foreign affairs with these words, spoken in excellent French:

"When you in the United States speak of defending democracy, it leaves us cold. For democracy here has been dead for twenty years and will not revive. There is no freedom of the press, no freedom of assembly; a ruling class of Spanish descent, which has supported all our dictators, still runs the country — and this is as it should be."

Next day another conservative remarked that it was fortunate that Apra, the outlawed opposition party, had come out in favor of co-operation with the United States. Why was this so fortunate if the party was suppressed? "Because Apra, though having no legal right to exist, is very strong among the people and has perhaps forty per cent or more of the country behind it," he replied.

Evidently there were some who still clung to at least the hope of democracy and who were perhaps not left cold when Americans used that word.

Late that night, after making an appointment by elaborately indirect means, I was driven to a house "somewhere in Peru" to meet the leader of this clandestine party which lives, politically, in the Catacombs. He had spent years in exile and months in prison. Some of his fellows were still living in Chile.

His name was Victor Raoul Haya de la Torre. He was shortish and rather plump, and his face beneath black hair beamed with animation, humor, and a kind of gay spirit of adventure as he talked. Like the party he had founded, he was a product of the post-war ferment of ideas and ideals of the nineteen-twenties (when Wilson and Lenin were both in vogue) which stirred up the student reform movement in universities in Argentina, Chile, and Peru. It was a movement for freer teaching, against the aristocratic spirit of the universities, against old and tired teachers, against class privilege. It swept through Latin-America; and when Señor Haya de la Torre, who led the Peruvian branch of it, staged a demonstration in Lima against the dictator of the time, Augusto Leguia, he was soon arrested and exiled.

He went to Panama, Mexico, Cuba, the United States, Europe, earning his way by writing for newspapers in Mexico and Argentina. In Mexico in 1924 he founded Apra — "*Alianza Populara Revolucionaria Americana* — dedicated to what he called the second American revolution which should spread democracy in those Latin lands and unite them, as Simon Bolivar had dreamed.

When Leguia fell in 1931, de la Torre returned to Peru to run for President. "The military candidate was counted in (though I think I won), and I was sent to prison for fifteen months," he said. "Later, in 1932, some six thousand Apristas were shot." In 1936 he wanted again to run for President, but his party was outlawed by the dictator, General Benavides, and has since been unable to hold meetings, though it publishes small newspapers secretly.

Señor de la Torre smiled in relating these episodes; in asserting that there was even an excess of democracy in the text of Peru's constitution though little outside that text; in remarking that Latin American governments were permeated with "Creole Fascism — the Fascism of Himmler rather than of Hitler."

This black-haired, Spanish-looking son of a journalist of Trujillo, flippant and witty though he could be, took democracy seriously. None who talked with him could doubt that he deeply believed in what Mr. James Truslow Adams called the American Dream, based upon faith in the potentialities of the average man and in the practicability of free government. Farther north it is an old and familiar dream. In Peru, in a still largely feudal environment, it has all the freshness of the eighteenth century and the Jacksonian period. It seemed to animate the faces of the devoted associates of de la Torre, who sat in the room while he talked.

Señor de la Torre believed that children should be educated — all of them — without distinction of race, religion, or the condition of servitude of their parents; and that those who can read and write should also vote, as the Peruvian Constitution provides. He believed in many other things, too, such as raising the standard of living and consuming power of the Peruvian people, even though three-fourths were Indian; such as a Pan-American co-operation which would take this economic concept of democracy as its starting point. He rejected the Nazi doctrine of race- or class-rule — a doctrine accepted by the conservative quoted above. He accepted the American creed of democracy, which that conservative coldly rejected.

"Where there is no democracy, schools are revolutionary centers," he said; adding that in Peru some 500,000 children were in school and more than 1,000,000 were not in school.

"Aprismo has grown out of Socialism and become a kind of co-operative movement," he continued. "We want nationalization, but not in the Mexican manner. It must not ruin economic life but must come gradually. It should not be against foreign capital, but should invite foreigners to collaborate in the development of the country. I propose a national economic congress or round table of capital, labor, and commerce, foreign and domestic, as a permanent advisory body for the government. But morality must come first; we need to clean up politics.

"United States capitalists should favor a program which would raise the purchasing power of the people, who are now so poor that they can buy little from the United States.

"The Good Neighbor policy is the best step the United States has taken in one hundred years. But we want to know whether it is permanent or subject to change with changes of government in Washington. Some say we have changed our attitude toward the United States, but it is United States policy that has changed.

"We should like guarantees of the permanence of the Good Neighbor policy — economic guarantees. Before the post-war economic battle starts between Europe and the United States in South America, we ought to make a beginning. We should have a single currency for Latin America, stabilized in relation to the dollar and based upon gold, silver, and raw materials. A single industrial bank for Latin America could handle exchanges of our raw materials against North American manufactures, which we badly need.

"It is said that the two continents of this hemisphere are not economically complementary, that neither could buy enough of the other's exports. This is just the question that should be studied by a Pan-American conference of specialists; otherwise Pan-Americanism may be like the League of Nations — good in peacetime only. The economic problem is the main one. We feel we are poor while you are rich, but that our standard of life might be greatly raised by proper use of our natural resources.

"When President Roosevelt denounces Hitler and Mussolini for suppressing civil liberties, people here applaud but are puzzled; for their own governments have likewise suppressed those liberties.

"The United States should encourage democracy in Latin-America by using its influence here. This would be a sort of moral intervention to which no objection could be taken.

"I would like to see an inter-American committee for the defense of democracy, with freedom of press and speech and assembly recognized as international principles, with a permanent inter-American court to uphold civil rights in each country. . . . But maybe that sounds a bit audacious."

It did. It seemed as audacious as the doctrine that all men were created equal and endowed with inalienable rights; as audacious as the American Dream which has found its way into the Andes.

Who Are Our American Allies?

HERE, THEN, is our dilemma in relation to Latin America: To whom are we to be a good neighbor — to the parties and groups in power, who may represent only a small military or feudal class, or to the masses of "forgotten men" who live at a low level and have not yet entered the twentieth century?

The technical, official answer is that we have abjured intervention and have no right to pass upon the odd manner in which governments get their hands on power in Latin America; that we as a government can collaborate only with other governments and must more or less close our eyes to the social foundations of their power. On the other hand, the United States stands for something in the world which is not technical or official but human — that strange and revolutionary doctrine enunciated by the Declaration of Independence. It is indeed revolutionary in Latin America, where the Bill of Rights is unknown to most of the population and unacceptable to some governments.

Some may say that this dilemma comes of too lavish expression of remote ideals in terms which may cause simple people to take them too literally or even to imagine they have something to do with living generations. Yet the dilemma is inherent in our traditional belief in what the French revolutionaries called the rights of man. For the Good Neighbor policy is simply the extension to the international field of the doctrine we ourselves asserted in 1776 — the doctrine that each people has the right to manage its own affairs. It would be natural to expect Americans to feel more friendly and good-neighborly towards states where freedom prevails than towards states ruled by military castes or feudal landlords, as some of our neighbors are. It would be logical to expect us to sympathize with efforts to overthrow oppressive régimes, in view of the right of revolution asserted in the Declaration.

Without going back to the eighteenth century, we may note — Latin Americans will note them — President Roosevelt's Four Freedoms, which include freedom of speech and of worship and freedom from want, and the Atlantic Charter, which proclaims the right of all peoples to choose the form of government under which they will live.

I do not go so far as to suggest that either of these admirable documents has any immediate relation to reality, but I would point out that both may logically be taken as American doctrines, especially since they harmonize so well with the Declaration. Some of the Latin American republics happen to be members of the United Nations, and as a matter of pure logic it would seem that they could hardly be excluded from the freedoms and rights which the President advocates for the whole world. It is ironical that at our own doorstep are nations that have not yet risen to a point where such rights can be considered attainable.

Yet our dilemma, while logically inescapable, is largely academic because of the rudimentary stage of democracy in Latin America. Between the Rio Grande and the borders of Chile and Argentina, Indians predominate and the majority of the people live at primitive levels and are illiterate. Until they reach what may be called a Western instead of an Oriental standard of life and education, anything that could be remotely called democracy in our sense of the word can hardly be possible, although the white upper element in Colombia, for example, has for itself what closely approaches a liberal régime. Possibly in Latin America democracy, if it develops, might begin by being of the ancient Greek type —

government by an educated class, necessarily limited — and gradually extend in scope as the native populations emerge from mud huts and jungles and feudalism into the modern era.

In discussing the possibility of democracy in Latin America with Latin Americans, I found that few would say it existed there, though the more optimistic would add, "possibly in Uruguay and Colombia." Argentina, one of the most advanced countries of all, cannot be counted a democracy because elections in most provinces are not free.[3] The same has been true of Mexico, the larger part of which is among the more backward regions of Latin America, though it lies at our door. In Chile the votes appear to have been counted in recent elections, but revolution is a constant possibility. Of all the countries to the south of us Uruguay is the most European, most liberal, most advanced socially, and to one who knows Europe its capital is among the most attractive of all. Argentina is the most opulent. Her comparative assets reflect the great poverty of the bulk of Latin America. Though Argentina's population is perhaps 10 per cent of that of Latin America, Argentina contains some 43 per cent of Latin American railway mileage, about one-third of the telephone and telegraph lines, about 40 per cent of the radio sets, 36 per cent of the motor cars. Her population, like those of Chile and Uruguay, is almost wholly of European descent, chiefly Italian and Spanish, with a large admixture of Germans and many British. She feels superior to the more mixed and far more Indian countries to the north of her and jealous of United States leadership in the hemisphere.

The Civilized Edge

SOUTH AMERICA is a huge but primitive continent whose surface and whose riches have as yet hardly been more than

[3] José Santos Gollán, one of the ablest of Argentina's political writers, says that fraudulent elections prevail in the Argentine provinces ruled by the conservatives and that these provinces number eleven in a total of fourteen provinces. (Article "El Enigma de la Argentina," in *Argentina Libre*, Buenos Aires, July 30, 1942.)

touched. It is so broken by mountains and so widely covered by jungle that movement, save by airplane, is extremely difficult, slow, and costly. Lack of transport is its greatest handicap. Of its 90,000,000 people the great majority live simply, consuming what they produce and having practically no purchasing power. Only around the edges has European civilization taken root in the continent — on the eastern coast of Brazil at Rio, São Paulo, Bahia, Porto Allegre, at Montevideo and Buenos Aires and nearby towns, across the Andes in Chile (a country that is hardly more than a seacoast), farther north at Lima, Quito, and Bogota; but hardly anywhere else. Great stretches on the western coast and across Brazil are arid, but the vast inland region of the Orinoco and the Amazon valleys remains a primitive wilderness whose mineral and vegetable possibilities are not even fully explored.

When one speaks of the overseas connections of South America, one speaks of the civilized rim, the most important part as regards human relations. Historically and culturally, this part of the continent has never made the sharp break from its European past which the United States made. Its heritage was not only Latin and Mediterranean; it was that of the feudal Europe which we long ago left behind us. Hence the islands of feudalism in Chile, Peru, and elsewhere which have been little affected by the modern world. Hence the slow growth of democratic ideas. Hence the suspicions of the United States, which to the ultra-conservative seems a very radical country. The newer Europe has also conspired to keep South and North America apart; for the main cultural influence south of Panama has been French, and certain recent French writers have severely criticized the trend of American capitalism.[4] Meanwhile the doctrines of Fascism, not always understood there, especially in their anti-Catholic and anti-religious aspects, have appealed to those who fear democracy.[5] Thus modern Europe, the overseas world which

[4] See the further reference to these French criticisms in Chapter III above.

[5] The odd phenomenon of North and South American Catholics who sympathized with the anti-clerical Fascism of Franco Spain is discussed in Chapter IX above.

South Americans know best and whose intellectual and political currents touch them closest, has joined with the feudal Europe of the past to create a barrier to South Americans' understanding of us and our understanding of them. Many of our less Good Neighbor activities of the past have likewise served to alienate that continent.

It happened that the foreign capital without which South America could not have developed came not from continental Europe, which seemed a kind of cultural home to those transplanted Europeans, but from Britain and the United States, which appeared permeated by an alien Protestantism and liberalism that were distasteful to those Catholic communities living mentally in the pre-democratic age. So the opposition to capitalism, or to foreign capitalism, which was vigorous in many quarters in South America when I visited it, and was reflected in such laws as that of Brazil terminating the rights of foreign banks and companies, was directed at the English-speaking powers whose cultural and political influences were regarded as foreign to those which South America had inherited from Southern Europe.[6] The resentment at the economically colonial character of their countries, dependent upon foreign capital and foreign markets and foreign manufactures, thus reinforces the resentment and fear towards what seem to South American conservatives to be the dangerous democratic principles of Britain and the United States. These basic "ideological" attitudes, derived from both tradition and current economic interests, are not unrelated to the complaints of British haughtiness and aloofness and of American casualness and arrogance in social and commercial relations with the Latin world. One finds all these feelings mingled in the often heard charges that we are trying to convert their peoples to Protestantism, to dominate their economic

[6] It is to be noted that while the predominant literary and intellectual influence in South America has been French, the political doctrines of the modern France created by the Revolution are anathema to the ruling classes of that continent, as they are to the French of Quebec who cling to and preserve the traditions of pre-Revolutionary France, just as the South Americans of the classes mentioned cling to those of the old Spanish Empire.

life, to overawe them with our military power, to upset their social systems by introducing democracy, which some look upon as being as subversive as Communism. The fact that in the war we have been allied with Russia has doubtless confirmed the long-standing impression in influential classes of Latin America that we "Anglo-Saxons," as Latins oddly call us, are generally a bad lot.[7]

"Dollar Diplomacy," New Style

THE FUTURE of Latin America will depend upon its relations with those more advanced parts of the world which, I trust, will be mainly under the influence, military and ideological,

[7] I happened to be in Brazil when Hitler attacked Russia in June 1941, and noted the singular fact that the Press and Propaganda Bureau of the government immediately issued to the press instructions regarding the attitude it was to take. The head of the Bureau, Dr. Lorivel Fontes (as he explained it to me afterward), told the press that as between Britain and Germany, Brazil was neutral, but that as between Russia and Germany, Brazil was for Germany. This effort to find an appropriate path among the conflicting ideologies of democracy, Fascism, and Communism was imposed by the fact that President Vargas, like the totalitarian leaders in Germany, Italy, and Spain, had justified his seizure of almost absolute power in Brazil by citing what he called the menace of Communism. He therefore could not very well take the side of Russia against Germany, or so he thought; though a year later he was to be at war with Germany and consequently more or less allied with Russia as well as with the democracies. Just how his Propaganda Bureau managed to explain that I do not know. But if there is anyone in Brazil who has tried to follow Vargas's ideological line in recent years he must have required the intellectual agility of the Communists, who were for Hitler until June 1941 and violently against him after that date.

When I met President Vargas I was favorably impressed by his good sense and realism, and I knew he would be on the right side even though his talk had been on the wrong side, as shown in the first footnote to this chapter (page 250). He was too intelligent to take seriously his own official ideology. But the trouble is that some do take it seriously in Brazil and throughout Latin America, and this fact is not the least of the obstacles to a mental attitude consistent with the real interests of that region and with a rapprochement with the United States.

of the British and Americans and receptive to the collaboration of Russia, assuming she can adopt a more accommodating attitude than she has so far done. I believe that after a time Latin Americans may become convinced that we as a nation are not conspiring to overthrow the Catholic Church in their countries or to impose Communism or even democracy upon them, assuming that these were possible. I believe they might be convinced that we do not intend to bully them with our armed forces or cheat them of their natural riches, and they might even come to understand that those riches are worthless unless dug out and refined and transported to the world markets with the aid of capital from countries that happen to have different philosophies.

They have operated during the war by what may be called a kind of state capitalism on the part of the United States, since it was our government that financed them, chiefly through the Export-Import Bank.[8] Here was a decidedly new version of "dollar diplomacy," for the dollars came from the United States Treasury and were invested for the industrialization of parts of Latin America which will reduce its dependence upon our exports. Some of the commitments run beyond the probable war period, and it seems likely we shall be financing our Good Neighbors in this way for years to come. The conception in Washington now is that such private capital as may flow into that region should henceforth go there not in the form of American companies but in companies in which local capital will also participate — companies which will therefore seem less alien and "Anglo-Saxon" and less calculated to offend the sensitive nationalism of the Latin countries.

But in whatever form it goes, private capital will require

[8] The statement of the Export-Import Bank shows that on June 30, 1943, it had lent to Latin American countries $173,411,376, that $86,814,844 had been repaid, that commitments as yet undisbursed amounted to $318,712,743. These sums seem small compared with our war expenditures, but for Latin America their proportions are immeasurably greater than they seem to us.

far better treatment than it has heretofore received in many places, notably Mexico, where some of it has been ruthlessly expropriated with the ultimate sanction of our government, which even helped finance the indemnity finally and grudgingly paid.[9] Latin Americans cannot have it both ways. Either they will deal reasonably and unemotionally with foreign capital, or they will not get it. Without it, they would remain in the economically backward "colonial" condition of which they so bitterly complain — unless the United States Treasury should supply them with enough capital to carry them from a primitive state to that of modern countries, which seems hardly likely and would in any case be a slower process than that with private capital. In the past, as in Mexico, they have tried to play one set of foreign capitalists against another, threatening the Americans by proposing to grant the richest concessions to Europeans, sometimes ending by expropriating both. Local political corruption has played a part in this process, a greater part than the long-range interests of the nations whose standards of life cannot be elevated except by unlocking their natural resources, which only foreign capital can do. Our Good Neighbor policy and the exigencies of wartime have caused our government to turn a blind eye to this basic fact and to the assertions of national dignity which consist in seizure of or discrimination against the wealth that Americans have invested in countries

[9] In 1942 the United States Government accepted on behalf of American oil companies a payment of $24,000,000 for the oil properties expropriated in Mexico for which settlement had not until then been made. Even this moderate payment was in effect indirectly financed by our government through loans and treaty-guaranteed silver purchases. The question of the subsoil rights which Mexican governments had granted to Americans was ignored in the official report forming the settlement, for the fact that these rights had first been recognized and later denied was a sensitive point which Mexicans preferred not to mention. I happened to be in Mexico City during those negotiations and know how sensitive it was. The fact that I, not being an official, felt free to mention it in my dispatches brought upon my head the fury of certain Mexican officials who in their speeches exalted the freedom of the press.

which, in some cases, have more sovereignty than they know how to exercise wisely.[10]

Not only since our entry into the war, which altered all standards, has there been a tendency to assume that our military and financial protection of Latin America called for more than abstention from trouble-making below the Rio Grande. This indispensable American aid to countries which could neither defend nor finance themselves was largely taken for granted and the Good Neighbor policy was accepted as a one-way affair. We should have earned greater respect, and possibly received greater collaboration, had we attached conditions to our largesse and required reciprocation in the form of fairer treatment of Americans and their property. Latin Americans would have understood that better than they understood our generosity. We have been so eagerly leaning backward to show respect for their sovereignty that we have done damage to our own. We have made such valiant but often inept efforts to understand them that we have quite forgotten the possibility that they might make a slight effort to understand us. We have striven so hard to live down our bad neighbor days of intervention that we have gone to the opposite extreme of abandoning hitherto recognized rights.

The above paragraph refers chiefly to the politicians who are the not always worthy custodians of the sovereignty which we now approach with such trepidation; not to the peoples, who in general are unable to exercise the right to choose the governments that rule them. Our official and business

[10] "The new dollar diplomacy . . . left the private creditors to fend for themselves as best they could against Latin American jurisprudence, with the feeble aid of the puny, disinherited and starving child of the State Department, the Foreign Bondholders' Protective Council, whilst it proceeded to grant public loans through . . . government agencies to the very Latin American governments which had defaulted on their dollar bonds and were 'squeezing' the direct investments of United States nationals with their ingenious and unchallenged national, social and economic legislation." Samuel Flagg Bemis: *The Latin American Policy of the United States* (New York, Harcourt, Brace & Co., 1943), p. 351.

contacts are mostly with the politicians, who often are military men, although in many cases the middle classes and the more advanced workers would come nearer to understanding this country if given a chance to do so. It is only such an understanding which can supply a sound foundation for the good relations we hope for in the future and for the economic co-operation which alone can bring the masses of Latin America into the modern world.

Appendix A

EXPORTS TO FRENCH NORTH AFRICA

PETROLEUM PRODUCTS:

Transported by French tankers *Frimaire*, *Shéhérazade*, and *Lorraine* in March, May, and October 1941, respectively.

Automobile gasoline	10,535 metric tons
Kerosene	11,235 " "
Gas oil	12,427 " "
Fuel oil	8,491 " "
Lubricating oils	813 " "

OTHER MERCHANDISE:

Transported by French freighters *Ile de Noirmoutier*, *Ile d'Ouessant*, *Ile de Ré*, and *Léopold L. D.* during the period from July 1 to November 15, 1941. Two voyages each were made by the *Ile de Noirmoutier* and the *Ile d'Ouessant*.

Sugar	14,095	metric tons
Coal	11,179	" "
Cotton fabrics	2,444.68	" "
Tea	1,414.40	" "
Condensed milk	1,359.61	" "
Tar	1,117	" "
Binder twine	1,113	" "
Tobacco	983.37	" "
Coke	896	" "
Paraffin	702.23	" "
Bags	178	" "
Copper sulphate	200	" "
Nails	105.55	" "
Wire	44.09	" "
Spare parts for farm machines	5.5	" "
Ready-made clothing	1.11	" "
Pharmaceutical products	1	" "
Glycerine	90	kilograms
Theobromine	3	"

APPENDIX A

Transported by French freighters—*Ile de Ré* and *Aldébaran* on January 28, 1942 and January 30, 1942, respectively.

Ile de Ré:
Coal	4,312 metric tons
Pitch briquettes	1,608 ″ ″

Aldébaran:
Refined sugar	5,115 ″ ″
Cotton textiles	1,497 ″ ″
Nails	245 ″ ″
Tobacco	205 ″ ″
Green tea	101 ″ ″
Copper sulphate	99 ″ ″
Black tea	55 ″ ″
Condensed milk	76 ″ ″
Iron wire (1,000 bundles)	45 ″ ″
Office furniture and food products, 153 cases	9 ″ ″
First aid material, 3 cases	272 kilograms
Medical products	168 ″
Oil essence	127 ″
Gauze for bandages	48 ″
Clothing, 1 case	23 ″
Miscellaneous (layettes, cotton lingerie, etc., 1 case)	8 ″

Transported by French freighters *Ile d'Ouessant* and *Ile de Noirmoutier* on August 9, 1942:

Ile d'Ouessant:
8,000 Empty drums } 24 Cartons of caps }	200 short tons
Coal	4,998 metric tons

Ile de Noirmoutier:
Sugar	2,288 metric tons
Cotton goods	1,257 ″ ″
Copper sulphate	499 ″ ″
Tobacco	349 ″ ″
Cotton thread	73 ″ ″
Fumogaz	″ ″
Gasoline	150 drums
Oil (for Armstrong Cork Company)	11 ″
Lubricating oil	2 ″
Office supplies, personal effects, and foodstuffs for American Consulate, Casablanca	251 cases

APPENDIX A 271

Personal effects, etc. for Monsieur Guerin	1 case
Cotton goods to be returned to U. S. under Hold Back Agreement	124 metric tons

IMPORTS FROM FRENCH NORTH AFRICA

Transported by the French freighter *Léopold L. D.* which arrived at Philadelphia July 23, 1941.

Cork	1,621 metric tons

Transported on the French freighter *Ile de Ré* which arrived at New York August 8, 1941.

Cork	1,213 metric tons
Red squill	51 " "
Tartar	201 " "

Transported on the French freighter *Ile de Noirmoutier* which arrived at New York October 23, 1941.

Cork	1,292 metric tons
Tartar	423 " "
Coriander	20 " "
Horehound	45 " "
Plants for perfume	15 " "
Snails	59 " "

Transported on the French freighter *Ile d'Ouessant* which arrived at New York October 25, 1941.

Cork	1,241 metric tons
Squills	10 " "
Tartar	145 " "
Essences for perfume	" "
Rough forms for briar pipes	20 " "

Transported on the French freighter *Léopold L. D.* which arrived at Philadelphia November 28, 1941.

Cork	1,623 metric tons
Rough forms for briar pipes	94 " "

Transported on the French freighter *Ile de Ré* which arrived at New York December 4, 1941.

Cork	1,330 metric tons
Tartar	224 " "
Essences for perfume	" "

APPENDIX A

Transported on the French freighter *Ile de Noirmoutier* which arrived at Philadelphia February 11, 1942 and at New York February 19, 1942.

Cork	1,290 metric tons
Tartar	299 " "

Transported on the French freighter *Ile d'Ouessant* which arrived at Philadelphia February 16, 1942 and at New York February 26, 1942.

Cork	1,032	metric tons
Tartar	552	" "
Horehound	24	" "
Plants for perfume	48	" "
Essences for perfume	.5	" "
Sandarac	10	" "
Caraway	28	" "
Ephedra	3	" "
Wild onions	14	" "

Transported on the French freighter *Ile de Ré* which sailed from Casablanca August 7, 1942.

Cork	985 metric tons
Tartreduvin	1,012 " "
Olive oil	218 " "
Briarwood	18 " "
Essential oils	7 " "
Iris root	3 " "
Horehound	4 " "
Rosebuds	2 " "
7 pieces of furniture from American Foreign Service Officers, addressed to the Despatch Agent, New York.	

Transported on the French freighter *Aldébaran* which sailed from Casablanca August 11, 1942.

Cork	1,816 metric tons
Locust beans	20 " "
Sandarac gum	15 " "
Thyme	6 " "
Wool	5 " "
Caraway seed	1 " "
79 Empty gasoline drums addressed to Standard Oil, Baytown, Texas.	

Appendix B

STATEMENT TO THE PRESS BY THE STATE DEPARTMENT, AUGUST 11, 1936

THE ACTING Secretary of State, Mr. William Phillips, on August 7 sent the following instruction to all representatives of this Government in Spain:

"While I realize that all of our officers have fully appreciated the necessity for maintaining a completely impartial attitude with regard to the disturbances in Spain, and that such an attitude has at all times been maintained by them, it may be well for them to have a summing up of what this Government's position thus far has been and will continue to be.

"It is clear that our Neutrality Law with respect to embargo of arms, ammunition and implements of war has no application in the present situation, since that applies only in the event of war *between or among nations.* On the other hand, in conformity with its well-established policy of non-interference with internal affairs in other countries, either in time of peace or in the event of civil strife, this Government will, of course, scrupulously refrain from any interference whatsoever in the unfortunate Spanish situation. We believe that American citizens, both at home and abroad, are patriotically observing this well-recognized American policy."

STATEMENT TO THE PRESS BY THE STATE DEPARTMENT, AUGUST 22, 1936

THE FOLLOWING is the text of a letter which was addressed to an American manufacturer in response to an inquiry with regard to the policy of this Government concerning the exportation of arms and ammunitions to Spain. Similar replies have been made to other oral inquiries on the same subject.

In reply to your inquiry, I beg to say that the attitude and policy of this Government relative to the question of intervention in the affairs of other sovereign nations has been well known especially since the conclusion of the Montevideo Treaty of 1933.

For your further information, I enclose a copy of a circular telegraphic instruction which was recently sent to certain consular representatives in Europe and which has not been made public up to the present.

I desire to call especial attention to the reference therein to our neutrality laws and to the fact that they have no application in the present Spanish situation, since they apply only in the event of war between or among nations.

Furthermore, I invite your attention with equal force to the reference, in the same circular instruction, to this Government's well established policy of non-interference with internal affairs in other countries, as well as to the statement that this Government will, of course, scrupulously refrain from any interference whatsoever in the unfortunate Spanish situation. At the same time the Department expressed the opinion that American citizens, both at home and abroad, are patriotically observing this recognized American policy.

In view of the above, it seems reasonable to assume that the sale of aeroplanes, regarding which you inquire, would not follow the spirit of the Government's policy.

Very truly yours,
WILLIAM PHILLIPS
Acting Secretary of State

TEXT OF A LETTER FROM THE SECRETARY OF STATE to *Senator Key Pittman of May 12, 1938, Made Public by the Chairman of the Committee on Foreign Relations on May 13, 1938*

May 12, 1938.

MY DEAR SENATOR PITTMAN:

I have received your letter of May 3, 1938, enclosing a copy of S. J. Resolution 288 "repealing the Joint Resolution to prohibit the export of arms, ammunition and implements of war from the United States to Spain, approved January 8, 1937, and conditionally raising the embargo against the Government of Spain," and requesting my comment.

In recent years this Government has consistently pursued a course calculated to prevent our becoming involved in war situations. In August, 1936, shortly after the beginning of the civil strife in Spain, it became evident that several of the great powers were projecting themselves into the struggle through the furnishing of arms and war materials and other aid to the contending sides, thus creating a real danger of a spread of the conflict into a European war, with the possible involvement of the United States. That there was such a real danger was realized by every thoughtful observer the world over. Twenty-seven Governments of Europe took special cognizance of that fact in setting up a committee designed to carry out a concerted policy of non-intervention in the conflict. In view of all these special and unusual circumstances, this Government declared its policy of strict non-interference in the struggle and at the same time announced that export of arms from the United States to Spain would be contrary to such policy.

The fundamental reason for the enactment of the Joint Resolution of January 8, 1937, was to implement this policy by legislation. This Joint Resolution was passed in the Senate unanimously and in the House of Representatives by a vote of 406 to 1.

In the form in which it is presented, the proposed legislation, if enacted, would lift the embargo, which is now being applied against both parties to the conflict in Spain, in respect to shipments of arms to one party while leaving in effect the embargo in respect to shipments to the other party. Even if the legislation applied to both parties, its enactment would still subject us to unnecessary risks we have so far avoided. We do not know what lies ahead in the Spanish situation. The original danger still exists. In view of the continued danger of international conflict arising from the circumstances of the struggle, any proposal which at this juncture contemplates a reversal of our policy of strict non-interference which we have thus far so scrupulously followed, and under the operation of which we have kept out of involvements, would offer a real possibility of complications. From the standpoint of the best interests of the United States in the circumstances which now prevail, I would not feel justified in recommending affirmative action on the Resolution under consideration.

Our first solicitude should be the peace and welfare of this country, and the real test of the advisability of making any changes in the statutes now in effect should be whether such changes would further tend to keep us from becoming involved directly or indirectly in a dangerous European situation.

Furthermore, if reconsideration is to be given to a revision of our neutrality legislation, it would be more useful to reconsider it in its broader aspects in the light of the practical experience gained during the past two or three years, rather than to rewrite it piecemeal in relation to a particular situation. It is evident that there is not sufficient time to give study to such questions in the closing days of this Congress.

Sincerely yours,
CORDELL HULL

APPENDIX B

(PUBLIC RESOLUTION—NO. 1—75TH CONGRESS)

(Chapter 1 — 1st Session)
(S. J. Res. 3)

JOINT RESOLUTION

To prohibit the exportation of arms, ammunition, and implements of war from the United States to Spain.

Resolved by the Senate and House of Representatives of the United States of America in Congress assembled, That during the existence of the state of civil strife now obtaining in Spain it shall, from and after the approval of this Resolution, be unlawful to export arms, ammunition, or implements of war from any place in the United States, or possessions of the United States, to Spain or to any other foreign country for transshipment to Spain or for use of either of the opposing forces in Spain. Arms, ammunition, or implements of war, the exportation of which is prohibited by this Resolution, are those enumerated in the President's Proclamation No. 2163 of April 10, 1936.

Licenses heretofore issued under existing law for the exportation of arms, ammunition, or implements of war to Spain shall, as to all future exportations thereunder, ipso facto be deemed to be cancelled.

Whoever in violation of any of the provisions of this Resolution shall export, or attempt to export, or cause to be exported either directly or indirectly, arms, ammunition, or implements of war from the United States or any of its possessions, shall be fined not more than ten thousand dollars or imprisoned not more than five years, or both.

When in the judgment of the President the conditions described in this Resolution have ceased to exist, he shall proclaim such fact, and the provisions hereof shall thereupon cease to apply.

Approved, January 8, 1937, at 12:30 P.M.

Appendix C

BRITAIN, RUSSIA, AND EUROPE

CONDITIONS OF CONTINENTAL SECURITY. THE LESSON OF HISTORY

(From the "Times," London, March 10, 1943)
From a Correspondent

DOES IT occur to American isolationists how English they are in their deep instinctive dislike of European entanglements and commitments? The Tory country gentlemen readily renounced the fruits of Marlborough's victories: they were weary of the Continent, and wished to be rid of it. The "wretched Electorate" of Hanover long remained a sore in British politics, and a reproach: it was a link with the Continent; its welcome loss favourably reacted on the position of the dynasty in this country. In the nineteenth century Continental alliances were shunned, and no policy could have been more English and more popular than "splendid isolation." The nation's energy and resources were not to be frittered away in unprofitable Continental squabbles.

This, in fact, is the natural attitude of a nation intent on developing an empire or a continent of its own. It is shared by America and by the great Empire of Russia, which in essence transcends Europe, and which over its inner development or Asiatic expansion is apt, at times, to forget even the Balkans, although to Russia, for a number of reasons, this is the most interesting region in Europe. No nation deeply engaged on the European Continent has managed to develop or retain wide extra-European territories; and no nation engaged in developing such territories willingly lets itself be drawn into Continental affairs. But what we call Continental, Americans call European; and this island being a link and transmitter between Europe and North America, the dislike of European entanglements is liable to receive an anti-British colouring (which certain American groups with strong European connexions try to enhance in their own un-American interest). Indeed the spiritual insularity of this country goes deeper than the professed ignorance of American isolationists who have too much of the European Continent in their midst.

Resistance to Unity

There is a tradition of spiritual unity in Europe, deriving from Rome. But whenever in the last three centuries a nation or dynasty tried to re-create this politically, by establishing its own predominance over Western Christendom, it met with the conscious and tenacious resistance of England; and in defeating these threats to her own freedom and independence, England has gained about half of White Man's land outside Europe for her language, culture, and tradition. Had Philip II of Spain been victorious, no English-speaking communities would have arisen in America. Had the Bourbons prevailed, New England and Virginia might have succumbed to Quebec and Louisiana, as New Amsterdam had to the English colonies. But so decisive was by 1806 Britain's naval superiority that the United States did not have to consider how the Napoleonic Empire would affect her own further development. In this century the German menace has placed our frontier on the Rhine, and America's at Dover: there are times when honest isolationists have to overcome their cherished (and well founded) dislikes.

Neither for good nor for evil has Europe ever been able to form a free union: not even against the conquering Turk, when religion and the common tradition seemed most to demand it. European cooperation can sometimes be achieved through a concert of the great Powers exercising a temperate measure of control. But integral European union would require coercion. Before 1795 attempts at universal dominion were unsuccessful, for there was a fair balance between the contending systems. In 1810, for the first time, the entire European Continent, from the Channel Ports to the frontiers of Russia, was under one ruler. Even so, potential centres of independent strength endured on the Continent, and in 1813–15 the two Germanic Powers played a part hardly inferior to that of Great Britain and Russia. In 1914–18 French resistance was of supreme importance; still, it was the joint weight of Russia and the two English-speaking Empires which accomplished Germany's defeat; the balance of population and power had already shifted to a marked degree against the purely European nations, and in favour of the extra-European Empires. But Russia's collapse, in the years 1917–20, was unfortunately allowed to obscure her past performance and her future importance, while the pacifist isolationism of the Anglo-Saxons well-nigh eliminated their influence from the European Continent.

After 1922 France, much inferior in her power-potential to any of the three Empires, as also to Germany, had the Continent to herself — a weight far beyond her strength to carry; and the system into which she now glided, during Russia's temporary eclipse, recalled that which had existed before Russia emerged as a great Power. In the seventeenth century Sweden, Poland, and Turkey were France's eastern counterpoise to the Greater Germany of the Habsburgs; but they changed into a liability when, under Peter the Great, Russia entered the European arena and engaged in conflict with the three. And when in the second half of the eighteenth century the two Germanic Powers joined hands with Russia, France withdrew; distant and single-handed she could not be effective. Napoleon's victories carried him into Eastern Europe — to his own destruction. He succumbed in the conflict with Russia, which he had tried his best to avoid. Experience proves, most emphatically, that no Western Power, however great, can safely act on the eastern flank of Germany except in a genuine and close understanding with Russia.

Divided Nations

The Continental nations, hopelessly divided, are now no match for Germany, especially if she manages to enlist the sympathy of one of the three extra-European white Empires. The League of Nations was to have supplied the framework of a peace system — but who was to work it? Russia, defeated and Bolshevist, estranged from her allies, was abandoned by them and mutilated by her neighbours; the United States withdrew from Europe; France, with an unresisting automatism, lapsed into that system from which, during the preceding 200 years, even in the days of her prepotency, she had consciously recoiled; and Great Britain, realizing the folly of the French system, tried to limit her commitments to Western Europe, as if international affairs, involving the balance of power on the Continent, could be transacted in watertight compartments.

Naturally every State tried to use the League of Nations for its own policies and purposes: France and her satellites, to collect a maximum of "binding" guarantees for the frontiers drawn by them in 1919 and 1920; Germany, to re-enter the concert of Europe as one of the great Powers; Russia, to construct a system of collective security against the Nazis, who noisily paraded their anti-Russian designs. Great Britain's purpose in the League was innocent and pathetic: to look wise and virtuous without much exertion — to attain the unbought ease of life. We were pacifists and isolationists — there is affinity between the desire for peace and the wish to be left alone. To escape Continental entanglements we went into the League of Nations — a paradoxical pursuit — and many a distinguished British champion of the League felt, deep down in his heart, how beautiful it would be were there no foreigners in it! Moreover, Parliamentary forms in League transactions were apt to reassure and mislead Englishmen — people seldom inquire how things work with which they have been familiar all their lives. On the Parliamentary analogy, an efficacy was subconsciously ascribed to votes and verdicts of Council and Assembly which could not have been reasonably asserted.

A Lasting Basis

The shams, illusions, and neglects of the 20 years 1919–1939 must not be reproduced after this war. If rest is to come to Europe, and a period of peaceful and productive development to the very much wider White Man's lands outside, if an end is now to be made of the German menace and Europe is to be resettled on a lasting basis, this basis must be sought in an association between the three great extra-European Empires and European nations which seek peace and not adventure; but the necessary antecedent to regional arrangements is a truly close collaboration between the three Empires. Disunion between them, and their withdrawal from Europe, annulled the victory of 1918.

SECURITY IN EUROPE
(From the "Times," London, March 10, 1943.)

Two lessons are to be drawn from the historical analysis of British policy in Europe which appears on this page this morning. The first is the familiar one that "splendid isolation" has ceased to be a safe or practicable policy for Great Britain now that the nineteenth-century balance of power within the continent itself has been destroyed — and, to all seeming, irrevocably destroyed — by the inexorable march of military and economic development towards larger and more complex forms of organization. The second and less familiar lesson relates specifically to Russia, and is two-sided. In the first place Russia's attempts to isolate herself from the troubles of the European continent — the last made as recently as 1939 — have proved as futile and as disastrous as similar attempts by Great Britain. Secondly, Britain has the same interest as Russia herself in active and effective Russian participation in continental affairs; for there can be no security in Western Europe unless there is also security in Eastern Europe, and security in Eastern Europe is unattainable unless it is buttressed by the military power of Russia. Security in Europe cannot be achieved by any single stroke however overwhelming. The proposition that it is impossible to exterminate the German people or destroy the German State has behind it the authority of M. STALIN himself. The realization of security will depend on the joint and continuous vigilance of Britain and Russia. If either one of them remains aloof or reverts to policies of isolation, the domination of Europe by Germany becomes once more inevitable.

A case so clear and cogent for close cooperation between Britain and Russia after the war cannot fail to carry conviction to any open and impartial mind. Yet its impact has undoubtedly been retarded and weakened on both sides by prejudices and suspicions left by recent history. To ignore them, or to pretend that they do not exist, is to render a poor service to Anglo-Russian friendship. There is a small minority of people in this country who, undeterred by the thought of playing into HITLER's hands, are still impressed by the "Bolshevist bogy," just as there is probably a small minority of Russians who still believe that British capitalism is a standing menace to Soviet Russia. Unfortunately the harm done by these minorities depends not on their numerical strength or on their influence, which is insignificant, but on the amount of suspicion which the mere fact of their existence can excite on the other side. HITLER's "Bolshevist bogy" propaganda is a two-edged weapon, more cunningly forged than appears at first sight. If he fails — as he has already failed — to induce Britain and America to abate an iota of their determination to crush and obliterate Hitlerism and all its works, he still hopes to sow distrust between his eastern and western foes by fanning Russian apprehensions that Britain and America will presently seek to rob Russia of the fruits of her victory. HITLER's chances of making mischief have been swollen by official hesitations both in Britain and in America to recognize that Russia will, at the moment of a victory so largely due to her outstanding effort, enjoy the same right as her allies to judge for herself of the conditions which she deems necessary for the security of her frontiers.

A study of the historical background serves to illuminate the character of Russian apprehensions and to make these apprehensions comprehensible to her allies. Russia as well as Germany was excluded from the last peace settlement; and the corollary was an attempt to build up security to the east of Germany on the basis of a combination of minor States under the aegis of the Western Powers. Excuses can be found for those who committed this cardinal blunder in 1919. There would be no excuse for advocating its repetition to-day. The sequel irrefutably proved that security in that region cannot be assured for any nation by any grouping of minor countries or by support given to any such grouping from the West. In the words of our correspondent, "no Western Power, however great, can safely act on the eastern flank of Germany except in a genuine and close understanding with Russia." The mere threat of intervention there by the Western Powers produced the Rapallo Treaty of 1922, just as the Franco-British undertaking to Poland given independently of Russia in April, 1939, led to the German-Russian agreement in August of that fatal year. It would be inexcusable — and in the long run suicidal — if British and American statesmen failed to read the lesson which these facts convey. To suppose that Britain and the United States, with the aid of some of the lesser European Powers, could maintain permanent security in Europe through a policy which alienated Russia and induced her to disinterest herself in continental affairs would be sheer madness.

These considerations point to two essential tasks which must engage British diplomacy at the present time. The first is to develop a spirit of growing confidence in relations between Britain and Russia. Success in this task will no doubt depend as much on military achievement as on diplomatic skill. But it will in no circumstances be complete or lasting unless ungrudging and unqualified agreement is attained between the two countries on the future conditions of security in Europe. Four Great Powers, as Mr. Eden said in his speech last December, will have "a virtual monopoly of armed strength" when the war ends: and this armed strength "must be used in the name of the United Nations to prevent a repetition of aggression." Of these four Powers only two are situated on the confines of Europe; and on these two rests a pre-eminent responsibility for European security. This is the sense and significance of the Eden-Molotov treaty of May last. If Britain's frontier is on the Rhine, it might just as pertinently be said — though it has not in fact been said — that Russia's frontier is on the Oder, and in the same sense. This does not mean that Russia any more than Britain desires to assail the independence of other countries or to control their domestic affairs. On the contrary it

APPENDIX C

must stand to reason that Russian security will best be served by an understanding with peoples who have themselves good cause to look to Russia for security against any repetition of the grim experience of Nazi domination and whose relations with the Soviet Union are founded upon a solid basis of contentment and good will. The sole interest of Russia is to assure herself that her outer defences are in sure hands; and this interest will be best served if the lands between her frontiers and those of Germany are held by governments and peoples friendly to herself. That is the one condition on which Russia must and will insist. Everything goes to show that she will be in a position after the war to shape the settlement on lines consistent with this conception of what her security demands. But it will make all the difference to the future of Anglo-Russian friendship whether these lines have been freely approved and welcomed by Britain in advance, or whether they are grudgingly accepted as a *fait accompli* after the victory has been won.

The other task of British foreign policy is to interpret to the United States the common interest of Britain and Russia in European security and in the means of attaining it. As MR. HERBERT MORRISON said in his recent speech, "we may be able to play a part in developing and cementing relations of friendship between our two great allies — the Russians and Americans." But this part cannot be passive. Differences, where they exist, will not be resolved or mitigated by the pusillanimity which refuses to make up its mind one way or the other. VICE-PRESIDENT WALLACE said bluntly on Monday that another world war is inevitable "unless the Western democracies and Russia come to a satisfactory understanding before the war ends." Both Britain and America have paid dearly for past indulgence in ignorant and wishful thinking about Europe; and if Britain has paid for it even more dearly than America — in the humiliations of the pre-war years and in the disasters of the war — this priority gives her both the duty and the right to speak out freely against the repetition of these errors. The issue of security in Europe will not be settled by the enunciation of general principles; it will not be settled by the acceptance of hypothetical obligations or by the establishment of loose machinery of consultation or cooperation; it will not be settled by any organization based on a conception of national independence which entails the partition of Europe among twenty separate and jarring military and economic sovereignties. It will be settled only if those who possess military and economic power on the largest scale, and are prepared to exercise it within the confines of Europe, organize that power in common for the fulfilment of common purposes and for the benefit of all. Russia's military achievements in the war have shown conclusively that no such organization can exist for a moment without her, and that those concerned for future security in Europe, both great and small, have an imperative need of her. This is the message of the events of the past eighteen months in Europe. It must be the decisive factor in shaping future British policy on the continent; and one of the main concerns of British statesmanship must be to reinforce the efforts of American leaders to promote American understanding and appreciation of it.

GREAT AND SMALL NATIONS
(From the "Times," London, March 23, 1943.)

It is no new discovery, though it has been made once more in the correspondence and comment inspired by a recent leading article in these columns on "Security in Europe," that the thorniest problem of international security turns on the relationship between great and small nations. The Congress of Vienna cut the Gordian knot by drawing a fixed line of demarcation between the Great Powers and the rest. The Great Powers, in virtue of their military strength, constituted the Concert of Europe and carried the burden and responsibility both of maintaining the international order and of waging international war when that order broke down from within or was assailed from without. The smaller countries enjoyed independence in the management of their domestic affairs — so long as these were not felt to threaten the general security — but were not expected to concern themselves in issues of high international policy. When the League of Nations was brought into being some of its more experienced advocates, such as LORD CECIL himself, proposed to create the Council of the League on the model of the Concert of Europe by confining its membership to the Great Powers.

Even had this counsel prevailed in 1919 it may be doubted whether the mere revival of a brilliant nineteenth-century improvisation would have met the needs of international security in the new age. It was not only that the destruction of old States, and the birth of new, had brought with it a fresh crop of problems. The evolution of military technique, the elimination of space, and the

APPENDIX C 285

development of policies of economic self-sufficiency had combined to render obsolete the notion of detached neutrality as a safe and desirable option for weaker countries. In modern conditions this status may still be open to a few countries which, like those of the Iberian Peninsula or Switzerland, owe their isolation to an exceptional geographical position. But for the vast majority of the smaller European States neutrality no longer offers any hope of security, whether in peace or in war. It can scarcely be supposed that any small European nation which has been swept into the vortex will be tempted after the war to take refuge once more in that policy of self-contained isolation which made it the easy prey of unscrupulous aggression; nor can there be room any longer for the nation which seeks to maintain a precarious and illusory independence by shifting its weight from side to side or by exploiting the rivalries of its more powerful neighbours. The balance of power in this sense is as dead as the policy of strict neutrality. Both belonged to a period of European history which came to an end — not before it had outlived its credit and its usefulness — in the fateful summer of 1940.

Security in Europe will not, then, be realized by restoring the *status quo ante bellum*. It demands not only a fresh adjustment and a new conception of relations between great and small Powers, designed to meet the essential and legitimate needs of both, but also a reinterpretation of what has been meant in the past, both for great and for small nations, by such terms as "self-determination" and "independence." This does not imply that there must be fewer separate and independent nations. There may be more — even in Europe; for there is no particular reason why the process of self-determination, so fruitful in stirring new nations to political consciousness over the past seventy or eighty years, should be arrested at the precise point which it had reached in 1919. But it does imply — and this conclusion is implicit in the Atlantic Charter — that independence must be tempered by interdependence, and must be interpreted in a way which enables a multiplicity of nations to occupy together a confined continental living space without constantly impinging on one another's security and well-being. The aim must be to extend rather than to restrict the diversity of national traditions, languages, and institutions which enrich Europe, and to encourage it to find full expression in a diversity of administrations. But ways must imperatively be found to reconcile independence, both for the great and for the small, with that increasing integration of military and economic power

APPENDIX C

on a basis of consent which is the only alternative to anarchy on the one hand or to Hitlerism on the other. The organization of the United Nations must provide a solid military and economic framework which alone can assure freedom from fear and freedom from want to the much tried peoples of Europe. National identity, national rights, and national development — whether of great or small nations — must not again assume forms incompatible with the discharge of this common obligation.

These principles have been broadly accepted by the United Nations for the conduct of the war. Units drawn from one nation are incorporated for operational purposes in the armed forces of another; armies, navies, and air forces of several nations fight under a commander drawn from one of them; bases are leased to one nation on another's territory. These forms of "mixing up" — the embryo of a true international force — far from being allowed to disappear, should be multiplied and extended more widely when the war ends, just as the joint economic machinery which is being created in the war should be further developed and expanded for the purposes of peace. So much is clear. The right policy is known and accepted in principle: it remains only to carry it out. But what form of political organization will ultimately best coordinate the power and resources of the four major countries for the common benefit of all, and regulate the crucial issue of relations between them and smaller nations, has still to be determined; and this issue is particularly acute in Europe. Americans have often put the tempting question why the States of Europe cannot federate as the thirteeen American colonies federated to found the United States. But perhaps a closer transatlantic parallel is provided by the twenty and more separate and independent countries of the two Americas with their diversities of origin, language, and tradition. This parallel is particularly worthy of study at a time when the original Monroe doctrine has deepened and broadened out into the good neighbour policy, and when relations between the American republics, which have had their stormy passages in the past, are more cordial and intimate than at any previous period. Nor is it irrelevant to recall that Great Britain has had her own Monroe doctrine in more than one region, and that this has proved no barrier to lasting friendship and mutually advantageous relations with the countries in whose destinies her own strategic security was involved.

Comparisons are always imperfect. Conditions in these regions differ widely from one another and from conditions in Eastern

Europe, whose particular problems of security have lately been under debate. But certain broad principles are applicable to all. The good neighbour policy in the Americas is firmly grounded in the Monroe doctrine and could not have flourished without it. It is rooted, on the one hand, in the recognition that the Government and people of the United States regard the immunity of any American territory from external attack as a condition of their own security and will cooperate to the full extent of their resources to uphold it; on the other hand, in the recognition that issues arising between the American nations shall be settled, not by coercion but by free discussion, untrammelled by extraneous intervention, between those nations themselves. These are the conditions precedent of a good neighbour policy based on mutual respect and mutual advantage. The present obstacle to their fulfilment in Eastern Europe is a lack of confidence, the historical causes of which are not difficult to discover. In the establishment of this essential confidence Russia has her part to play; and she has begun to play it by proclaiming her desire to see the countries of the United Nations in Eastern Europe strong and independent and by renouncing any ambition to influence the ideological complexion of their governments. Much remains to be done on her side. But in the meanwhile Russia's principal allies must also make their contribution by allaying the Russian apprehensions, also rooted in history, that they may be unwilling to accord to Russia the rights of full and equal partnership in the future settlement and the same voice in issues vitally affecting her security as they claim for themselves in issues affecting their own.

This argument, cogent as it is, may lead, and has sometimes led, to misconceptions which it is necessary to remove. It does not invite Russia to ride roughshod over the interests and aspirations of smaller nations; on the contrary, it suggests the conditions in which a good neighbour policy, based on a sense of security and of assurance against external intervention, may become a reality in Eastern Europe. It does not involve a balancing of Britain's friendship with Russia against Britain's friendship with the United States; on the contrary, it is inspired by the profound and anxious conviction that Europe, and not only Europe, will perish unless threefold concord between the United States, Russia, and Britain is fully maintained. It does not rest on the anticipation of a withdrawal of American military strength from Europe after the war — and still less on the desire for it; on the contrary, nothing is more earnestly hoped for by Great Britain than permanent participation by the United States in strategic commitments and military establishments on this side of the Atlantic and on the European continent. It does not imply acceptance of the dangerous regional principle as the foundation of an international society. But in any future world organization of security reasonable account will have to be taken of geographical proximity. Common sense would protest against any system of pooled security which did not leave the defence of, say, the Panama Canal in predominantly American hands; and while the organization of security in Eastern Europe, as throughout the world, will remain a matter of common and world-wide concern, the nucleus of military and economic power, which is the only effective instrument of security, must in that region, within the general framework, be provided primarily by Russia — the sole country east of Germany possessing industrial resources and development on a scale in any way equal to the task. This is a hard fact which cannot be overcome by wishful thinking or overlooked without dire peril. It is a fact of which the British and American peoples have become increasingly aware in recent months. Recognition of its implications and consequences is a condition of the establishment of relations of lasting confidence with Russia, and must form an essential part both of British and of American policy.

ACKNOWLEDGMENTS

Acknowledgments are hereby made to the following for permission to use material quoted in this book:

Alfred A. Knopf, Inc. for permission to quote from NIGHT OVER EUROPE by Frederick L. Schuman, and APPEASEMENT'S CHILD by Thomas J. Hamilton.

The Macmillan Company for permission to quote from CONDITIONS OF PEACE by E. H. Carr.

Henry Holt & Company for permission to quote from A DIPLOMATIC HISTORY OF THE U. S. by Samuel Flagg Bemis.

Harcourt Brace & Co. for permission to quote from THE LATIN AMERICAN POLICY OF THE U. S. by Samuel Flagg Bemis.

The New Republic for permission to quote from two editorials in April 26, 1943 and May 3, 1943 issues.

Longmans Green Co. for permission to quote from ESSAYS ON FAITH AND MORALS by William James.

PM for permission to quote from an editorial published on June 11, 1943. Copyright 1943 by Field Publications, released through PM Syndicate.

Houghton Mifflin Co. for permission to quote from A HISTORY OF EUROPE by H. A. L. Fisher.

Simon & Schuster, Inc. for permission to quote from ONE WORLD by Wendell Willkie.

Oxford University Press, London, for permission to quote from A STUDY OF HISTORY by Arnold Toynbee.

The Editor of the *Times* of London for permission to reproduce three articles from that newspaper.

The Editors of *Punch* for permission to reproduce a verse by "Evoe."

Index

Adams, James Truslow, 169
Adams, John, 238
Africa, North, Chapters IV, V, VI, VII, 111; American supplies, 36 *et seq.*; German infiltration, 43; German supplies from, 50 *et seq.*; politics in, 58 *et seq.*, 111; as American frontier, 34-6; British policy towards, 39-41, 42-45, 47, Chapter VI; American policy towards, 60 *et seq.*, Chapter VI
Age of Conflict, 120 footnote
Air France, 54
Aleutian Islands, 13
Algeria, 56, 62
America, isolation from war, 14; as a menace, 24-5
America Comes of Age, 24 footnote
"American Dream," 169
American Policy, towards North Africa, Chapters IV, V, VI, 113, 115; towards Spain, 118 *et seq.*; towards Japan, 151, 155-7, 163-5; to avoid war, 157; effect on Germany, 159; towards Britain, 218; towards Russia, 206, 210, 241
Anti-Comintern Pact, 150
Appeasement policy, 154-5
Argentina, 254; opulence, 261; elections, 261
Asia, 18, 34, 132
Atlantic Charter, 22, 111, 219, 233
Axis, positive aims, 7-8; and Africa, 35, 43-4, 48, 50-1, 55

Badoglio, 106-7
Bainville, Jacques, 184
Baldwin, Lord, 14, 138, 140
Baltic States, 201, 205, 218
Bases, leased from Britain, 220
Bastille, de Gaulle on, 75
Baudoin, 81
Beaumarchais, 238

Berle, A. A., 47
Béthouart, General, 54, 72
Bismarck, 181, 192
Boisson, Pierre, 97
Bolshevism, Hitler on, 117
Borah, Senator W. E., 215
Bracken, Brendan, 197
Brazil, as defensive point, 248
Briand, Aristide, 145
Briand-Kellogg Pact, 152, 220
Britain, and U. S., 212 *et seq.*; and Russia, 20, 22, 216 *et seq.*; Constitution, 223; civilization, 195, 222-3; character, 233; homogeneity, 196; use of power, 224; losses in war, 213-4
Britain, contribution to American war industry, 214-5 footnote; contribution to our Good Neighbor Policy, 250
Britain, isolation of, 14; no longer an island, 14-5; and Germany, 19-20; our aid to, 169, 170, 172; social legislation, 170
British Commitments, 135, 152
British Navy, 160
British policy in North Africa, 39 *et seq.*, 42-3, 47, 79, 87-90
British Radio and de Gaulle, 90
British Treasury and de Gaulle, 60
Brussels Conference, 165
Buenos Aires, 262

Canada, 12
Carlists (Requetés) in Spain, 124, 127
Carr, E. H., quoted, 27, 185, 216
Casablanca, 37, 38, 42, 43, 44, 46, 62, 64, 90
Cassidy, Henry W., 204
Castillo, Ramon, 254
Catalonia, 126
Catholic Sovereigns, 125

INDEX

Catholics, and Spain, 124, 126
Chamber of Commerce, 31
Chamberlain, Neville, 137; on "people of whom we know nothing," 155
Chamberlain, William H., 212
Chatel, Ives, 54
China, as a power, 16; territorial integrity, 152, 156, 165
Church, in Spain, 125-6
Churchill, Winston, 64, 86, 90, 91, 104, 106, 107-11; on U. S. Vichy policy, 120; address to Congress, 173; on Atlantic Charter, 233; on Council of Europe, 230; as source of news, 108-9; American views of, 109-10; Harvard speech on Combined Chiefs of Staff, 244
Clark, General Mark, 67, 68, 72, 73
Coalition, of powers, 19; of Allies collapsed, 131
"Collaborators" in North Africa, 98
Collective security, 24, 219, 245; American opinion on, 245
Colombia, 261
Combined Chiefs of Staff Committee, 244
Communism, and Nazis, 5-6, 117, 135, 143; in Spain, 126
Conant, President of Harvard, 174
Congress, and President, 235-6
Conseils généraux, 99
Conservatives, attitude to Communism, 135, 136
Constitutions, British and American contrasted, 236-7
Cordon Sanitaire, 207
Council of Europe, 217-8; of Asia, 218
Crémieux Decree, 166 footnote
Czechoslovakia, 137, 138, 203

Daily Worker, 209
Dakar, 37, 43, 44, 46, 97
Darlan, Admiral, 40, 58, 61, 67-8, 70, 72, 73, 79, 80, 87, 89, 114
Davis, Norman H., 165
Deane, Silas, 238
Debts owed to U. S., 174 footnote; in default, 175 footnote
Democracies, power of, 4, 23-4

Democracy, and Diplomacy, 111
De Valera, 168
Dewey, Governor, 244
Dibelius, on Britain, 224
Dilemma of Diplomacy, 102
Diplomacy, and Democracy, 111
Disarmament, 24
Duhamel, Georges, 24 footnote
Duranty, Walter, 212

Ebbutt, Norman, 144 footnote
Economics and peace, viii
Economist, The, 144
Eden, Anthony, 90
Eisenhower, General Dwight D., 59, 63, 89
Employment, full, 245
Epic of America, 169
Europe, its role in the future, 16, 17, 30; unity of, 242
l'Europe ou l'Amérique, 24 footnote

Falange in Spain, its aims, 124, 125, 126
Fascism, in North Africa, 71
Fascist powers, 117
Fenard, Admiral, 54
Fighting French, 88, 91
Finland, and Russia, 201, 206, 217, 240-1
Fisher, H. A. L., 211
Flynn, John T., 170
Foreign policy of U. S., vii
Fossoyeurs, Les, 72, 80
"Four Freedoms," 260
"Fourteen Points," 232
France, 3, 4, Chapters V, VII; limited power of, 145-6; appeal to U. S., 167; effect on U. S. of fall of, 168; "National revolution," 57, 97
Franco, General Francisco, 69-70, 117, 118, 124
Franklin, Benjamin, 238
French Army, 67, 75, 98, 101
French Fleet, 35, 52, 80-85; merchant fleet, 42
French funds in U. S., 41
French independence, 62, 63, 73, 94, 95
French problem, 56 et seq., 73
French Revolution, 74

INDEX

Gaulle, General de, 53, 57, 59, 60, 65, 67, 69, 70, 73, 74, 75, 79; nationalism of, 73–6; official U. S. attitude to, 85 *et seq.*; and Britain, 60, 87–8
Gaullism, American de, 69 *et seq.*
Gensoul, Vice-Admiral, 81
Germany, 4 *et seq.*, Chapter XIII; youth, 5, 27, 188; American loans to, 134; British sympathy for, 132, 133, 134, 141 *et seq.*
Germany, Disarmament of, 22, 184; bombardment of, 197; birth rate, 199; dismemberment of, 184; lack of unity, 185, 192
Germany, hopes in case of defeat, 130
Germany, as problem, 180 *et seq.*; Prof. Schmitt on, 183–4; Bainville on, 184; E. H. Carr on, 185; her aims, 190 *et seq.*; living space, 191; idea of freedom, 192–3; admiration for British, 195
Giraud, General, 57, 59, 61, 62, 64, 65, 66, 67, 68, 76, 79, 89, 90, 93, 95, 97, 98 *et seq.*; on Peyrouton, 64
Godfroy, Vice-Admiral, 81
Gollán, José Santos, 261
Good Neighbor Policy, 35, 221, 248–9; Britain's role in, 250
Grafton, Samuel, 106
Greenland, 12
Grey, Sir Edward, 139
Guam, 220
Guérin, Paul, 42

Habsburgs, 112
Hamilton, Thomas J., 154 footnote
Hanotaux, Gabriel, 184
Havana, Treaty of, 118, 122
Henry-Haye, 82
Herriot, Edouard, 61
Hitler, 5, 135, 137, 138, 139, 142, 144, 145, 146, 150, 151, 154, 155, 157, 164, 166, 167, 175, 181–2, 189, 190–1; his conquest of Germany, 5, 175; "had a case," 134; an interview with, 189
Hitler period, 150 *et seq.*
Hitler's missed opportunity, 138, 181–2

Holy Roman Empire, 138
House of Commons, 110
Hull, Cordell, 35, 36, 82, 84; policy on Spain, 119–20, 122, 123; foresaw war danger, 158, 159, 161, 162, 164; on futility of isolation, 162

Ideals, lack of, 23–4, 26–7
Ideology and foreign policy, 177
Intervention, Allied in North Africa, 62 *et seq.*
Isolation, U. S., 171, 173; various forms of, 177
Italy, 166–7; armistice with, 102 *et seq.*

James, William, 32
Japan, 7, 8, 16, 20, 21, 131, 132, 148; alliance with Germany, 150; and Manchuria, 151–2, 155–6
Jay, John, 231

Kemper, James S., 170
Kennedy, John F., quoted, 132 footnote, 147
King of Italy, 106
Knox, E. V., 137, 144
Krock, Arthur, 159

Latin America, economic links with Europe, 253; Germans in, 253; feudalism, 255; our dilemma there, 259; democracy, 261; standard of living, 257; French cultural influence, 263
Latin America, Fascism, 250; foreign capital, 265–6; view of "Anglo-Saxons," 264; new "dollar diplomacy," 264; Chapters III, XVI; non-intervention in, Chapter VIII, 10, 16; as defensive responsibility of U. S., Chapter XVI
Laval, Pierre, 49, 52
League of Nations, 28, 135, 139, 151, 174, 218
Légion des Combattants, 98
Lend-lease, and de Gaulle, 86, 87; and Britain, 170, 172, 213; and future economic policy, 239, 243; and Argentina, 254

INDEX

Lend-lease Act, 170, 172, 213
Lenin, on plebiscites, 207
Lewis, Sir Wilmot, 213
Liberty, 8 footnote
Lindbergh, Charles, 229
Lippmann, Walter, 17, 19, 160, 215
Luther, Dr., 164
Lytton Report on Manchuria, 151

Maginot Line, 145
Manchester Guardian, 144
Manchuria, and Russia, 212
Map, new conception of, 11
Mast, General, 54
Mediterranean, 34, 35, 102
Mediterranean Commission, 109
Mers-el-Kebir, 81
Mexico, oil settlement, 266; attitude to U. S., 253-4
Ministry of Economic Warfare, 37
Miquelon, 86
Mitchell, Wesley C., 246
Molotov, 204
Monroe, President, 230-1
Monroe Doctrine, 238
Montevideo, 262
Moral Equivalent of War, 32
Moral Suasion, 163, 165, 167
Morocco, 38, 40, 41, 42, 53
Moscow agreement of October, 1943, 210, 212
Mowrer, E. A., 115 footnote
Munich agreement, 138, 139
Murmansk, 12, 205
Murphy, Robert D., 37, 38, 41, 43, 44, 59
Murphy-Weygand Agreement, 41; results, Appendix A
Mussolini, 106, 166-7

National Income, 245
National Resources Planning Board, 245
Nationalism, in United States, Chapter XII
Naval treaty, 132
Nazis, movement, 5 *et seq.*, 27, 188 *et seq.*
Neutrality Act, 141, 158, 160, 169; amended, 158-9; handicap to our diplomacy, 159, 162

New Deal, *vii*, 29
New Republic, on State Dept., 115
News-Chronicle, 64
New Statesman, 144
New Zealand, 12
Night Over Europe, 27
Nine-power pact, 156, 165
Noguès, General, 38, 97
"Normalcy," 28, 33
North Africa (see Africa, North)

Office of War Information, 106
One World, by Wendell Willkie, 88
Otto, Archduke, 112
Oxford students, 31

Pacific, 4, 18, 35; Japan's power in, 132
Panama Canal, 35
Pan-American Conferences, 248
Panay, 154, 157, 165
Parti Populaire Français, 53
Peace, 23, 28, 31, 32; Roosevelt on possibility of, 161
Peace Conference of 1919, 232
Pearl Harbor, 18, 147-8
Pertinax, 72, 80
Pessimism, after last war, 24, 26-7
Pétain, Marshal, 39, 43, 45, 57, 59, 67
Peyrouton, Marcel, 62, 63, 64, 89, 97
Phillips, William, 118-9
Poland, 131, 145, 169, 201, 203, 206
Pole, North, and air traffic, 11
Polish Corridor, 134
Pope Alexander VI, 151
"Power politics," 219
Powers, great, 16
Pravda, 205
Preventive war, 15
Punch, 137, 144
"Purge" in North Africa, 97, 100

Ramirez, Pedro, 254
Red Army, 205
Reformation, 192
Republican Party, 31, 171; post-war conference, 244
Requetés in Spain, 124, 127

INDEX

Revolution, of Nazis, 5; and geography, 11
Reynaud, Paul, 167
Rhineland, 15, 133, 135, 141, 200; commission, 131
Ribbentrop, Joachim von, 201, 202
Rogers, Will, 238
Romier, Lucien, 24
Rommel, Marshal, 48, 51, 52
Roosevelt, President, F. D., as economic nationalist, 175–7; as political leader, 234; attitude to French, 60; on our neutrality, 158–9, 162; warns of war danger, 158, 161; "quarantine" speech, 162
Royal Air Force, 251
Ruhr, 131
Rumania, 201, 203
Russia, 4, 16, 18, 19, 21, 22, Chapter XIV; and U. S., 18, 25, 207, 209, 211; compared to U. S., 25
Russia, British and American views of, 210 et seq.
Russia, pact with Hitler, 201; and Baltic States, 203; and Atlantic Charter, 22, 202, 207; "second front, 1942," 204; relations with Allies, 204 et seq.; territorial claims, 205–10, 217; policy towards Germany, 208–9; and Far East, 212; and Britain, 216 et seq.; Moscow Agreement, 210, 212

St. Pierre, 86
Santayana, George, 193
Scandinavia, 240
Schacht, Hjalmar, 164
Schmitt, Prof. Bernadotte, 183–4
Schuman, Prof. Frederick, 27
Second World War, vii
Self-sufficiency, 242
Senate of U. S., 236
Service d'Ordre de la Légion, 53
Siegfried, André, 24
Simon, Sir John, 132, 156
Socialism, British, 30, 170
South America, and Spain, 126
Space, changed proportions, 12, 15
Spain, civil war, 69, Chap. IX, 150; British policy, 136; American policy, 118 et seq.; and European war, 38, 41, 44, 117, 120, 150; and North Africa, 38, 41, 44, 123
Spectator, 144
Spengler, Oswald, 24, 193
Spitzbergen, 12
Stalin, Joseph, 22, 202, 204, 205, 208, 209, 210, 211, 212; on "second front," 204–5; on Poland, 241
State, Department of, 47, 48, 50, 51, 105, 220; criticism of, 114–6
Sterne, Laurence, 14
Stimson, Henry L., 152, 156, 220
Stolper, Gustav, 194
Stohrer, von, 125
Storni, Admiral, 254
Sullivan, Mark, 170
Syria, 84

Tariff, U. S., 175
Third Republic, 74
Thirty Years' War, 192
Time and Tide, 144
The Times of London, 144; on Russian-British relations, 211, Appendix C
Torre, Haya de la, 256
Toynbee, Prof. Arnold, 26
Two-thirds rule in Senate, 236–7
Tyrrell, Lord, 133

Unconditional Surrender, 210
United States, as an enigma, 236 et seq.; negative policies, 230; Constitution, 234–7; as a conservative nation, 247; outlines of future policy, 239
United States, Far Eastern diplomacy, 152; tradition and foreign policy, 218; and Britain, Chapter XV
United States, legend of her incompetence in foreign affairs, 237
United States, and foreign war, 14; smallest great power, 18; security requirements, 21; and Russia, 18; mass production, 24 et seq.; as a menace, 24; depression, 23; policy in North Africa, Chapters IV, V and VI.
"Universality," as American Doctrine, 218
Uruguay, 261

INDEX

Vargas, Getulio, 250, 264
Veblen, Thorstein, 183, 193
Vichy Government, 39, 41, 43, 44, 45, 47, 49; and U. S., 81 et seq., 98
Victory, 3
Victory of 1918, 4, 131
Visions de la Vie Future, 24
Voigt, F. A., 144

Wallace, Vice-President, 233
Washington, George, 231

Weber, Max, 194
Welles, Sumner, 166, 245
Wells, H. G., 31
Weygand, General, 38, 39, 41, 43, 46, 49
Whidden, Howard P., quoted, 131
Willkie, Wendell, on de Gaulle, 88
Wilson, Woodrow, 211, 218, 232-3
Wilsonian Europe, 211, 233
Wood, Sir Kingsley, 245
World War, Second, 14

For Product Safety Concerns and Information please contact our EU
representative GPSR@taylorandfrancis.com
Taylor & Francis Verlag GmbH, Kaufingerstraße 24, 80331 München, Germany

www.ingramcontent.com/pod-product-compliance
Lightning Source LLC
Chambersburg PA
CBHW071346290426
44108CB00014B/1452